The Romance

OF

The Colorado River

The Story of its Discovery in 1540, with an Account
of the Later Explorations, and with Special Reference to the Voyages of Powell through
the Line of the Great Canyons

By

Frederick S. Dellenbaugh

Member of the United States Colorado River Expedition of
1871 and 1872

"No sluggish tide congenial to the glooms :
This, as it frothed by, might have been a bath
For the fiend's glowing hoof—"

BROWNING

DOVER PUBLICATIONS, INC.
Mineola, New York

Bibliographical Note

This Dover edition, first published in 1998, is an unabridged republication of the work originally published in 1902 by G. P. Putnam's Sons, New York.

Library of Congress Cataloging-in-Publication Data

Dellenbaugh, Frederick Samuel, 1853–1935.
The romance of the Colorado River : the story of its discovery in 1540, with an account of the later explorations, and with special reference to the voyages of Powell through the line of the great canyons / by Frederick S. Dellenbaugh.
p.   cm.
Originally published: New York : G. P. Putnam's Sons, 1902.
Includes index.
ISBN 0-486-40439-0 (pbk.)
1. Colorado River—Description and travel.   2. Colorado River Valley—Description and travel.   3. Grand Canyon (Ariz.)—Description and travel.   4. Powell, John Wesley, 1834–1902.   5. Colorado River—Discovery and exploration.   6. Colorado River Valley—Discovery and exploration.   7. Grand Canyon (Ariz.)—Discovery and exploration.   I. Title.
F788.D37   1998
917.91'3044—dc21   98-35346
                                                                    CIP

Manufactured in the United States of America
Dover Publications, Inc., 31 East 2nd Street, Mineola, N.Y. 11501

TO
MY FRIENDS AND COMRADES
OF THE
COLORADO RIVER EXPEDITION OF 1871 AND 1872
IN GRATEFUL REMEMBRANCE

PREFACE

EARLY in 1871, when Major Powell[1] was preparing for his second descent through the canyons of the Green and Colorado rivers, he was besieged by men eager to accompany him; some even offered to pay well for the privilege. It was for me, therefore, a piece of great good fortune when, after an interview in Chicago with the eminent explorer, he decided to add me to his small party. I was very young at the time, but muscular and healthy, and familiar with the handling of small boats. The Major remarked that in the business before us it was not so much age and strength that were needed as "nerve," and he evidently believed I had enough of this to carry me through. Certainly in the two-years, continuous work on the river and in the adjacent country I had some opportunity to develop this desirable quality. I shall never cease to feel grateful to him for the confidence reposed in me. It gave me one of the unique experiences of my life,—an experience which, on exactly the same lines, can never be repeated within our borders. Now, these thirty years after, I review that experience with satisfaction and pleasure, recalling, with deep affection, the kind and generous companions of that wild and memorable journey. No party of men thrown together, without external contact for months at a time, could have been more harmonious; and never once did any member of that party show the white feather. I desire to acknowledge here, also, my indebtedness to Prof. A. H. Thompson, Major Powell's associate in his second expedition, for many kindnesses.

When his report to Congress was published, Major Powell,

[1] I use the title Major for the reason that he was so widely known for so long a period by it. He was a volunteer officer during the Civil War, holding the rank of Colonel at the end. The title Major, then, has no military significance in this connection.

perhaps for the sake of dramatic unity, concluded to omit mention of the personnel of the second expedition, awarding credit, for all that was accomplished, to the men of his first wonderful voyage of 1869. And these men surely deserved all that could be bestowed on them. They had, under the Major's clear-sighted guidance and cool judgment, performed one of the distinguished feats of history. They had faced unknown dangers. They had determined that the forbidding torrent could be mastered. But it has always seemed to me that the men of the second party, who made the same journey, who mapped and explored the river and much of the country round-about, doing a large amount of difficult work in the scientific line, should have been accorded some recognition. The absence of this has sometimes been embarrassing for the reason that when statements of members of the second party were referred to the official report, their names were found missing from the list. This inclined to produce an unfavourable impression concerning these individuals. In order to provide in my own case against any unpleasant circumstance owing to this omission, I wrote to Major Powell on the subject and received the following highly satisfactory answer:

WASHINGTON, D. C., January 18, 1888.

MY DEAR DELLENBAUGH :

Replying to your note of the 14th instant, it gives me great pleasure to state that you were a member of my second party of exploration down the Colorado, during the years 1871 and 1872, that you occupied a place in my own boat and rendered valuable services to the expedition, and that it was with regret on my part that your connection with the Survey ceased.

Yours cordially,
J. W. POWELL.

Recently, when I informed him of my intention to publish this volume, he very kindly wrote as follows:

WASHINGTON, January 6, 1902.

DEAR DELLENBAUGH :

I am pleased to hear that you are engaged in writing a book on the Colorado Canyon. I hope that you will put on record the second trip, and the gentlemen who were members of that expedition. No other trip has been made since that time, though many have tried to follow us. One party, that headed by Mr. Stanton, went through the Grand Canyon on its second attempt, but many persons have lost their lives in attempting to follow us through the whole length of the canyons. I shall be very glad to write a short introduction to your book.   Yours cordially,

                                            J. W. Powell.

In complying with this request to put on record the second expedition and the gentlemen who composed it, I feel all the greater pleasure, because, at the same time, I seem to be fulfilling a duty towards my old comrades.

No party, as noted by the Major, has since made the entire passage through the whole line of canyons: those of the upper region are, even now, quite unknown to the outer world. Yet there have been some who appear to be inclined to withhold from Major Powell the full credit which is his for solving the great problem of the Southwest, and who, therefore, make much of the flimsy story of White, and even assume on faint evidence that others fathomed the mystery even before White. There is, in my opinion, no ground for such assumptions. Several trappers, like Pattic and Carson, had gained a considerable knowledge of the general course and character of the river as early as 1830, but to Major Powell and his two parties undoubtedly belongs the high honour of being the first to explore and explain the truth about it and its extraordinary canyon environment.

If danger, difficulty, and disaster mean romance, then assuredly the Colorado of the West is entitled to first rank, for seldom has any human being touched its borderland even, without some bitter or fatal experience. Never is the Colorado twice alike, and each new experience is different from the last. Once acknowledge this and the dangers, however, and approach it in a humble and reverent spirit, albeit firmly, and death need seldom be the penalty of a voyage on its restless waters.

I have endeavoured to present the history of the river, and

immediate environment, so far as I have been able to learn it, but within the limits of a single volume of this size much must necessarily be omitted.   Reference to the admirable works of Powell, Gilbert, and Dutton will give the reader full information concerning the geology and topography; *Garces*, by Elliott Coues, gives the story of the friars; and the excellent memoir of Chittenden, *The American Fur Trade of the Far West*, will give a complete understanding of the travels and exploits of the real pioneers of the Rocky Mountain country. I differ with this author, however, as to the wise and commendable nature of the early trappers' dealings with the natives, and this will be explained in the pages on that subject. He also says in his preface that "no feature of western geography was ever discovered by government explorers after 1840." While this is correct in the main, it gives an erroneous impression so far as the canyons of the Colorado are concerned.   These canyons were "discovered," as mentioned above, by some of the trappers, but their interior character was not known, except in the vaguest way, so that the discovery was much like discovering a range of mountains on the horizon and not entering beyond the foothills.

For the titles of works of reference, of the narratives of trappers, etc., I refer to the works of H. H. Bancroft; to Warren's *Memoirs*, vol. i. Pacific Railroad reports; and to the first volume of Lieut. Geo. M. Wheeler's report on Explorations West of the 100th Meridian.   The trappers and prospectors who had some experience on the Green and the Colorado have left either no records or very incomplete ones.   It seems tolerably certain, however, that no experience of importance has escaped notice.   So far as attempts at descent are concerned, they invariably met with speedy disaster and were given up.

In writing the Spanish and other foreign proper names I have in no case translated, because such translations result in needless confusion.   To translate "Rio del Tizon " as Firebrand River is making another name of it.   Few would recognise the Colorado River under the title of Red River, as used, for example, in Pattie's narrative.   While Colorado means red, it is quite another matter as a *name*. Nor do I approve of hyphenating native words, as is so frequently done. It is no easier to understand Mis-sis-sip-pi than Mississippi. My thanks are due to Mr. Thomas Moran, the distinguished painter, for the admirable sketch from nature he has so kindly permitted a reproduction of for a frontispiece. Mr. Moran has been identified as a painter of the Grand Canyon ever since 1873, when he went there with one of Powell's parties and made sketches from the end of the Kaibab Plateau which afterwards resulted in the splendid picture of the Grand Canyon now owned by the Government.

I am indebted to Prof. A. H. Thompson for the use of his river diary as a check upon my own, and also for many photographs now difficult to obtain; and to Dr. G. K. Gilbert, Mr. E. E. Howell, Dr. T. Mitchell Prudden, and Mr. Delancy Gill for the use of special photographs. Other debts in this line I acknowledge in each instance and hence will not repeat here. I had hoped to have an opportunity of again reading over the diary which "Jack" Sumner kept on the first Powell expedition, and which I have not seen since the time of the second expedition, but the serious illness of Major Powell prevented my requesting the use of it.

F. S. Dellenbaugh.

New York, October, 1902.

NOTE ON THE AUTHOR'S ITINERARY IN THE BASIN OF THE COLORADO RIVER AND ADJACENT TERRITORY

(Except where otherwise stated journeys were on horseback.)

1871—By boat from the Union Pacific Railway crossing of Green River, down the Green and Colorado to the mouth of the Paria, Lee's Ferry. Numerous side trips on foot. Lee's Ferry to House Rock Valley, and across north end of the Kaibab Plateau to the village of Kanab.

1872—Kanab to House Rock Valley and Paria Plateau. To Kanab. To southern part of Kaibab Plateau. To Kanab *via* Shinumo Canyon and Kanab Canyon. To Pipe Spring. To the Uinkaret Mountains and the Grand Canyon at the foot of the Toroweap Valley. To Berry Spring near St. George, along the edge of the Hurricane Ledge. To the Uinkaret Mountains *via* Diamond Butte. To the bottom of the Grand Canyon at the foot of the Toroweap. To Berry Spring *via* Diamond Butte and along the foot of the Hurricane Ledge. To St. George. To the Virgen Mountains and summit of Mt. Bangs. To Kanab *via* St. George. To the Aquarius Plateau *via* Potato Valley. To and across the Henry Mountains. To the Colorado at the mouth of Frémont River. By boat to the mouth of the Paria. To Kanab and return across the Kaibab. By boat down the Colorado to the mouth of the Kanab. To Kanab *via* the Kanab Canyon. To the Uinkaret Mountains. To Kanab *via* Pipe Spring.

1873—To Salt Lake City, *via* Long Valley and the Sevier River.

1875—To terminus of Utah Southern Railway, about at Spanish Forks, by rail. To Kanab *via* Sevier River and Upper

Kanab. To the Kaibab Plateau, De Motte Park, and the rim of the Grand Canyon. To the bottom of the Grand Canyon *via* Shinumo and Kanab Canyons. To Kanab *via* Kanab Canyon. To the Uinkaret Mountains *via* Pipe Spring and the Wild Band Pockets. To the Grand Canyon at the foot of the Toroweap.

1876—To St. George across the Uinkaret Plateau. To Las Vegas, Nevada, *via* Beaver Dam, Virgen River, the Muddy, and the desert. To St. George, by the desert and the old "St. Joe" road across the Beaver Dam Mountains. To the rim of the Grand Canyon, *via* Hidden Spring, the Copper Mine, and Mt. Dellenbaugh. To a red paint cave on the side of the canyon, about twenty-five hundred feet down. To St. George *via* same route. To Ivanpah, California, *via* the old desert road, the Muddy, Las Vegas, and Good Spring. To St. George *via* same route. To Kanab *via* Short Creek and Pipe Spring. To the Uinkaret Mountains *via* Pipe Spring and Antelope Valley. Across to the Shewits Plateau and to Ambush Waterpocket south of Mt. Dellenbaugh.¹ To the bottom of the Grand Canyon on the east side of the Shewits Plateau. To St. George *via* Mt. Dellenbaugh and Hidden Spring. To Kanab *via* Berry Spring and Pipe Spring. To Salt Lake City *via* Upper Kanab and the Sevier Valley.

1885—By rail to Ft. Wingate, New Mexico. By rail to Flagstaff. To Flagstaff *via* circuit of, and summit of, San Francisco Mountain and the Turkey Tanks. By rail to the Needles, California. By rail to Manuelito, New Mexico. To Ft. Defiance. By buckboard to Keam's Canyon. To the East Mesa of the Moki. To Keam's Canyon. By buckboard *via* Pueblo, Colorado, to Ft. Defiance. To the San Juan River at the "Four Corners," *via* Lukachukai Pass and the summit of the Carisso Mountains. To Ft. Defiance *via* the crest of the Tunicha Plateau. By buckboard to Keam's and to the East Mesa of the Moki. To Mishongnuvi and back.

---

¹ This waterpocket, which is a very large one, has, so far as I am aware, never had an English name and I do not know the Amerind one. I have called it "Ambush" because it was the place where three of Powell's men were shot by the Shewits in 1869.

By waggon to Keam's. To Oraibe *via* Tewa. To Keam's *via* Shimopavi and Tewa. To Holbrook by buckboard.

1899—By rail west across Green River Valley. By rail down Price River, east across Gunnison Valley, up Grand River, and over the Continental Divide.

CONTENTS

CHAPTER I

Contents

Contents

CHAPTER XIV

ILLUSTRATIONS

Illustrations

Illustrations xxiii

Illustrations

Illustrations

Illustrations

Illustrations

THE ROMANCE
OF THE COLORADO RIVER

CHAPTER I

The Secret of the Gulf—Ulloa (1539), One of the Captains of Cortes, Almost Solves it, but Turns Back without Discovering—Alarçon (1540) Conquers.

IN every country the great rivers have presented attractive pathways for interior exploration — gateways for settlement. Eventually they have grown to be highroads where the rich cargoes of development, profiting by favouring tides, floated to the outer world. Man, during all his wanderings in the struggle for subsistence, has universally found them his friends and allies. They have yielded to him as a conquering stranger; they have at last become for him foster-parents. Their verdant banks have sheltered and protected him; their skies have smiled upon his crops. With grateful memories, therefore, is clothed for us the sound of such river names as Thames, Danube, Hudson, Mississippi. Through the centuries their kindly waters have borne down ancestral argosies of profit without number, establishing thus the wealth and happiness of the people. Well have rivers been termed the "Arteries of Commerce"; well, also, may they be considered the binding links of civilisation.

Then, by contrast, it is all the more remarkable to meet with one great river which is none of these helpful things, but

which, on the contrary, is a veritable dragon, loud in its dangerous lair, defiant, fierce, opposing utility everywhere, refusing absolutely to be bridled by Commerce, perpetuating a
wilderness, prohibiting mankind's encroachments, and in its

In Glen Canyon.
Walls of homogeneous sandstone 1000 feet high.
Photograph by J. FENNEMORE, U. S. Colorado River Expedition.

immediate tide presenting a formidable host of snarling waters
whose angry roar, reverberating wildly league after league between giant rock-walls carved through the bowels of the earth,
heralds the impossibility of human conquest and smothers
hope.   From the tiny rivulets of its snowy birth to the fero-

Looking into the First Granite Gorge, Grand Canyon foot of Bright Angel Trail.
Canyon 300 miles long.   River 1000 feet below point of view.   Total depth between 5000
and 6000 feet.
Photograph by HALL.

cious tidal bore where it dies in the sea, it wages a ceaseless
battle as sublime as it is terrible and unique.

Such is the great Colorado River of the West, rising amidst
the fountains of the beautiful Wind River Mountains of
Wyoming, where also are brought forth the gentler Columbia
and the mighty, far-reaching Missouri. Whirling down ten
thousand feet in some two thousand miles, it meets the hot
level of the Red Sea, once the Sea of Cortes, now the Gulf of
California, in tumult and turmoil. In this long run it is cliff-
bound nine-tenths of the way, and the whole country drained
by it and its tributaries has been wrought by the waters and
winds of ages into multitudinous plateaus and canyons. The
canyons of its tributaries often rival in grandeur those of the
main stream itself, and the tributaries receive other canyons
equally magnificent, so that we see here a stupendous system
of gorges and tributary gorges, which, even now bewildering,
were to the early pioneer practically prohibitory. Water is the
master sculptor in this weird, wonderful land, yet one could
there die easily of thirst. Notwithstanding the gigantic work
accomplished, water, except on the river, is scarce. Often for
months the soil of the valleys and plains never feels rain; even
dew is unknown. In this arid region much of the vegetation
is set with thorns, and some of the animals are made to match
the vegetation. A knowledge of this forbidding area, now
robbed of some of its old terrors by the facilities in transportation, has been finally gained only by a long series of persistent
efforts, attended by dangers, privations, reverses, discourage-
ments, and disasters innumerable.

The Amerind,[1] the red man, roamed its wild valleys.
Some tribes built stone houses whose ruins are now found
overlooking its waters, even in the depths of the Grand Canyon
itself, or in the cliffs along the more accessible tributaries,
cultivating in the bottoms their crops. Lands were also tilled
along the extreme lower reaches, where the great rock-walls fall
back and alluvial soils border the stream. Here and there the
Amerind also crossed it, when occasion required, on the great

[1] This name is a substitute for the misnomer "Indian." Its use avoids
confusion.

5

The Inner Gorge of the Grand Canyon at the foot of Toroweap.

Depth from point of view about 3000 feet.   Total depth about 4500 feet.   Width about 3500 feet from brink to brink.
Negative 20x24 by J. K. HILLERS, U. S. Geol. Survey.

intertribal highways which are found in all districts, but it was neither one thing nor another to him.

So the river rolled on through its solemn canyons in primeval freedom, unvexed by the tampering and meddling of man. The Spaniards after the picturesque conquest of the luckless Aztecs, were eagerly searching for new fields of profitable battle, and then they dreamed of finding among the mysteries of the alluring northland, stretching so far away into the Unknown, a repetition of towns as populous, as wealthy in pure gold, as those of the valley of Mexico whose despoiled treasures had fired the cupidity of Europe and had crammed the strong boxes of the Spanish king. And there might be towns even richer! Who could say? An Amerind named Tejo, who belonged to Guzman when he was president of New Spain, that is, about 1530, told of journeys he had made

House Ruins on Cliff of Glen Canyon.
There were habitations also under the heavy top ledge.
Photograph by J. FENNEMORE, U. S. Geol. Survey.

with his father, when a boy, to trade in the far north where he saw very large villages like Mexico, especially seven large towns full of silver-workers, forty days' journey through the wilderness. This welcome story was fuel to the fire. Guzman organised a party and started for these wonderful seven cities, but numerous difficulties prevented the fulfilment of his plans, and caused a halt after traversing but a small portion of the distance. Cortes had now also returned from a visit to Spain, and he and

Guzman were at the point of the sword. Then shortly arrived from the north (1536), after incredible wanderings between the Mississippi and the Rio Grande, that man of wonderful endurance, Alvar Nuñez Cabeza de Vaca,[1] with his surviving companions, Dorantes, Maldonado, and Estevan. The latter, a negro, was afterwards very prominent by his connection with the fatal expedition sent out under the Friar Marcos to investigate the north country. The negro, if not the other men, gave a highly colored account of the lands they had traversed, and especially of what they had heard, so that more fuel was added to the fire, and the desire to explore the mysteries burned into execution. Cortes, harassed by his numerous enemies in Mexico and Spain, determined on a new effort to carry out his cherished plan of reaping further glories in the fascinating regions of the north so full of possibilities. There consequently sailed from Acapulco, July 8, 1539, a fleet of three vessels under Francisco de Ulloa. Cortes was prevented by circumstances from going with this expedition. After many difficulties Ulloa at length found himself at the very head of the Sea of Cortes in shallow water.

" And thus sailing [he writes] we always found more shallow water, and the sea thick, black, and very muddy, and came at length into five fathom water; and seeing this we determined to pass over to the land which we had seen on the other side, and here likewise we found as little depth or less, whereupon we rode all night in five fathom water, and we perceived the sea to run with so great a rage into the land that it was a thing much to be marvelled at; and with the like fury it returned back again with the ebb, during which time we found eleven fathom water, and the flood and ebb continued from five to six hours."

The next day

" the captain and the pilot went up to the ship's top and saw all the land full of sand in a great round compass and joining itself with the other shore; and it was so low that whereas we were a league

[1] For a full account of the experiences of Alvar Nuñez, see the translation of Buckingham Smith. Also Bandelier, *Contributions to the History of the Southwestern Portions of the United States.*

from the same we could not discern it, and it seemed there was an inlet of the mouths of certain lakes, whereby the sea went in and out. There were divers opinions amongst us, and some thought that that current entered into these lakes, and also that some great river there might be the cause thereof."[1]

This seems to have been the very first visit of Europeans to the mouth of the Colorado, but as Ulloa did not see the river, and only surmised that there might be one there, it cannot be considered in any way a discovery. It has been supposed by some that Friar Juan de la Asumpcion, in 1538, might have reached the Colorado in his deep river which he could not cross, but this river was more likely a branch of the Yaqui, for the friar was told that ten days beyond, to the north, there was another larger river settled by many people, whose houses had three stories, and whose villages were enclosed. This describes the Rio Grande and its southern settlements perfectly, so that, had he been on the Colorado, or even the Gila, the Rio Grande could not have been described as "ten days to the north." Ulloa took possession formally, according to Spanish custom, and then sailed southward again. Though he had not found the great river, he had determined one important geographical point: that Lower California was not, as had been supposed, an island, but was a peninsula; nevertheless for a full century thereafter it was considered an island. Had Ulloa followed up the rush of the current he would have been the discoverer of the Colorado River, but in spite of his marvelling at the fury of it he did not seem to consider an investigation worth while; or he may have been afraid of wrecking his ships. His inertia left it for a bolder man, who was soon in his wake. But the intrepid soul of Cortes must have been sorely disappointed at the meagre results of this, his last expedition, which had cost him a large sum, and compelled the pawning of his wife's jewels. The discovery of the mouth of a great river would have bestowed on this voyage a more romantic importance, and would consequently have been somewhat healing to his injured pride, if not to his depleted purse; but his sun was set-

---

[1] From Hakluyt's *Voyages*. The spelling has been modernised.

ting.   This voyage of Ulloa was its last expiring ray.   With
an artistic adjustment to the situation that seems remarkable,
Ulloa, after turning the end of the peninsula and sailing up the
Lower Californian coast, sent home one solitary vessel, and vanished then forever.   Financially wrecked, and exasperated to
the last degree by the slights and indignities of his enemies and
of the Mendoza government, Cortes left for Spain early in
1540 with the hope of retrieving his power by appearing in

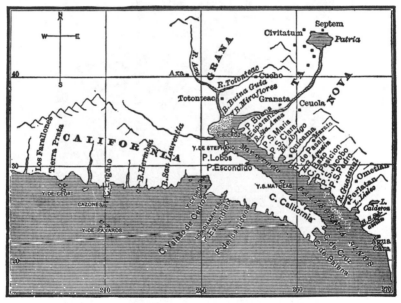

Wytfliet-Ptolemy Map of 1597.
From BANCROFT'S *History of Arizona and New Mexico.*

person before the monarch.   As in the case of Columbus, scant
satisfaction was his, and the end was that the gallant captain,
whose romantic career in the New World seems like a fairy
tale, never again saw the scene of his conquests.

Mendoza, the new viceroy of New Spain, a man of fine
character but utterly without sympathy for Cortes, and who
was instrumental in bringing about his downfall, now determined on an expedition of great magnitude: an expedition that

should proceed by both land and water to the wonderful Seven Cities of Cibola, believed to be rich beyond computation. The negro Estevan had lately been sent back to the marvellous northland he so glowingly described, guiding Marcos, the Franciscan monk of Savoyard birth, who was to investigate carefully, as far as possible, the glories recounted and speedily report. They were in the north about the same time (summer of 1539) that Ulloa was sailing up the Sea of Cortes. The

The Ancient Ruin on the Cliff.
Glen Canyon.
Photograph by J. FENNEMORE, U. S. Colo. Riv. Exp.

negro, who had by arrangement proceeded there some days in advance of Marcos, was killed at the first Pueblo village, and Marcos, afraid of his life, and before he had seen anything of the wonderful cities except a frightened glimpse from a distant hill, beat a precipitate retreat to New Galicia, the province just north of New Spain, and of which Francis Vasquez de Coronado had recently been made governor. Here he astonished Coronado with a description of the vast wealth and beauty of the Seven Cities of Cibola; a description that does credit to his powers of imagination. Coronado lost no time in accompanying Marcos to Mexico, where a conference with Mendoza resulted in the promotion of the monk, and the immediate organisation of the great expedition mentioned. Coronado was made general of the land forces, and Hernando de Alarçon was placed in charge of the ships. Having a land march to make Coronado, started in February, 1540, while Alarçon sailed in May. Coronado proceeded to San Miguel de Culiacan, the last settlement toward the north, near the coast, whence he took a direction slightly east of north.

Alarçon, with his ships the *San Pedro* and the *Santa Catalina*, laid a course for the haven of Sant Iago. They were caught in a severe storm which so greatly frightened the men on the *Santa Catalina*, "more afraid than was need," remarks Alarçon, that they cast overboard nine pieces of ordnance, two anchors, one cable, and "many other things as needful for the enterprise wherein we went as the ship itself." At Sant Iago he repaired his losses, took on stores and some members of his company, and sailed for Aguaiauall, the seaport of San Miguel de Culiacan, where Coronado was to turn his back on the outposts of civilisation. The general had already gone when Alarçon arrived, but they expected to hold communication with each other, if not actually to meet, farther on; and it seems from this that they must have felt confidence in finding a river by which Alarçon might sail into the interior. As early as 1531 there were vague reports of a large river, the mouth of which was closed by the Amerinds living there by means of a huge cable stretched across from side to side. There may also have been other rumours of a large river besides the surmises of the Ulloa party. At any rate, Alarçon and Coronado fully expected to be in touch much of the time. This expectation appears absurd to us now when we understand the geography, but there was nothing out of the way about the supposition at that time. As it happened, the two divisions never met, nor were they able to communicate even once. So far as rendering Coronado any assistance was concerned, Alarçon might as well have been on the coast of Africa. The farther they proceeded

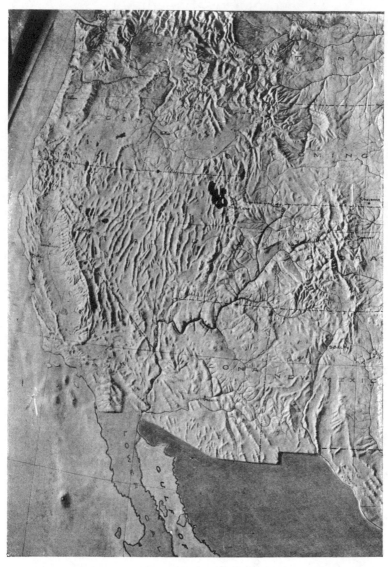

Western Part United States.
Relief map by E. E. Howell.

12

the farther apart they were, but Alarçon kept a constant and faithful lookout for the other party the whole time, never losing an opportunity to inquire its whereabouts.

Coronado had left a well-provisioned ship, the *San Gabriel*, at Aguaiauall, for Alarçon to bring along. These supplies were for the use of the army when the two parties should meet

Gulf of California at the Mouth of the Colorado.
Photograph by DELANCY GILL.

in the north from time to time. Alarçon added the vessel to his fleet and proceeded along up the coast, keeping as near the land as the water would permit, and constantly on the lookout for signals from the other party, or for Amerinds who might be able to give information concerning the position of the general. Thus, at last, he came to the very head of the gulf where Ulloa had wondered at the rush of waters and had turned away without investigation. "And when we were come," he says,

"to the flats and shoals from whence the aforesaid fleet returned, it seemed to me, as to the rest, that we had the firm
land before us, and that those shoals were so perilous and fearful that it was a thing to be considered whether with our skiffs
we could enter in among them: and the pilots and the rest of
the company would have had us do as Captain Ulloa did, and
have returned back again." But Alarçon was not of a retreat-
ing disposition; the fierce Colorado had now met its first conqueror. It must be remembered, for Ulloa's sake, that there
was not the same incentive for him to risk his ships and the
lives of his men in an attempt to examine the shoals and currents of this dangerous place. Alarçon was looking for and
expecting to meet Coronado at any time. He knew that Coronado was depending on the supplies carried by the *San
Gabriel*, and it would have been rank cowardice on the part of
Alarçon to have backed out at the first difficulty. But he had
no intention of retiring from the contest, for he says:

" But because your Lordship commanded me that I should bring
you the secret of that gulf, I resolved that although I had known
I should have lost the ships, I would not have ceased for anything
to have seen the head thereof, and therefore I commanded Nicolas
Zamorano, Pilot Major, and Dominico del Castello that each of them
should take a boat, and lead in their hands, and run in among those
shoals, to see if they could find out a channel whereby the ships
might enter in ; to whom it seemed that the ships might sail up
higher (although with great travail and danger), and in this sort I
and he began to follow our way which they had taken, and within
a short while after we found ourselves fast on the sands with all our
three ships, in such sort that one could not help another, neither could
the boats succour us because the current was so great that it was
impossible for one of us to come to another. Whereupon we were
in such great jeopardy that the deck of the Admiral was oftentimes
under water ; and if a great surge of the sea had not come and
driven our ship right up and gave her leave, as it were, to breathe
awhile, we had there been drowned ; and likewise the other two
ships found themselves in very great hazard, yet because they were
lesser and drew less water their danger was not so great as ours.
Now it pleased God upon the return of the flood that the ships

15

Alarçon's Ships Struggling With the Great Bore of the Colorado—1540.
Drawing by F. S. DELLENBAUGH.

came on float, and so we went forward. And although the company would have returned back, yet for all this I determined to go forward and to pursue our attempted voyage. And we passed forward with much ado, turning our stems now this way, now that way, to seek and find the channel. And it pleased God that after this sort we came to the very bottom of the bay, where we found a very mighty river, which ran with so great fury of a stream, that we could hardly sail against it."

Here, then, began the acquaintance between the European and the river now known as the Colorado of the West. The experience of Alarçon was immediately typical of much that was to follow in the centuries of endeavour to arrive at an intimate knowledge of this savage torrent.

CHAPTER II

The Unknown River—Alarçon Ascends it Eighty-five Leagues and Names it the Rio de Buena Guia—Melchior Diaz Arrives at its Banks Later and Calls it the Rio del Tizon—Cardenas Discovers the Grand Canyon.

HAVING triumphed over the fierce tidal bore which renders the mouth of the Colorado dangerous, Alarçon secured a safe anchorage for his vessels and began immediate preparations for following up the river into the distant interior, both to gain a knowledge of it and to seek for information of the position of Coronado. Leaving one of his small boats for the use of those who remained in charge of the ships, he took the other two, and, placing in them some light cannon, prepared them as well as he could for any emergency that might be encountered. His party consisted of twenty soldiers, sailors, and helpers, besides his treasurer, Rodrigo Maldonado, and Gaspar de Castilleia, comptroller. Alarçon possessed the qualities of a successful explorer. He was bold yet cautious, determined but not reckless, with safe judgment and quick adaptability. His first command was that, no matter what happened in case of meeting with natives, all his company were to remain silent and inactive. With this wise provision, which kept the control in his own hands, the party left the ships behind on Thursday, August 26th [1] (1540), apparently the same day as the arrival. The current was so strong that the men were obliged to tow the boats from the bank, rendering progress slow and difficult, but nevertheless they were able, before night and fatigue compelled a halt, to advance about six leagues. Though constantly on the lookout for natives in the wide barren stretches of lowland on each side of the river, none were seen till early next

[1] Hakluyt gives "25th," but it is a misprint, as this Thursday in 1540 was the 26th.

morning, when, soon after starting, a number of huts were discovered near the river bank.   The occupants rushed forth in
great excitement at the sudden appearance of these singular-
looking people in their equally singular boats, and no wonder!
Years and the ages had slipped away and never yet had any
people but their own kind appeared on their horizon.   Opposition was the natural impulse, and they signed for the Spaniards
to go back, threatening attack.   The effect of this on Alarçon
was a command to anchor the boats out of reach in the middle

Native Ladies of the Lower Colorado.

of the river, though the rapidly
augmenting numbers of the
people on the shore soon inspired the others of the expedition with a desire to beat a retreat
towards the ships.   Alarçon,
however, was not of this mind.
The natives were, of course,
armed only with the bow-and-
arrow and similar primitive
weapons, while the Spaniards,
though few in number, possessed the advantage of firearms,
of which the natives had no
comprehension whatever.   The
interpreter, being a native from
down the coast, understood not
a word of this language, but the
presence among the strangers
of one of their own kind some-
what pacified the natives, and Alarçon did all he could by
signs to express his peaceful intentions, throwing his arms to
the bottom of the boat and putting his foot on them, at the
same time ordering the boats to be placed nearer shore.   After
much manœuvring they finally brought about some trifling intercourse and then proceeded up the river, the natives following along the shore.   Repeatedly they signalled for the
Spaniards to land, but Alarçon, fearful of treachery, declined,
and spent the night in the middle of the stream.   Nor was the

appearance of the natives reassuring, for they had their faces hideously painted, some all over and others only half, while still others carried painted masks before them. In their nostrils they wore pendants, and their ears were pierced with holes wherein they hung bones and shells. Their only clothing was a sort of girdle around the waist.

Gradually, intercourse increased, and presents of trinkets seemed to incline all the natives in Alarçon's favour. At length he discovered that they reverenced the sun, and without compunction he proclaimed that he came from that orb. This deception served him well. Henceforth no service was too great for the natives to perform for these sacred beings. Everything was placed at their disposal. Alarçon's word was their law. They relieved the men entirely of the wearisome task of towing the boats, striving with each other for the privilege.

Freaks of Erosion.

Without this help it would have been impossible for Alarçon to have proceeded far up the river, and he fully appreciated this, though the chief reward bestowed on the helpers and all the natives was crosses made of sticks and of paper. These, he informed them by signs, were precious, and he distributed them in large numbers. The morning after he proclaimed himself as coming from the sun, many swam out to

20   One of the Cocopa Giants.   Height, 6 feet, 4 inches.
         The costume in early days was " nothing."
              Photograph by DELANCY GILL.

where the boat was anchored, contending for the privilege of securing the rope with which the boat was towed. "And we gave it to them," says Alarçon, ".with a good will, thanking God for the good provision which He gave us to go up the river."

The interpreter frequently addressed the natives as he went forward, and at last, on Tuesday night, a man was discovered who understood him. This man was taken into the boat, and Alarçon, always true to his trust, asked him whether he had seen or heard of any people in the country like himself, hoping to secure some clue to Coronado. "He answered me no, saying that he had some time heard of old men that very far from that country there were other white men, and with beards like us, and that he knew nothing else. I asked him also whether he knew a place called Cibola and a river called Totonteac, and he answered me no."

Komohoats.
A Pai Ute Boy—S. W. Nevada.
Photograph by J. K. Hillers, U. S. Geol. Sur.

Coronado meanwhile had arrived at Cibola on July 7th (or 10th) and had therefore been among the villages of the Rio Grande del Norte nearly two months. The route to these towns from the lower Colorado, that is, by the great inter-tribal highway of southern Arizona, followed the Gila River, destined afterwards to be traversed by the wandering trappers, by the weary gold-seeker bound for California, and finally, for a considerable distance, by the steam locomotive. But it was an unknown quantity at the time of Alarçon's visit, so far as

white men were concerned.   Farther up, Alarçon met with another man who understood his interpreter, and this man said
he had been to Cibola, or Cevola,[1] as Alarçon writes it, and
that it was a month's journey, "by a path that went along that
river."   Alarçon must now have been about at the mouth of the
Gila, and the river referred to was, of course, the Gila.   This
man described the towns of Cibola as all who had seen them
described them; that is, large towns of three- or four-storey
houses, with windows on the sides,[2] and encompassed by walls
some seven or eight feet in height.   The pueblos of the Rio
Grande valley were well known in every direction and for long
distances.   The Apaches, harassing the villagers on every side,
and having themselves a wide range, alone carried the knowledge of them to the four winds.   In every tribe, too, there are
born travellers who constantly visit distant regions, bringing
back detailed descriptions of their adventures and the sights
beheld, with which to regale an admiring crowd during the
winter evenings.   Their descriptions are usually fairly accurate
from the standpoint of their own understanding.   In this case
the native gave a good description of the Cibola towns, and
the Tusayan people had meanwhile given Cardenas a description of these very natives on the lower Colorado.   A day or
two later Alarçon received further information of Cibola, and
this informant told about a chief who had four green earthen
plates like Alarçon's, except in color, and also a dog like Alarçon's, as well as other things, which a black man had brought
into the country.   This black man was Estevan, who had been
killed about a year before.   The news of this man and his execution had travelled rapidly, showing frequent intercourse
with the pueblos beyond the mountains.   Still farther on he
met another man who had been at Cibola, and who also told
him of a great river in which there were crocodiles.   This was

---

[1] The old Spaniards used "v" and "b" interchangeably, so that Cibola and
Cevola would be pronounced the same.   Other letters were used in the same loose
way.

[2] Windows on the sides of the houses, *not* of the *walls*, as one writer has put it.
The villages of the lower part of New Mexico had these walls of circumvallation,
but to the northward such walls appear to have been rare.

the Mississippi, of course, and the crocodiles were alligators. As Alarçon had never seen an alligator he took the description to mean crocodile. A little farther and he heard of the negro Estevan again and the reason why the Cibolans had killed him, which was to prevent the Spaniards, whom he described, from finding their way into the Cibola country. This man also described the bison and a people who lived in painted tents in summer and in winter in houses of wood two or three storeys high. And thus the expedition continued up the river, inquiring as they went on all subjects. On September 6th the old man who had been a particular friend and interpreter was called on shore by the natives, and there was immediately an animated discussion which Alarçon discovered related to himself. Information had come from Cibola that there were there men like these Spaniards who said they were Christians. These had been warlike, and it was proposed to kill all of Alarçon's party to prevent the others from gaining a knowledge of this country. But the old man declared Alarçon to be the son of the sun and took his part. Finally it was decided to ask him whether he were a Christian or the son of the sun. Alarçon pretended great wonder at men like himself being at Cibola, but they assured him it was true, as two men who had come from there reported that they had beards and guns and swords just the same. Alarçon still insisted that he was the son of the sun. They said the men at Cibola said the same, to which Alarçon replied that it might well be, and if so they need have no fear, for the sons of the sun would be his brothers and would treat them as he had done. This seemed to pacify them. He inquired now how far it was to Cibola, and they answered ten days through an uninhabited country, with no account of the rest of the way because it was inhabited.

Alarçon was now more than ever desirous of informing Coronado of his whereabouts, and tried to persuade some of his men to go to Cibola with a message, promising fine rewards. Only one, a negro slave, and he with reluctance, offered to attempt the journey. Alarçon tried to get the old man to give him guides and provisions, but without success, as the old man seemed to desire to induce Alarçon to help them fight their battles with the Cumanas, saying, if he would end this war, he could have their company to Cibola. Alarçon was determined to go, and sent a man back to the ships to inform those there of his purpose, but he changed his mind soon after, concluding to go to the ships himself and return, leaving there his sick, and rearranging his company. The man who had been sent to the ships overland was overtaken and brought back by the natives, but was obliged to remain with them till Alarçon came up

Professor McGee and a Group of Cocopas.
Originally the Cocopas wore no clothing.
Photograph by DELANCY GILL.

again. The descent from here was made in two and a half days, though it had taken fifteen to come up. Arriving at the ships all was found to have gone well except a few minor accidents, and, directing repairs to be made, Alarçon turned about and started up-river once more, first calling the whole company together, telling them what he had learned of Cibola, and that, as Coronado might now have been informed by natives of his presence, he hoped to find means of reaching him. There was much objection to this plan, but he proceeded to carry it out, taking all three boats this time, loaded with "wares of exchange, with corn and other seeds, with hens and cocks of Castile." This region he called the Province of Campanna de la Cruz, and he left orders for the building of an oratory or chapel to be named the Chapel of Our Lady de la Buena Guia. The river he called the Rio de Buena Guia (good guidance) from the motto on the viceroy Mendoza's coat of arms. It was Tuesday, the 14th of September, when he started, taking with him Nicolas Zamorano, chief pilot, to record the latitudes. He soon arrived again among the Quicomas,[1] and then among the Coamas, where he found his man who had been left behind on the first trip. This man had been so well treated that he was entirely content to remain till the party should come back down the river. This was the highest point reached on the first visit. Everywhere the people were treasuring the crosses which had been given them, kneeling before them at sunrise. Alarçon kept on up the river till he "entered between certain very high mountains, through which this river passeth with a straight channel, and the boats went up against the stream very hardly for want of men to draw the same." From this it may be inferred that the Coamas did not strive with each other for the privilege of towing the boats of these children of the sun as those below had done. Now an enchanter from the Cumanas tried to destroy the party by setting magic reeds in the water on both sides, but the spell failed and the explorers went on to the home of the old man who had been so good a friend and guide to them. At this, Alarçon's farthest point, he caused a very high cross to be erected, on which words were carved to the effect that he had reached the place, so that if Coronado's men chanced to come that way they might see it. Nothing is said about burying letters, yet Diaz later mentions finding letters buried at the foot of a tree, apparently nearer the sea. Deciding that he could not at this time accomplish

---

[1] The tribes and bands spoken of by Alarçon cannot be identified, but these Quicomas, or Quicamas, were doubtless the same as the Quiquimas mentioned by Kino, 1701, and Garces, 1775. They were probably of Yuman stock. The Cumanas were possibly Mohaves.

The Colorado at the Junction of the Gila.

Looking up stream—Gila right hand lower corner. Colorado about 500 yards wide.

Photograph by DELANCY GILL.

his purpose of opening communication with the army, Alarçon
concluded to return to the ships, but with the intention of trying once more. The second day after starting down he arrived
at the place where the Spaniard had remained. He told him
that he had gone "above thirty leagues into the country" beyond. It had taken him, before, two and a half days to reach
the river mouth from here, so that it seems he was about four
days going down from his farthest point. Roughly estimating
his progress at six miles an hour for twelve hours a day, in four
days the distance covered would be about 288 miles. He says
he went up eighty-five leagues (this would be fifty-five the first
time and thirty more the second), which, counting in Mexican
leagues of two and three quarter miles each, gives a distance of
233¾ miles, or about one hundred miles above the mouth of the
Gila. This stream he does not mention. He may have taken
it for a mere bayou, but it appears to be certain that he passed
beyond it. He says Ulloa was mistaken by two degrees as to
his northernmost point, and that he sailed four degrees beyond
him. The meaning of this may be that he went four degrees
beyond Ulloa's false reckoning, or actually two degrees above
the shoals where Ulloa turned back. This would take him
to the 34th parallel, and would coincide with his eighty-five
leagues, and also with the position of the first mountains met
with in going up the river, the Chocolate range. Alarçon was
not so inexperienced that he would have represented eighty-
five leagues on the course of the river as equalling four degrees
of latitude. Had he gone to the 36th degree he would have
passed through Black Canyon, and this is so extraordinary a
feature that he could not have failed to note it specially.
When Alarçon arrived at the ships again he evidently had
strong reason for abandoning his intention of returning for
another attempt to communicate with Coronado, and he set
sail for home. Another document says the torredo was de-
stroying the ships, and this is very probable. He coasted
down the gulf, landing frequently, and going long distances
into the interior searching for news of Coronado, but he
learned nothing beyond what he heard on the river.

While he was striving to find a way of reaching the main

body of the expedition, which during this time was compla-
cently robbing the Puebloans on the Rio Grande, two officers
of that expedition were marching through the wilderness endeavouring to find him, and a third was travelling toward the
Grand Canyon.　One of these was Don Rodrigo Maldonado,
thus bearing exactly the same name as one of Alarçon's officers; another was Captain Melchior Diaz, and the third Don
Lopez de Cardenas, who distinguished himself on the Rio
Grande by particular brutality toward the villagers.　Don
Rodrigo went in search of the ships down the river to the coast
from the valley of Corazones, but obtained no information of
them, though he met with giant natives and brought back with
him one very tall man as a specimen.　The main army of Coronado had not yet gone from this valley of Corazones, where
the settlement called San Hieronimo had been established, and
the best man in it reached only to the chest of this native
giant.

　　The army moved on to another valley, where a halt was
made to await orders from the general.　At length, about the
middle of September, Melchior Diaz came back from Cibola,
with dispatches, accompanied by Juan Gallegos, who bore a
message for the viceroy.　In their company also was the miserable Friar Marcos, pursuing his dismal return to New Spain
by direction of the general, who considered it unsafe for him to
remain with the army now that the glorious bubble of his imagination had been exploded.　Melchior Diaz was an excellent
officer, and already had an experience in this northern region
extending over some four years.　It was he, also, who had
been sent, the previous November, as far as the place called
Chichilticalli, in an attempt to verify the friar's tale, and had
reported that the natives were good for nothing except to
make into Christians.　The main army, which was in command
of Don Tristan de Arellano, in accordance with the orders received from Coronado, now advanced toward Cibola.　Maldonado, who had been to the coast, went with it.　Diaz retained
eighty men, part of whom were to defend the settlement of
San Hieronimo, and twenty-five were to accompany him on his
expedition in search of Alarçon.　He started north and then

went west, following native guides for 150 leagues (412½ miles) in all, and at length reached a country inhabited by giant natives who, in order to keep warm in the chill autumn air, carried about with them a firebrand. From this circumstance, Diaz called the large river he found here the Rio del Tizon.

An Arizona Landscape.
There are Navajo Gardens in the bottom of this canyon.
Photograph by E. O. BEAMAN.

This was the Buena Guia of Alarçon. The natives were prodigiously strong, one man being able to lift and carry with ease on his head a heavy log which six of the soldiers could not transport to the camp. Here Diaz heard that boats had come up the river to a point three days' journey below, and he went there to find out about it, doubtless expecting to get on the track of Alarçon. But the latter had departed from the mouth

of the river at least two or three weeks before; one writer says
two months.[1] The same writer states that Diaz reached the
river thirty leagues above the mouth, and that Alarçon went
as far again above. This coincides very well with Alarçon's
estimate of eighty-five leagues, for Diaz did not follow the
windings of the stream as Alarçon was forced to do with his

Cocopa Tule Raft.
Photograph by DELANCY GILL.

boats. At the place down the river, Diaz found a tree bearing
an inscription: "Alarçon reached this point; there are letters
at the foot of this tree." Alarçon does not, as before noted,
mention burying letters, and these were found at the foot of a

[1] *Relacion del Suceso.* Alarçon must have reached his highest point about
October 5th or 6th, and the ships on the return about the 10th. Diaz probably
arrived at the river about November 1st.

tree, so that Diaz evidently failed to reach the cross erected at Alarçon's highest point.

Diaz now proceeded up the river again, looking for a place where he could safely cross to explore the country on the opposite side. After ascending from the spot where he found the letters for five or six days, he concluded they could cross by means of rafts. In the construction of these rafts he invited the help of the natives of the neighbourhood. He was probably up near the Chocolate Mountains and the Cumanas, who were hostile to Alarçon, and whose sorcerer had attempted to destroy him by means of the magic reeds. They had been merely waiting for an opportunity to attack Diaz, and they perceived their chance in this assistance in crossing the river. They readily agreed to help make the rafts, and even to assist in the crossing. But while the work was in progress a soldier who had gone out from the camp was surprised to observe a large number of them stealing off to a mountain on the other side. When he reported this, Diaz caused one of the natives to be secured, without the others being aware of it. He was tortured till he confessed that the plan was to begin the attack when some of the Spaniards were across the river, some in the water, and the others on the near bank. Thus separated they believed they could easily be destroyed. The native, as a reward for this valuable confession, was secretly killed, and that night, with a heavy weight tied to him, was cast into the deep water. But the others evidently suspected the trick, for the next day they showered arrows upon the camp. The Spaniards pursued them and by means of their superior arms soon drove them into the mountains. Diaz was then able to cross without molestation, his faithful Amerind allies of another tribe assisting.

Alarçon had conveyed in his letters the nature of the gulf and coast, so Diaz struck westward to see what he could find in that direction. The country was desolate and forbidding, in places the sand being like hot ashes and the earth trembling. Four days of this satisfied them, and the captain concluded to return to San Hieronimo. The subsequent fate of Diaz is another illustration of how a man may go the world round, escaping many great dangers, and then be annihilated by a simple accident that would seem impossible. A dog belonging to the camp pursued the little flock of sheep that had been driven along to supply the men with meat, and Diaz on his horse dashed toward it, at the same time hurling a spear. The spear stuck up in the ground instead of striking the dog, and the butt penetrated the captain's abdomen, inflicting, under the conditions, a mortal wound. The men could do nothing for him except to carry him along, which for twenty days they did, fighting hostile natives all the time. Then he died. On the 18th of January they arrived without their leader at the settlement from which they had started some three months before.

Cardenas with twelve men had meanwhile gone from Cibola to a place called Tusayan, or Tucano, situated some twenty or twenty-five leagues north-westerly from Cibola, from whence he was to strike out toward the great river these natives had described to Don Pedro de Tobar, who recently had paid them a visit, and incidentally shot a few of them to invite submission. Cardenas was kindly received by the people of Tusayan, who readily supplied him with guides. Having lived in the country for centuries, they of course knew it and the many trails very well. They knew the highway down the Gila to the Colorado, and they told Cardenas about the tall natives living on the lower part of it, the same whom Alarçon and Diaz had met. In the direction in which Cardenas was to go they said it was twenty days' journey through an unpopulated country, when people would again be met with. After the party had travelled for twenty days they arrived at a great canyon of the Colorado River, apparently not having met with the people mentioned. If Cardenas started from the Moki towns, as has generally been believed, where would he have arrived by a journey of twenty days, when an able-bodied man can easily walk to the brink of Marble Canyon from there in three or four days? Why did the guides, if they belonged in the Moki towns, conduct Cardenas so far to show him a river which was so near? The solution seems to be that he started from some locality other than the present Moki towns. That is to say,

The Grand Canyon from Bright Angel Hotel.
12 miles to opposite rim.
Total depth here between 5000 and 6000 feet.
Photograph by HALL.

there has been an error, and these Moki towns are not Tusayan.   Where Cardenas reached the great canyon the river came
from the *north-east* and turned to the *south-south-west*.   There
are but two places where the canyoned river in Arizona con-
forms to this course, one at Lee's Ferry, and the other the
stretch from Diamond Creek to the Kanab Canyon.   The
walls being low at Lee's Ferry, that locality may be excluded,
for where Cardenas first looked into the canyon it was so deep
that the river appeared like a brook, though the natives declared it to be half a league wide.   Three of the most agile
men, after the party had followed along the rim for three days
hunting for a favourable place, tried to descend to the water,
but were unable to go more than one-third of the way.   Yet
from the place they reached, the stream looked very large, and
buttes that from above seemed no higher than a man were
found to be taller than the great tower of Seville.   There can
be no doubt that this was the gorge we now call the Grand
Canyon.   No other answers the description.   Cardenas said
the width at the top, that is, the "outer" gorge with its
broken line, was three or four leagues or more in an air line.[1]
This is the case at both great bends of the river.   The point
he reached has usually been put, without definite reason, at
about opposite Bright Angel River, say near the letter "L" of
the word "Colorado" on the relief map, page 41 *op.*, but here
the river comes from the *south-east* and turns to the *north-west*,
directly the reverse of what Cardenas observed.   The actual
place then must have been about midway of the stretch referred
to, that is, near the letter "A" of the word "Cañon" on the
relief map.   Where he started from to arrive at this part of
the canyon cannot be discussed here for want of space, but the
writer believes the place was some three hundred miles south-
east, say near Four Peaks on the new Mexican line.[2]   Cardenas

[1] " A las barrancas del rio que puestos a el bado [lado?] de ellas parecia al
otro bordo que auia mas de tres o quatro leguas por el ayre."—Castañeda, in
Winship's monograph, *Fourteenth Ann. Rep. Bureau of Ethnology*, p. 429.

[2] For the author's views on Coronado's route see the *Bulletin* of the American
Geographical Society, December, 1897.   Those views have been confirmed by
later study, the only change being the shifting of Cibola from the Florida Mountains north-westerly to the region of the Gila, perhaps near old Fort West.

was, therefore, guided along the southerly edge of the great Colorado Plateau, through the superb Coconino Forest, where he had wood, water, and grass in abundance. The locality he reached was very dry, and they were obliged to go each night a long distance back from the brink to procure water. For this reason, Cardenas gave up trying to follow the canyon, and returned again, by way of Tusayan, to Cibola, passing on the way a waterfall, which possibly was in the Havasupai (Cataract) Canyon. Castañeda, the chief chronicler of the Coronado expedition, says the river Cardenas found was the Tizon, "much nearer its source than where Melchior Diaz crossed it," thus showing that its identity was well surmised, if not understood, at that time. Nothing, however, was known of its upper course; at least there is no evidence of any such knowledge, though the natives had doubtless given the Spaniards some information regarding it. The special record of the Cardenas expedition was kept by one Pedro de Sotomayor, but it has apparently never been seen in modern times. It is probably in the archives of Spain or Mexico, and its discovery would throw needed light on the location of Tusayan and the course Cardenas followed.[1] The distance of this whole region from a convenient base of supplies, and its repellent character, prevented further operations at this period, and when these explorers traced their disappointed way homeward, the Colorado was not seen again by white men for over half a century; and it was more than two hundred years before European eyes again looked upon the Grand Canyon.

Coronado proceeded eastward to about the western line of Missouri, and, finding colonisation anywhere in the regions visited out of the question, he returned in 1542 to Mexico, with his entire army excepting a couple of padres.

[1] It may be noted here with reference to the location of Cibola, Tiguex, Tusayan, etc., that too much heretofore has been *assumed*. The explanations presented are often very lame and unsatisfactory when critically examined. So many writers are now committed to the errors on this subject that it will be a hard matter to arrive at the truth.

CHAPTER III

The Grand Canyon—Character of the Colorado River—The Water-Gods ; Erosion and Corrasion — The Natives and their Highways — The " Green River Valley" of the Old Trappers—The Strange Vegetation and Some Singular Animals.

THE stupendous chasm known as the Grand Canyon, discovered by Cardenas in the autumn of 1540, is the most remarkable feature of this extraordinary river, and at the same time is one of the marvels of the world. Though discovered so long ago that we make friends with the conquistadores when we approach its history, it remained, with the other canyons of the river, a problem for 329 years thereafter, that is, till 1869. Discovery does not mean knowledge, and knowledge does not mean publicity. In the case of this gorge, with its immense length and countless tributary chasms, the view Cardenas obtained was akin to a dog's discovery of the moon. It has practically been several times re-discovered. Indeed, each person who first looks into the abyss has a sensation of being a discoverer, for the scene is so weird and lonely and so incomprehensible in its novelty that one feels that it could never have been viewed before. And it *is* rather a discovery for each individual, because no amount of verbal or pictorial description can ever fully prepare the spectator for the sublime reality. Even when one becomes familiar with the incomparable spectacle it never ceases to astonish. A recent writer has well said : "The sublimity of the Pyramids is endurable, but at the rim of the Grand Canyon we feel outdone." [1] Outdone is exactly the right word. Nowhere else can man's insignificance be so

[1] Harriet Monroe, *Atlantic Monthly*, June, 1902.

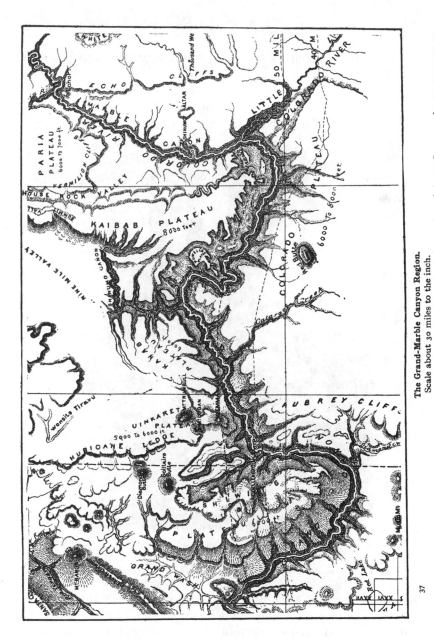

The Grand-Marble Canyon Region.
Scale about 30 miles to the inch.
This is not as accurate as the map opposite page 41, but is given as an aid to the understanding of that. Compare also map on page 12.

37

burned into his soul as here, where his ingenuity and power
count for naught.

Cardenas, after all, was only one of the discoverers. He was
merely the first *white* man who saw it. When was it that the
first *man* recoiled from the edge of that then actually unknown

The Work of Erosion.
The Witch of Endor and Cerberus.
Photograph by J. K. HILLERS, U. S. Geol. Survey.

masterpiece of the Water-gods, who so persistently plied their
tools in the forgotten ages? He was the real discoverer and he
will never be known. As applied to new countries—new to
our race—the term "unknown" is relative. Each fresh explorer considers his the deed that shall permanently be re-

corded, no matter who has gone before, and the Patties and the Jedediah Smiths are forgotten. In these later years some who have dared the terrors of the merciless river in the Grand Canyon spoke of it as the "Great Unknown," forgetting the

The Work of Corrasion.

Parunuweap Canyon of the Virgen River, Southern Utah.   20 to 30
feet wide and 1500 feet deep and 18 miles long.
Photograph by J. K. HILLERS, U. S. Geol. Survey.

deed of Powell; and when Lieutenant Wheeler laboriously succeeded in dragging his boats up to the mouth of Diamond Creek, he said: "*Now* the exploration is completed." *He* forgot the deed of Powell. A recent writer mentions the north-

western corner of Arizona as a "mysterious wilderness." [1] He
forgot that it was thoroughly explored years ago.   Wilderness
it may be, if that means sparsely settled, but mysterious?—no.
It is all known and on record.

The Grand Canyon may be likened to an inverted mountain
range.   Imagine a great mountain chain cast upside down in
plaster.   Then all the former ridges and spurs of the range
become tributary canyons and gulches running back twenty or
thirty miles into the surrounding country, growing shallower
and shallower as the distance increases from the central core,
just as the great spurs and ridges of a mountain range, descending, melt finally into the plain.   Often there are parts where
the central gorge is narrow and precipitous, just as a mountain
range frequently possesses mighty precipices.   But it is an
error to think of great canyons as mere slits in the ground,
dark and gloomy, like a deep well from whose depths stars
may be sighted at midday.   Minor canyons sometimes approach this character, as, for example, the canyon of the upper
Virgen, called Parunuweap, fifteen hundred feet deep and no
more than twenty to thirty feet wide, with vertical walls, but I
have never been in a canyon from which stars were visible in
daylight, nor have I ever known anyone who had.   The light
is about the same as that at the bottom of a narrow street
flanked by very high buildings.   The walls may sometimes be
gloomy from their colour, or may seem so from the circumstances under which one views them, but aside from the fact
that any deep, shut-in valley or canyon may become oppressive,
there is nothing specially gloomy about a deep canyon.   The
sun usually falls more or less in every canyon, no matter how
narrow or deep.   It may fall to the very bottom most of the
day, or only for an hour or two, depending on the trend of
the canyon with reference to the sun's course.   At the bottom
of the Kanab where it joins the Grand, the sunlight in November remains in the bottom just two hours, but outside in the
main gorge the time is very much longer.

The walls of a great canyon, and usually a small one, are terraced; seldom are they wholly vertical for their entire height,

[1] Ray Stannard Baker, *Century Magazine*, May, 1902.

The Grand Cañon and Terrace Plateau Region.

This covers an area in Southern Utah and Northern Arizona 144 miles square, containing more marvels than any other part of the globe of equal extent. In the lower right-hand corner are the Yosemite Valley and the Gorge of Niagara on the same scale. The scale of this reduction is about 14 miles to one inch. The vertical and horizontal scales are the same. The black ribbon on the left at Virgen and Beaver Dam Mountains is to represent Archean formation. The Shiwits Plateau and Uinkaret Mts. are basaltic. The Kaibab and the Colorado Plateau are Carboniferous. Paria Plateau and Vermilion Cliffs are Triassic. The Markagunt and Paunsagunt Plateaus are Tertiary. Cardenas reached the canyon about at letter "A" of the word "Cañon." Tourists now come to the river about half way between the letters "L" and "O" of the word "Colorado." The largest settlement is the charming little Mormon city of St. George, on the Virgen, north of the letter "A" of the word "Arizona." Grand and Marble Canyons form a continuous gorge about 300 miles long, a complete barrier to travel for this distance as its walls are precipitous and reach a height of between 5000 and 6000 feet—4000 being about the average. The lowest portion is toward Lee's Ferry, upper right-hand side of the map, where the walls begin at a couple of hundred feet and rise very rapidly, the river cutting down also. The relief map from which this photograph was made was modelled by E. E. HOWELL for the U. S. Geological Survey and is 6 x 6 feet.

though occasionally they may approach this condition on one side or the other, and more rarely on both sides at once, depending on the geological formations of the locality. Owing to the immense height of the walls of such canyons as those on the Colorado, the cliffs frequently appear perpendicular

The " Hole in the Wall," near Ft. Defiance, Arizona.
This kind of sandstone has the peculiarity of weathering in this way, sometimes producing larger arches, alcoves, etc.
Photograph by BEN WITTICK.

when they are far from it, just as a mountain peak often seems to tower over one's head when in reality it may be a considerable distance off. In the nature of the formation and development of canyons, they could not long retain continuous vertical walls. What Powell calls the "recession of cliffs" comes into play. The erosive and corrasive power of water

being the chief land sculptors, it is evident that there will be a
continual wearing away of the faces of the bounding cliffs.
The softer beds will be cut away faster than the harder, and
where these underlie the harder the latter will be undermined
and fall.   Every canyon is always widening at its top and
sides, through the action of rain, frost, and wind, as well as
deepening through the action of its flowing stream.   *Erosion*
is this power which carves away the cliffs, and *corrasion* the
one which saws at the bottom, the latter term, in geological
nomenclature, meaning the cutting power of running water.[1]
This cutting power varies according to the declivity and the
amount of sediment carried in suspension.   It is plain that a
stream having great declivity will be able to carry more sediment than one having little, and in a barren country would
always be highly charged with sand, which would cut and scour
the bed of the channel like a grindstone.   As Dutton says, a
river cuts, however, only its own width, the rest of a canyon
being the work of the forces of erosion, the wind, frost, and
rain.   That is why we have canyons.   The powers of erosion
are far slower than those of corrasion, especially in an arid
region, because they are intermittent.   Where rocks take a
polish, as in Marble Canyon, the scouring and polishing work
of corrasion is seen in the shining bright surface as far as the
water rises.   This all belongs to the romance of the Water-
gods, those marvellous land sculptors.

   To produce canyons like those of the Colorado, peculiar
and unusual conditions are necessary.   There must exist a vast
region lying high above sea-level.   This region must be arid.
Out of it must rise separated mountain masses to such heights
that they shall be well watered.   These most elevated regions
alone having abundant rain- and snowfall, torrential streams
are generated and poured down upon the arid wastes, where
they persistently scour their beds, ploughing deep channels below the level of their surroundings.   The perpendicularity of
the walls of these channels, or canyons as they are called, de-

---

[1] The introduction of this subject may seem unnecessary to the general reader,
but no just comprehension of this river can be reached without some knowledge
of the forces creating its chasms.

Looking down upon Glen Canyon.
Cut through homogeneous sandstone.
Photograph by J. K. HILLERS, U. S. Colo. Riv. Exp.

43

pends on the volume and continuity of the flowing stream, on the aridity of the country through which they are cut, and on the rock-formation. A fierce and continuous torrent, where the rainfall is at the minimum, will so speedily outrival the forces of erosion that the canyon will have vertical walls. An example is seen in those frequent "mud" canyons found in arid regions, where some brook, having its source in highlands, cuts a channel through clay or dry earth with vertical sides, that stand for years. As long as the surface of the adjacent lands is undisturbed, it acts like a roof, throwing off the water that falls upon it into the main stream.[1] Thus the foundations of these walls are not assailed from *behind*, which is their weakest point. If the land surface is broken up, permitting the rains to soak in and saturate the clay or earth, the whole mass becomes softened and will speedily fall and slide out into the canyon.[2] The sides of all canyons in an arid region are more or less protected in the same way. That is, the rains fall suddenly, rarely continuously for any length of time, and are collected and conducted away immediately, not having a chance to enter the ground. Homogeneous sandstone preserves its perpendicularity better than other rocks, one reason being that it does not invite percolation, and usually offers, for a considerable distance on each side of the canyon, barren and impervious surfaces to the rains. Where strata rest on exposed softer beds, these are undermined from the front, and in this way recession is brought about.

In the basin of the Colorado are found in perfection all the extraordinary conditions that are needed to bring forth mammoth canyons. The headwaters of all the important tributaries are *invariably in the highest regions* and at a long distance from their mouths, so that the flood waters have many miles of opportunity to run a race with the comparatively feeble

[1] Just as wheat flour getting wet on the surface protects the portion below from dampness. The rainfall is often so slight, also, that a surface is unchanged for years. I once saw some wagon tracks that were made by our party *three* years before. From peculiar circumstances I was able to identify them.

[2] Robert Brewster Stanton explained this very clearly in his investigations for the Canadian Pacific Railway into the causes of land-slides on that line.

erosive forces of desert lands.   The main stream-courses are
thus in the lower arid regions and in sedimentary formations,
while their water-supply comes from far away.   The deepest
gorges, therefore, will be found where the rainfall is least, unless diminishing altitude interferes.   Thus the greatest gorge
of the whole basin, the Grand Canyon, is the one farthest from

Pinnacle in the Canyon de Chelly.
About 1500 feet high.   It is much wider from the side.
Photograph by BEN WITTICK.

the sources of supply, and in the driest area, but one, of the
whole drainage system.   It ends abruptly with the termination
of the high arid plateau which made it possible, but had this
plateau extended farther, the Grand Canyon would also have
extended a similar distance.   It is plain then that the cutting
of these canyons depends on the amount of water (snow is

included) which may fall in the high mountains, the canyons themselves being in the drier districts. It is also clear that if, by some chance, the precipitation of the high sources should increase, the corrasion of the stream-beds in the canyons would likewise increase and outrun with still greater ease the erosion of their immediate surroundings. On the other hand, if the precipitation in the arid surroundings should increase, the wearing down of the side walls would for a time—till covered by débris and vegetation—go on more rapidly till, instead of canyons of the Colorado River type, there would be deep, sharp valleys, or wide valleys, according to the amount of difference between the precipitation of the low lands and the high. Where the two were nearly the same, that is, a balance of precipitation,[1] the slopes might be rounded and verdure-clad, though this would depend on the *amount* of precipitation. On lower Snake River a change seems to be going on. The former canyon-cliffs are covered by débris and vegetation, but in places the old dry cliff-lines can be discerned beneath like a skeleton. The precipitation there has not been great enough to destroy the old lines—only enough to mask them.

The "inner gorge" of the Grand Canyon appears to have been cut far more rapidly than the outer one, and at a much later period. Were this not the case there would be no inner gorge. It is a singular fact that some side canyons, the Kanab, for example, while now possessing no running water, or at best a puny rivulet, and depending for their corrasion on intermittent floods, meet on equal terms the great Colorado, the giant that never for a second ceases its ferocious attack. Admitting that the sharper declivity of the Kanab would enhance its power of corrasion, nevertheless we should expect to see it approach the Grand Canyon by leaps and bounds, like the Havasupai farther down, but, on the contrary, there are parts that appear to be at a standstill in corrasion, or even filling up, and its floor is a regular descent, except for the last three or four miles where the canyon is clogged by huge rocks that seem to have fallen from above. The maximum height of

[1] There could be a balance of precipitation and still very little snow- or rainfall, or they might be very great.

its present flood-waters is about six feet, proved by a fern-cov-
ered calcareous deposit, projecting some fifteen feet, caused by
a spring (Shower-Bath Spring) on the side of the wall, seven or
eight miles above the mouth, which is never permitted by the
floods to build nearer the floor of the canyon. A suspicion
arises, on contemplating some of these apparent discrepancies,
that the prevailing conditions of corrasion are not what they
were at some earlier period, when they were such that it was

Bad Lands on Black's Fork of Green River.
Photograph by U S. Geol. Survey

rendered more rapid and violent; that there was perhaps an
epoch when these deep-cut tributary canyons carried perennial
streams, and when the volume of the Colorado itself was many
times greater, possessing a multiplied corrasive power, while
the adjacent areas were about as arid as now. At such a time,
perhaps, the Colorado performed the main work of the inner
gorge, the Kanab, and similar affluents, their deep now rather
evenly graded canyons. Such an increase of volume, if we
suppose the aridity to remain as now, could have come about

only by an increase of precipitation on the mountain summits. During the Glacial Epoch, the Rocky Mountain summits were considerably glaciated, the amount varying according to altitude and latitude. The general topography of the Colorado River was about as it is to-day, and the rainfall in the valleys probably nearly the same, or at least only a little greater. In other words, the conditions were those of to-day intensified. In summer, then, the amount of water seeking outlet by these drainage channels to the sea was enormously multiplied, and the corrasive power was correspondingly augmented. When the ice caps finally began to permanently diminish, the summer floods were doubtless terrific. The waters of the Colorado now rise in the Grand Canyon, on the melt-

In Lower Kanab Canyon.
Width about 75 feet, depth 2500 to 3000.
Photograph by E O BEAMAN

ing of the snows in the distant mountains, from forty to one hundred feet; the rise must then have amounted to from one hundred to four hundred or more. The Kanab heads in two very high regions—the Pink Cliffs and the Kaibab. Though probably not high enough to be heavily glaciated they were high enough to receive an increased snowfall and to hold it, or a portion of it, over from one year to another. Thus the canyons having their origin on these high regions would be given perennial streams, with torrential floods each summer, compared with which anything that now comes down the Kanab would be a mere rivulet. The summit of the Kaibab is covered with peculiar pocket-like basins having no apparent outlets. These were possibly glacial sinks, conducting away some of the surplus water from the melting snow and ice by subterranean channels. It seems probable, therefore, that glacial flood-waters were an important factor in the formation of the canyons of the Colorado. If this supposition is correct it would account, at least

The Pink Cliffs.
Southern end of High Plateaus.
Photograph by J. K. HILLERS, U. S. Geol. Survey.

in a measure, for that distinct impression of arrested activity one receives from the present conditions obtaining there.[1]

The drainage at the edges of most canyons is back and away from the gorge itself. The reason is that the rains cannot flow

[1] Some canyon floors, where there is no permanent large stream, appear to have altogether ceased descending. Dutton says of those which drain the Terrace Plateaus: '' Many of them are actually filling up, the floods being unable to carry away all the sand and clay which the infrequent rains wash into them."— *Tertiary History*, p. 50. See also pp. 196 and 228 *Ib*.

evenly over a canyon brink, owing to irregularities of surface, and once an irregular drainage is established, the water seeks the easiest road. A side canyon is formed, draining a certain area. Another is formed elsewhere, and another, and so on till all drainage is through these tributaries and *away* from the brink, by more or less circuitous channels to the main stream. This backward drainage leaves the immediate brink, or "rim," till the last, in its work of erosion and corrasion, and the rim consequently is left higher than the region away from it. This effect of a backward drainage is very plain on both sides of the Grand Canyon, though it is somewhat assisted, on the north at

Towers at Short Creek. Southern Utah.
This is a part of the great line of the Vermilion Cliffs. The region here represented possesses some of the most magnificent scenery of the whole West.
Outline drawing by W. H. Holmes.

least, by the backward dip of the strata. It may be modified by other conditions, so that it would not always be the case.

The basin of the Colorado, excepting that part below the mouth of the Virgen and a portion among the "parks" of the western slope of the Rocky Mountain range, is almost entirely a plateau region. Some of the plateaus are very dry; others rise above the arid zone and are well watered. The latter are called the "High Plateaus." They reach an altitude of eleven thousand feet above the sea. They are east of the Great Basin, and with the other plateaus form an area called by Powell "The Plateau Province." Eastward still the plateaus merge

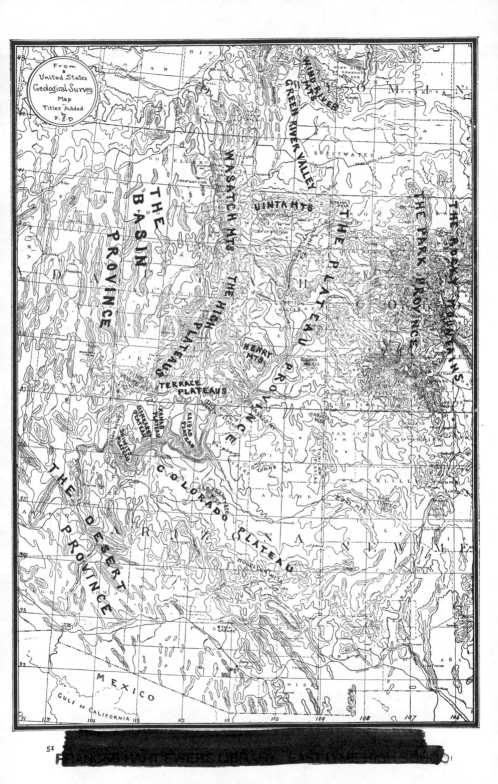

into the "parks." The High Plateaus, as a topographical feature, are a southern continuation of the Wasatch Mountains. They terminate on the south in the Markagunt, the Paunsagunt, and the Aquarius Plateaus. The extreme southern extremities of the two former are composed of mighty precipices of columnarly eroded limestone called the Pink Cliffs. Here is the beginning of the Terrace Plateaus, likewise bounded by vertical, barren cliffs. Between the High Plateaus

Gray's Peak, 14,341 feet.   Torrey's Peak, 14,336 feet.
Tip-top of the Continental Divide whence the Colorado derives flood waters
Photograph by U. S. Geol. Survey.

and the parks, the plateaus may be called, for convenience, Mesa Plateaus, as they are generally outlined by vertical cliffs. This is the case also south of the end of the High Plateaus where, stepping down the great terraces, we arrive at the region immediately adjacent to the Grand Canyon, composed of four plateaus, three of them of mesa character, the Shevwits, Uinkaret, Kanab, and Kaibab; and up at the head of Marble Canyon a fifth, the Paria, while still farther to the north-eastward is the Kaiparowitz. The edges of these Mesa Plateaus,

precipitous cliffs, stretch for many miles across the arid land like mountain ranges split asunder. This region, lying between the High Plateaus, the Grand Wash, the Henry Mountains, and the Colorado, is perhaps the most fascinating of all the basin. The relief map at page 41 gives the larger part of it.

Balanced Rock.
On Trail from House Rock Valley to Lee's Ferry.
Photograph by E. O. BEAMAN.

In the basin there are also great mountain masses, the fountainheads of the waters which have carved the canyons. These are Uinta, Zuñi, San Francisco, Henry, Pine Valley, Uinkaret, Beaver Dam, Virgen, Navajo, La Sal, and others, some reaching an altitude of more than twelve thousand feet. The highest peaks of these, and of course those of the Continental Divide on the east, which furnish a large proportion of the water of the Colorado, and the Wind River Mountains on the extreme north, show snow-banks throughout the summer. To show how dependent the Colorado is on the high peaks for its flood-waters, I will mention that it is not till the snows of these high altitudes are fiercely attacked by the sun in May and June that the river has its annual great rise. It would take only a slight lowering of the mean annual temperature now to furnish these peaks with ice caps. The rainfall in the lower arid regions is from three to ten inches, increasing northward to fifteen and twenty-five. On the peaks, of course, it is much greater. Almost any climate can be had, from the hot arid to the wet frigid. On the lower stretches, from Mohave down, the thermometer in summer stands around 112° F. a great deal of the time, and reaches 118° F. Yet Dr. Coues said he felt it no more than he did the summer heat of New York or Washington.[1] In winter the temperature at the bottom of the Grand Canyon is very mild, and flowers bloom most of the time. One November I descended from the snow-covered top of the Kaibab to the Grand Canyon at the mouth of the Kanab, where I was able to bathe in the open air with entire comfort.

There are six chief topographical features, canyons, cliffs, valleys, mesa plateaus, high plateaus, mountains. There are two grand divisions: the lowland or desert, below the Virgen, and the plateau, but the topography of the immediate river course separates itself into four parts, the Green River Valley, the canyon, the valley-canyon, and the alluvial. The canyon part is the longest, occupying about two-thirds of the whole, or about 1200 miles. It is cut mainly through the plateaus. The last of these southward is the Colorado, a vast upheaval reaching from the lower end of the Grand Canyon south-east to about where the 34th parallel crosses the western line of New Mexico. Lieutenant Wheeler several times claims the honour of naming it (1868–71), but the name occurs on Lieutenant Ives's map of 1858. This plateau breaks sharply along its south-west line to the lowland district, and on its

[1] I was at the Needles one summer for a brief time, and the air seemed very oppressive to me.

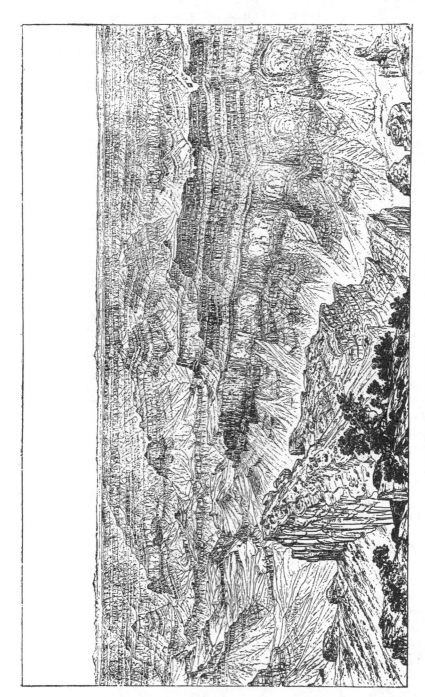

Outline Sketch of the Grand Canyon from Point Sublime.

Drawn by W. H. Holmes.

north-westerly edge slopes to the Little Colorado. It bears a
noble pine forest, and from its summit rise to over 12,000 feet
the volcanic peaks of the San Francisco Mountains. Its northern edge is the Grand Canyon, which separates it from its kin-
dred on the other side. These and the Colorado Plateau rise

Character of the Mountains and High Plateau Regions of the Basin of the Colorado.
Photograph by J. K. Hillers.

to from 6000 to 8000 feet above sea-level, and it is through this
huge mass that the river has ground out the Grand Canyon, by
corrading its bed down tremendously, the bottom at the end
being only 840 feet above the sea, whereas the start at the
mouth of the Little Colorado is 2690. Yet here it is already

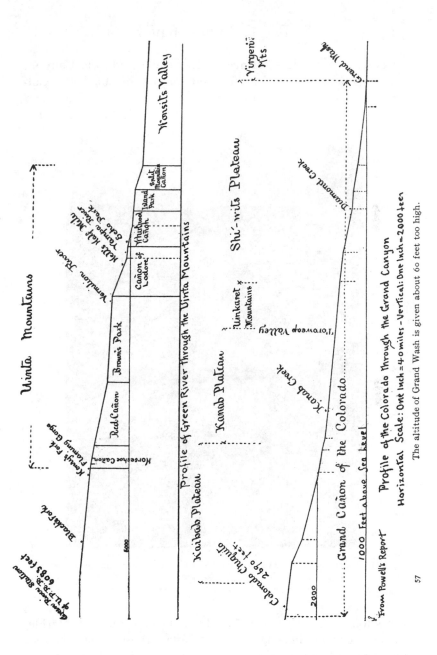

Uinta Mountains

Green River Station of U.P.R.R. 6083 feet

Blacks Fork

Kenaty Fork Flaming Gorge

Horseshoe Cañon

Red Cañon

6000

Brown's Park

Vermilion River

Cañon of Lodore

Wells Half Mile Yampa River Echo Park

Whirlpool Cañon

Island Park

Split Mountain Cañon

Wonsits Valley

Profile of Green River Through the Uinta Mountains

Kaibab Plateau

Kanab Plateau

Shi'-wits Plateau

Colorado Chiquito 2690 feet

Unkaret Mountains

Toroweap Valley

Kanab Creek

Diamond Creek

Yungerü Mts

Grand Wash

2000

1000 feet above Sea level

Grand Cañon of the Colorado

From Powell's Report

Profile of the Colorado through the Grand Canyon
Horizontal Scale: One Inch = 40 miles – Vertical: One Inch = 2000 feet

The altitude of Grand Wash is given about 60 feet too high.

3500 feet below the surface at the end of Marble Canyon,
which, separated only by the deep canyon of the Little Colorado, is practically a northward continuation of the Grand
Canyon itself. As the river runs, the Grand Canyon is $217\frac{1}{2}$

Looking across the Grand Canyon (Inner Gorge) near the Foot of the Toroweap.
Depth 3000 feet.
Photograph by J. K. HILLERS, U. S. Geol. Survey.

miles long. To this may be added the $65\frac{1}{2}$ miles of Marble,
giving a continuous chasm of 283 miles, the longest, deepest,
and most difficult of passage in every direction of any canyon
in the world. The depth begins with a couple of hundred feet

at Lee's Ferry (mouth of the Paria), the head of Marble Canyon, and steadily deepens to some 3500 feet near the Little Colorado, where the sudden uplift of the Kaibab lends about 2000 feet more to the already magnificent gorge. Along the end of the Kaibab the walls, for a long distance, reach their greatest height, about 6000° feet, but the other side is considerably lower than the north all the way through. At the mouth of the Kanab the altitude of the river-bed is 1800 feet above the sea, showing a fall in the interval of 890 feet. The greatest declivity is about 210 feet in 10 miles, in what is termed the Kaibab division, extending from a point 10 miles below the Little Colorado to a point 58 miles farther down. Here the smooth stretches of river are long, the rapids short and violent. Here, also, is the "granite," making the walls sombre, as the colour is slaty to black. At the mouth of Diamond Creek the river is still 1300 feet higher than the sea, giving a fall of 500 feet from the Kanab. There is another descent of 460 feet to the Grand Wash, and then 149 to the mouth of the Virgen. Next to the Kaibab division of the Grand Canyon, the greatest declivity occurs in the Uinta region, in the Canyon of Lodore. The profile of the river in these two districts is approximately given on page 57. The average depth of the Grand Canyon is about 4000 feet. Its width at the top varies from 4½ to 12 miles. This is the extreme outer cliff-line. The inner gorge is much narrower, at the Toroweap being only about 3500 feet. The river varies in width from 500 or 600 feet to 75 or 100. In this canyon is water-power enough to run the machinery of the world, and there is as much more in the canyons above.

Joining Marble Canyon on the north is Glen, 135 miles long, from the Paria to Fremont River. It has but one rapid of consequence. At high water, with the exception of this rapid, the tide sweeps smoothly and swiftly down with a majestic flow. The walls are homogeneous sandstone, in places absolutely perpendicular for about a thousand feet. I have stood on the brink and *dropped* a stone into the river. The highest walls are 1600 feet. Next is Narrow Canyon, about 9 miles long, 1300 feet deep, and no rapids. It is hardly more

than the finish of Cataract, a superb gorge about 40 miles long
with a depth of 2700 feet, often nearly vertical.   The rapids
here are many and violent, the total fall being about 450 feet.
At its head is the mouth of the Grand River.   The altitude of
the junction is 3860 feet.[1]   Following up the Green, we have
first Stillwater, then Labyrinth Canyon, much alike, the first
42$\frac{3}{4}$ and the second 62$\frac{1}{2}$ miles in length.   The walls of sandstone are 1300 feet.   Their names well describe them, though
the stillwater of the first is very swift and straight.   There are
no rapids in either.   All these canyon names, from Green River
Valley to the Grand Wash, were applied by Powell.   Between
Labyrinth and the next canyon, Gray, so called from the
colour of its walls, 2000 feet high, is Gunnison Valley, where
the river may first be easily crossed.   Here the unfortunate
Captain Gunnison, in 1853, passed over on his way to his
doom, and here, too, the Old Spanish Trail led the traveller in
former days toward Los Angeles.   The Denver and Rio Grande
Western Railway has taken advantage of the same place to
cross.   The 36 miles of Gray are hardly more than a continuation of the Canyon of Desolation's 97 miles.   Desolation is a
fine chasm, whose walls are 2400 feet.   The view on page 206
gives an excellent idea of their average character.   The mouth
of the Uinta River, not far above its head, is 4670 feet above
the sea, while Gunnison Valley is 4083, showing a descent for
the river, in Desolation and Gray, together of 587 feet.   Desolation is full of rapids, some of them bad.   Wonsits Valley,
which succeeds Desolation, is the longest of the few valleys,
being about 87 miles, with a width of 6 or 8 miles.   There is a
considerable amount of arable land, and along the river bank
large groves of cottonwood trees.   The river course is winding,
the current sluggish, the width being 600 to 800 feet.   At the
head of this valley is Split-Mountain Canyon, 8 miles long,
with ragged, craggy walls 2700 feet high.   It contains a number
of medium rapids.   Island Park separates it from Whirlpool
Canyon.   It is a charming little valley, full of islands, a mere

[1] The character of the Grand River is similar to that of the Green, but the
canyons above the mouth of the Dolores are not so long nor so deep.   The river
also carries less water.

expansion of the walls, 9 miles long,—9 miles of rainbow, for the surrounding rocks and marls are of every hue. Whirlpool, 2400 feet deep, is about 14 miles in length and contains a number of rapids, but the whirlpools depend on the stage of water. Then

Pinnacles in Split Mountain Canyon.
Photograph by E. O. BEAMAN, U. S. Colo. Riv. Exp.

comes the beautiful little Echo Park, really only the head of Whirlpool. Its name is derived from a wonderful echo of ten words returned from the smooth wall seen in the cut on page 203. It is only a mile long with walls of 600 feet. At its head enter the Yampa River and Canyon, which mark the foot of

Lodore, the most striking gorge, next to the Grand Canyon, on the whole river.   Lodore is only 20 miles long, but it
is 20 miles of concentrated water-power energy and grandeur,

Head of the Canyon of Lodore just inside the " Gate."
Walls 2500 feet high; river 300 feet wide.
Photograph by E. O. BEAMAN, U. S. Colo. Riv. Exp.

the fall being about 400 feet, the walls 2700.   Never for a moment does it relax its assault, and the voyager on its restless,
relentless tide, especially at high water, is kept on the alert.
The waters indeed come rushing down with fearful impetu-

osity, recalling to Powell the poem of Southey, on the Lodore *he* knew, hence the name. The beginning of the gorge is at the foot of Brown's Park through what is called the Gate of Lodore, an abrupt gash in the Uinta Mountains 2000 feet deep. In viewing this entrance the ordinary spectator is at a loss to comprehend how the stream could have begun its attack upon

this precipitous ridge. The theory that the river was there before the upheaval formed the mountain does not entirely satisfy, for it would seem in that case that the canyon walls would long ago have become much more broken down than they are. But the walls have a strikingly fresh look, as if formed recently, compared with the time of the original upheaval. It seems possible that there may have been in this region some great lake which lifted the waters up to the top of

Pot-hole in Intermittent Water Course, Glen Canyon.
Homogeneous sandstone. These holes are often 10 to 15 feet deep, with the stones which ground them lying in the bottom.
Photograph by J. FENNEMORE, U. S. Colo Riv. Exp.

the ridge to begin their work of corrasion. Such lakes did exist; but lack of space forbids the further pursuit of this discussion here.

Brown's Park, originally called Brown's Hole, after one of the early trappers, is a fine valley about 35 miles long and 5 or

6 miles wide.   It is, like the few other valleys, an expansion of
the canyon walls.   There is considerable arable land, and the
place possesses a remarkable climate.   Though its general level
is so high, around 5500 feet, it receives hardly any snow, and
for this reason was long a favourite place for wintering cattle
on the drive from Texas to California.   It was a great rendezvous, also, for the early trappers and traders, and here stood

Looking up Green River Valley from below Union Pacific Railway Bridge.
Photograph by C. R. SAVAGE.

Fort Davy Crockett, in those days famous.   It was one of
those necessary places of refuge and meeting, established when
the trappers were pursuing their extermination of the beaver,
which once were so numerous in all the Western country.   The
river enters this park from the solitudes of Red Canyon, a
splendid chasm, 25 miles long, 2500 feet deep, and abounding
in plunging waters.   The name is from the colour of the sandstone walls.   Above it are three short canyons, Kingfisher,

Horseshoe, and Flaming Gorge, aggregating about 10 miles. There are there no rapids worth mentioning, but the scenic beauty is entrancing. The walls are from 1200 to 1600 feet, in places extremely precipitous. Flaming Gorge, with walls 1300 feet, is particularly distinguished by being the beginning of the long series of close canyons. The river enters suddenly from Green River Valley, repeating on a smaller scale the conditions at the entrance to Lodore. From here on up to the Wind River Range the stream is flanked by occasional cliffs and buttes, but the country is comparatively open, and the many tributaries often have fine grassy bottoms. This was the locality of the great rendezvous of the period from 1825 to 1835, and even later.

Specimen of a Navajo.
Photograph by J. K. HILLERS, U. S. Geol. Survey.

Green River Valley is an elevated region, from six thousand to seven thousand feet above sea. It stretches from the Wind River Mountains on the north to the Uintas on the south, and is bounded westwardly by the Wyoming Range, and on the east merges into the Laramie Plains. The drainage exit is through the Uintas, as noted, by means of the canyons heading at Flaming Gorge. There are here opportunities for extensive farming by irrigation. The only other chance for agriculture on the river, except Wonsits Valley, Brown's Park, and a few minor places, is below Black Canyon, in the stretches I have called the alluvial and the canyon-valley divisions. In the latter short canyons separate extensive valleys with wide alluvial bottoms capable of high cultivation, though often subject to overflow. Almost anything will grow there. Vast groves of cottonwood and mesquite exist. In the alluvial

Young Warriors of the North.
Photograph by C. R. Savage.

division, the last stretch of the river, from the Gila down, cotton and sugar cane would probably grow. This is the only division where the water of the river can be extensively diverted. At the mouth of the Gila an old emigrant road to California crossed, and another here in this Green River Valley. A third route of travel was by way of Gunnison's Crossing; and a fourth, though this was seldom traversed, was by the Crossing of the Fathers, some thirty-five miles above the present Lee's Ferry. In Green River Valley, Bonneville built his

Fort Nonsense, and the region was for many years the best known of any place beyond the mountains. The routes of trappers and prospectors frequently followed old native trails, which crossed and recrossed the country in every direction, except where the canyons of the Green and Colorado were approached, when few lines of traverse were open across, and none along the course of the water.

The Joshua Tree.
Clistoyucca Arborescens.   Southern Nevada.
Photograph by C. R. SAVAGE.

On the headwaters of Green River lived the Crows, who called it the Seedskedee Agie or Prairie Hen River. The Snakes and Utes living farther down called it the Bitter-root. Fremont called it the Rio Verde of the Spaniards, but apparently without good authority. It was also spoken of as Spanish River, from the report that Spaniards occupied its lower valleys. Colorado was also one of its names, and this is what it should have remained. The commonest appellation was Green, supposed to have been derived from a trapper of that name.   Just when the term "Colorado" was first applied to the lower river is not now known.   It bore several names, but finally Colorado took first place because of its appropriateness. Both the walls and the water are usually red, though the name is undoubtedly derived from the colour of the water.   Green River is frequently as red as any river could be.   After a storm in the headwaters of Vermilion Creek I have seen the Green a positively bright vermilion.

A Pai Ute Family at Home.
Photograph by J. K. HILLERS, U. S. Colo. Riv. Exp.

The Arapahos were said to range into Brown's Park; the Utes were all along the Wonsits Valley and below it on both sides of the river.   Then came the Navajos, ranging up to the San Juan and above.[1]   On the north side, below the San Juan, were the various bands of Pai Utes, while on the south were the Puebloan tribes, with the Apaches, Suppais, Wallapais, etc., while still below came the Mohaves, Cocopas, and Yumas, with, on the Gila, the Pimas, Papagos, and Maricopas.   The 250,000 square miles of the basin were variously apportioned

[1] For notes on the distribution of tribes see the *Seventh Ann. Rep. Bu. Ethnology; Wheeler's Report*, vol. i. ; *Report of Lieut. Ives, Works of H. H. Bancroft*, and *Garces*, by Elliott Coues.

amongst these tribes, but their territorial claims were usually well defined.

The vegetation of the area, especially that of the lower half, possesses singular characteristics quite in keeping with the extraordinary to-pography. Here flourishes the cac-tus, that rose of the desert, its lovely blossoms red, yel-low, and white, il-luminating in spring the arid wastes. The soft green of its stems and the multiplicity of its forms and species, are a constant de-light. It writhes and struggles across the hot earth, or spreads out silver-spined branches in-to a tree-like bush, or, in the great pitahaya, rises in fierce dignity like a monitor against the deep blue sky. And the yuccas are quite as beautiful, with their tall central

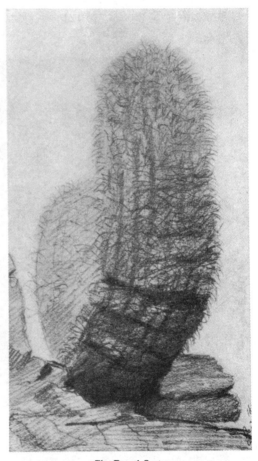

The Barrel Cactus.
Pencil sketch by F. S. DELLENBAUGH.

rods so richly crowned with bell-like blossoms, the fantastic *Clistoyucca arborescens*, or Joshua tree, being more in harmony with the archaic landscape than any other plant there. As the traveller crosses one of the open forests of this tree, which

is often twenty-five feet high, the more distant ones appear
to beckon like some uncanny desert octopus yearning to draw
him within reach of those scrawny arms.   The blossom of
this monstrous growth is a revelation, so unexpected is it.   A
group as large as one's head, pure white, on the extremity of
a dagger-covered bough, it is like an angel amidst bayonets.

Vegetation of the Southwest.
Photograph by E. O. BEAMAN.

The pitahaya, often more than thirty feet high and twelve to
twenty-four inches diameter, is a fit companion for the Joshua,
with an equally startling blossom.

" To go out on the desert . . . and meet these cacti is like
whispering into the ear of the Sphinx, and listening at her locked
lips, . . . and to go out in April and see them suddenly abloom

is as though the lips of the Sphinx should part and utter solemn words. A bunch of white flowers at the tip of the obelisk, flowers springing white and wonderful out of this dead, gaunt, prickly thing—is not that Nature's consummate miracle, a symbol of resurrection more profound than the lily of the fields." [1]

Then there is the glorious ocotillo, waving its long, slender wands from the ground-centre, each green with its myriad little lance-shaped leaves, and bursting at the end into a scarlet flame of blossoms dazzling in the burning sunlight. Near by springs up the Barrel cactus, a forbidding column no one dares touch. A little farther is the "yant" of the Pai Ute, with leaves fringed with teeth like its kind, the Agaves. This is a source of food for the native, who roasts the asparagus-like tip starting up in the spring, and he also takes the whole head, and, trimming off the outer leaves, bakes it in pits, whereby it is full of sweetness like thick molasses. The inner pulp is dried in sheets and laid away. Near by, the Pinyon tree in the autumn sheds its delicious nuts by the bushel, and meanwhile there are many full, nutritious grass seeds, the kind called "ak" by the Pai Utes almost equalling wheat in the size of its kernel. In the lowlands grows the stolid mesquite tree, more underground than above, whose roots furnish excellent firewood,—albeit they must be broken up with a sledge hammer, for no axe will stand the impact. Near it may be seen huge bunches of grass (or perhaps straw would describe it better), which the white man gathers for hay with a huge hoe. Then there is the ever-present, friendly sage-brush, miniature oak trees, with branch and trunk so beautiful. It grows, as a rule, about two feet high, but I have seen it higher than my head; that is, at least six feet. Beneath its spreading shade in the south lurks the Gila Monster, terrible in name at any rate, a fearful object to look upon, a remnant of antediluvian times, a huge, clumsy, two-foot lizard. The horned toad is quite as forbidding in appearance, but he is a harmless little thing.

Here we are in the rattlesnake's paradise. Nine species are found along the Mexican border; and no wonder. The

[1] Harriet Monroe, *Atlantic Monthly*, June, 1902.

country seems made for them,—the rocks, cliffs, canyons, pit-
ahayas, Joshuas, and all the rest of it.   Notwithstanding their
venom they have beauty, and when one is seen at the bottom
of some lonely, unfrequented canyon, tail buzzing, head erect,
and defiant, glistening eyes, a man feels like apologising for the
intrusion.   Above in the limpid sunlight floats the great eagle,
deadly enemy of the rattlesnake; from a near-by bush the exquisite song of the mocking-bird trills out, and far up the rocks

A Kaibab Pai Ute.
Posed by THOMAS MORAN.
Photograph by J. K. HILLERS, U. S. Geol. Survey.

the hoof-strokes
of the mountain
sheep strike with
a rattle of stones
that seems music
in the crystal air.
Yonder the wild
turkey calls from
the pine trees, or
we hark to the
whir of the grouse
or the pine-hen.
Noisy magpies
startle the silence
of the northern
districts, and the
sage-hen and the
rabbit everywhere
break the solitude
of your walk.
Turn up a stone
and sometimes

you see a revengeful scorpion: anon the huge tarantula
comes forth to look at the camp-fire.   As one sits resting
on a barren ledge, the little swifts come out to make his acquaintance.   Whistle softly and a bright-coated fellow will run
up even upon your shoulder to show his appreciation of the
Swan Song.   Antelope dart scornfully away across the open
plains, and the little coyote halts in his course to turn the in-
quisitive gaze of his pretty bright eyes upon this new animal

crossing his path. The timber wolf, not satisfied with staring, follows, perhaps, as if enjoying company, at the same time occasionally licking his chaps. When the sun goes down his long-drawn bark rolls out into the clear winter sky like a song

Side Canyon of Glen Canyon.
Homogeneous Sandstone.
Photograph by J. FENNEMORE, U. S. Colo. Riv. Exp.

to the evening star, rendering the blaze of the camp-fire all the more comfortable. Under the moonlight the sharper bark of the coyote swells a chorus from the cliffs, and the rich note of the night-storm is accentuated by the long screech of the puma prowling on the heights.   In daylight his brother, the wild-cat, reminds one of Tabby at home by the fireside.   There is the lynx, too, among the rocks; and on the higher planes the deer, elk, and bear have their homes.   In Green River Valley once roamed thousands of bison.   The more arid districts have the fewest large animals, and conversely the more humid the most, though in the latter districts the fauna and flora approach that of the eastern part of the continent, while as the former are approached the difference grows wider and wider, till in the southern lowlands there is no resemblance to eastern types at all.   Once the streams everywhere had thousands of happy beaver, with their homes in the river banks, or in waters deepened by their clever dams.   Otter, too, were there.   The larger rivers are not favourable for fish on account of the vast amount of sediment, but in the smaller, especially in the mountain streams, trout were abundant.   In Green River occurs a salmon-trout attaining a length of at least four feet.   This is also found in the Colorado proper, where another fish, with a humpback, is to be caught.   I do not know the name of this, but imagine it the same as has in latter days been called "squaw-fish."

All over the region the rocks are seamed by mineral veins. Some of these have already poured forth millions of dollars, while others await a discoverer.   On the river itself gold is found in the sands; and the small alluvial bottoms that occur in Glen Canyon, and a few gravel bars in the Grand, have been somewhat profitably worked, though necessarily on a small scale.   The granite walls of the Grand Canyon bear innumerable veins, but as prospecting is there so difficult it will be many a long year before the best are found.   The search for mineral veins has done much to make the farther parts known, just as the earlier search for beaver took white men for the first time into the fastnesses of the great mountains, and earlier the effort to save the souls of the natives marked their main trails into the wilderness.

This sketch of the Basin of the Colorado is most inadequate, but the scope of this volume prevents amplification in this direction.   These few pages, however, will better enable the reader to comprehend the labours of the padres, the trappers, and the explorers, some account of whose doings is presented in the following chapters.[1]

[1] In connection with the subject of erosion and corrasion the reader is advised to study the following works, which are the standards : *The Exploration of the Colorado of the West,* and the *Geology of the Uinta Mountains,* by J. W. Powell ; *The Henry Mountains,* by G. K. Gilbert ; *The Geology of the High Plateaus of Utah,* and *The Tertiary History of the Grand Canyon District,* by C. E. Dutton.

CHAPTER IV

IN the historical development of the Basin of the Colorado four chief epochs are apparent. The discovery of the river, as already outlined in previous chapters, is the first; second, the entradas of the padres; third, the wanderings of the trappers; and fourth, the expeditions of the explorers. These epochs are replete with interesting and romantic incidents, new discoveries; starvations; battles; massacres; lonely, dangerous journeys, etc., which can only be touched upon in a volume of the present size. Dr. Coues placed the diary of Garces, one of the chief actors of this great four-act life-drama, in accessible shape, and had not his lamented death interfered he would have put students under further obligation to him.

Preliminary to the entradas of the padres, Don Antonio de Espejo, in 1583, went from the Rio Grande to Moki and westward to a mountain, probably one of the San Francisco group, but he did not see the Colorado. Twenty-one years elapsed before a white man again ventured into this region. In 1604, Don Juan de Oñate, the wealthy governor of New Mexico, determined to cross from his headquarters at the village of San Juan on the Rio Grande, by this route to the South Sea, and, accompanied by thirty soldiers and two padres, he set forth, passing west by way of the pueblo of Zuñi, and probably not seeing at that time the celebrated Inscription Rock,[1] for, though his name is said to be first of European marks, the date is 1606.

Entrance to Acoma, N. M.
The town is on top of a mesa, and was a prominent point on the highway from the Rio Grande to Zuñi.
Photograph by BEN WITTICK.

From Zuñi he went to the Moki towns, then five in number, and possibly somewhat south of the present place.   Beyond

[1] This is a quadrangular mass of sandstone about a mile long, thirty-five miles east of Zuñi. On its base at the eastern end are a number of native and European inscriptions, the oldest, of the European dates according to Simpson, being 1606, recording a visit by Oñate. The rock, or, more properly, mesa, is also called the Morro. Chas. F. Lummis has also written on this subject.

Moki ten leagues, they crossed a stream flowing north-westerly, which was called Colorado from the colour of its water,—the first use of the name so far traced. This was what we now call the Little Colorado. They understood it to discharge into the South Sea (Pacific), and probably Oñate took it for the very headwaters of the Buena Guia which Alarçon had discovered over sixty years before. As yet no white man had been north of Moki in the Basin of the Colorado, and the only source of information concerning the far northern region was the natives, who were not always understood, however honestly they might try to convey a knowledge of the country.

Skirting the southern edge of the beautiful San Francisco Mountain region, through the superb forest of pine trees, Oñate finally descended from the Colorado Plateau to the headwaters of the Verde, where he met a tribe called Cruzados, because they wore little crosses from the hair of the forehead, a relic, no doubt, of the time when Alarçon had so freely distributed these emblems among the tribes he encountered on the Colorado, friends probably of these Cruzados. The latter reported the sea twenty days distant by way of a small river running into a greater, which flowed to the salt water. The small river was Bill Williams Fork, and on striking it Oñate began to see the remarkable pitahaya adorning the landscape with its tall, stately columns; and all the strange lowland vegetation followed. The San Andreas, as he called this stream, later named Santa Maria by Garces, he followed down to the large river into which it emptied, the Colorado, which he called the Rio Grande de Buena Esperanza, or River of Good Hope, evidently deciding that it merited a more distinguished title than had been awarded it at the supposed headwaters. He appears to have well understood what river this was, and we wonder why he gave it a new name when it had already received two. Sometimes in new lands explorers like to have their own way. They went down the Colorado, after a party had examined the river a little above the mouth of the Bill Williams Fork, meeting with various bands of friendly natives, among whom we recognise the Mohaves and the Cocopas. Not far below where Oñate reached the Esperanza he entered the Great

Across the House Tops of Zuñi.
Photograph by J. K. Hillers.

Colorado Valley and soon crossed the highest point attained by Alarçon in 1540, probably near the upper end of the valley. He now doubled Alarçon's and presently also Melchior Diaz's paths, and arrived at the mouth of the river on the 25th of January, 1604, the first white man in over sixty years. A large harbour which struck his fancy was named in honour of the saint's day, Puerto de la Conversion de San Pablo, for the sun seldom went down without a Spaniard of those days thus propitiating a saint. We are more prone to honour the devil in these matters. The Gila they called Rio del Nombre de Jesus, a name never used again. So it often happens with names bestowed by explorers. The ones they regard most highly vanish, while some they apply thoughtlessly adhere forever.

All the tribes of this region, being familiar with the Californian coast, described it in a way that caused Oñate to believe that the gulf was the South Sea, extending indefinitely beyond the mouth of the Colorado northwards, and thus the persistent error that Lower California was an island received further confirmation. Without going across to the sea beyond the mountains, which would have dispelled the error, Oñate returned to the Rio Grande by the outward route, suffering so greatly for food that the party were forced to eat some of their horses, a source of relief often resorted to in future days in this arid country. A few years after Oñate's expedition Zalvidar (1618), with Padre Jiminez and forty-seven soldiers, went out to Moki, and from there fifteen leagues to the Rio de Buena Esperanza, but they evidently encountered Marble Canyon, and soon returned.

Another name closely linked with the early history of the Colorado is that of Padre Eusibio Francisco Kino,[1] an Austrian by birth and a member of the Jesuit order. This indefatigable enthusiast travelled back and forth, time and again, over the whole of northern Sonora and the southern half of Arizona, then comprised in Pimeria Alta, the upper land of the Pimas, and Papagueria, the land of the Papagos. His base of opera-

---

[1] The name is written Kühn, Kühne, Quino, and in several other ways. Humboldt used Kühn, and either this or Kühne is probably the correct form, but long usage gives preference to Kino.

81

Ruin called Casa Grande, Arizona.

From a photograph by Cosmos Mindeleff, U. S. Bu. Eth.

tions was a mission he established in Sonora; the mission of Dolores, founded in 1687. For some thirty years Kino laboured in this field with tireless energy, flinching before no danger or difficulty. He was the first white man to see the extraordinary ruin called Casa Grande, near the present town of Florence, and on the occasion of his first visit he took advantage of the structure to say mass within its thick adobe walls. This is probably the most remarkable ancient building within the limits of the United States. For a long time it was called the House of Montezuma, though, of course, Montezuma never heard of it. A similar ruin, called Casas Grandes, exists in Sonora. The construction is what is called cajon, that is, adobe clay rammed into a box or frame, which is lifted for each successive course as the work advances. In the dry air of that region such walls become extremely hard, and will endure for ages if the foundations are not sapped.[1] Kino paid a second visit to the ruin of Casa Grande in 1697, this time accompanied by Captain Juan Mateo Mange, an officer detailed with his command to escort the padres on their perilous journeys.

The method of the authorities was to establish a military post, called a presidio, at some convenient point, from which protection would be extended to several missions. The soldiers in the field wore a sort of buckskin armour, with a double-visored helmet and a leathern buckler on the left arm. Kino was as often without as with the guardianship of these warriors, and seems to have had very little trouble with the natives. The Apaches, then and always, were the worst of all. In his numerous entradas he explored the region of his labours pretty thoroughly, reaching, in 1698, a hill from which he saw how the gulf ended at the mouth of the Colorado; and the following year he was again down the Gila, which he called Rio de los Apostoles, to the Colorado, now blessed with a fourth name, the Rio de los Martires. "Buena Guia," "del Tizon,"

[1] See *The North Americans of Yesterday*, by F. S. Dellenbaugh, p. 234; and for complete details see papers by Cosmos Mindeleff, *Thirteenth An. Rep. Bu. Eth.* and *Fifteenth An. Rep. Bu. Eth.*; also Font's description in Coues's *Garces*, p. 93.

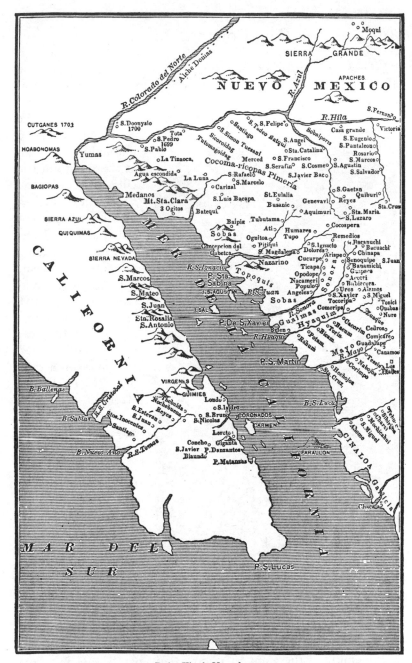

Padre Kino's Map of 1701.

The first map giving the head of the Gulf correctly.

From BANCROFT'S *History of Arizona and New Mexico*.

83

"Esperanza," and "los Martires," all in about a century and a half, and still the great Tiger of Waters was not only untamed but unknown.   Kino kept up his endeavours to inaugurate somewhere a religious centre, but without success.   The

A Lateral Canyon of Escalante River.
Photograph by J. K. HILLERS, U S Colo Riv Exp

San Dionisio marked on his map at the mouth of the Gila was only the name he gave a Yuma village at that point, and was never anything more.   On November 21, 1701, Kino reached a point only one day's journey above the sea, where he crossed the river on a raft, but he made no attempt to go to the mouth.   At last, however, on March 7, 1702, he actually set foot on the barren sands where the waters, gathered from a hundred mountain peaks of the far interior, are hurled against the sea-tide, the first white visitor since Oñate, ninety-eight years before.   Visits of Europeans to this region were then counted by centuries and half-centuries, yet on the far Atlantic shore of the continent they were swarming in the cradle of the giant that should ultimately rule from sea to sea, annihilating the desert.   But even the desert has its

The Moki Town of Wolpi, Arizona.
700 feet above the valley.
Photograph by J. K. HILLERS, U. S. Geol. Survey.

charms.   One seems to inhale fresh vitality from its unpeopled immensity.   I never could understand why a desert is not generally considered beautiful; the kind, at least, we have in the South-west, with all the cacti, the yucca, and the other flowering plants unfamiliar to European or Eastern eyes, and the lines of coloured cliffs and the deep canyons.   There is far more beauty and variety of colour than in the summer meadow-stretches and hills of the Atlantic States.   So the good Padre Kino, after all, was perhaps to be congratulated on having those thirty years, interesting years, before the wilds could be made commonplace.

Arizona did not seem to yield kindly to the civilisers; indeed, it was like the Colorado River, repellent and unbreakable. The padres crossed it and recrossed it on the southwestern corner, but they made no impression.   After Kino's death in 1711 there was a lull in the entradas to the Colorado, though Ugarte, coming up along the eastern coast of Lower California, sailed to the mouth of the river in July, 1721.   Twenty-four years later (1744) Padre Jacobo Sedelmair went down the Gila from Casa Grande to the great bend, and from there cut across to the Colorado at about the mouth of Bill Williams Fork, but his journey was no more fruitful than those of his predecessors in the last two centuries.   It seems extraordinary in these days that men could traverse a country, even so infrequently, during two whole centuries and yet know almost nothing about it. Two years after Sedelmair touched the Colorado, Fernando Consag, looking for mission sites, came up the gulf to its mouth, and when he had sailed away there was another long interval before the river was again visited by Europeans.   This time it was over a quarter of a century, but the activity then begun was far greater than ever before, and the two padres who now became the foremost characters in the drama that so slowly moved upon the mighty and diversified stage of the South-west, were quite the equals in tireless energy of the Jesuit Kino.   These two padres were Garces and Escalante, more closely associated with the history of the Basin of the Colorado than any one who had gone before.   Francisco Garces, as well as Escalante, was of the Franciscan order, and this order, superseding the Jesuit, was making settlements, 1769–70, at San Diego and Monterey, as well as taking a prominent part in those already long established on the Rio Grande. There was no overland connection between the California missions and those of Sonora and the Rio Grande, and the desire to explore routes for such communication was one of the incentives of both Garces and Escalante, in their long entradas. But it seemed to be the habit of those days, either never to seek information as to what had previously been accomplished, or to forget it, for the expedition of Oñate might as well never have been made so far as its effect on succeeding travels was concerned. He had crossed Arizona by the very best route, yet Escalante, 172 years afterward, goes searching for one by way of Utah Lake! Coming from the west, the Moki Towns were ever the objective point, for they were well known and offered a refuge in the midst of the general desolation. Garces had his headquarters at the mission of San Xavier del Bac, or Bac, as it was commonly called, nine miles south of the present town of Tucson. Here Kino had begun a church in 1699, and at a later period another better one was started near by. This was finished in 1797 and to-day stands the finest monument in the South-west of the epoch of the padres. It is a really beautiful specimen of the Mexico-Spanish church architecture of that time. No better testimony could there be of the indefatigable spiritual energy of the padres than this artistic structure standing now amidst a few adobe houses, and once completely abandoned to the elements. Such a building should never be permitted to perish, and it well merits government protection. Its striking contrast to Casa Grande, the massive relic of an unknown time, standing but a few leagues distant, will always render this region of exceptional interest to the artist, the archæologist, and the general traveller.

From Bac, under the protection of the presidio of Tubac, some thirty miles farther south, later transferred (1776) to the present Tucson, Garces carried on his work. He made five great entradas from the time of his arrival in June, 1768. The first was in that same year, the second in 1770, but in these he did not reach the Colorado, and we will pass them by. In the third, 1771, he went down the Gila to the Colorado and descended the latter stream along its banks perhaps to the mouth. On the fourth, 1774, he went with Captain Anza to the Colorado and farther on to the mission of San Gabriel in California, near Los Angeles, and in his fifth, and most important one, 1775–76, he again accompanied Captain Anza, who was

Church of San Xavier del Bac, near Tucson.
Drawing by F. S. DELLENBAUGH, after a photograph.

bound for the present site of San Francisco, there to establish a mission.   Padre Font was Anza's chaplain, and with Garces's aid later made a map of the country.[1]   At Yuma Garces left the Anza party, went down to the mouth of the Colorado, and then up along the river to Mohave, and after another trip out to San Gabriel, he started on the most important part of all his

[1] Font says of Garces : " He seems just like an Indian himself . . . and though the food of the Indians is as nasty and disgusting as their dirty selves the padre eats it with great gusto."   Dr. Coues had planned to publish a translation of Font's important diary.   See *Garces*, by Elliot Coues, p. 172.

journeys, from Mohave to the Moki Towns, the objective point of all entradas eastward from the Colorado. The importance attached at that time to the towns of the Moki probably seems absurd to the reader, but it must not be forgotten that the Moki were cultivators of the soil and always held a store of food-stuffs in reserve. They were also builders of very comfortable houses, as I can testify from personal experience.

Cocopa Woman Grinding Corn.
Photograph by DELANCY GILL.

Thus they assumed a prominence, amidst the desolation of the early centuries, of which the railway in the nineteenth speedily robbed them.

Garces, like most of his kind, was an enthusiast on the subject of saving the souls of the natives. "It made him sick at heart," says Coues, "to see so many of them going to hell for lack of the three drops of water he would sprinkle over them if only they would let him do it." With this idea ever in mind he toiled up and down the lower Colorado, and received assistance from a Yuma chief called Captain Palma. Once when he came up the river to Yuma, where he had left Padre Eisarc, the report the latter gave was so encouraging that Garces exclaims: "I gave a thousand thanks to God to hear them sing psalms divine that the padre had taught them." He further declared that Captain Palma would put to the blush for observing the forms of piety, "many veteran Christians, by the reverence and humility with which he assisted at the holy sacrifice." But alas for the padre's fond hopes!

The Yumas called the Colorado Javill or Hahweel according to Garces; and he also says the name Colorado was given because, as the whole country is coloured, its waters are tinged in the month of April, when the snows are melting, but that they are not always red, which is exactly the case. The name is also said to be a translation of the Piman title "buqui aquimuti."

Leaving Mohave June 4, 1776, Garces struck eastward across Arizona, guided by some Wallapais, but with no white companion. These people had told him about the distance to Moki and the nature of the intervening region. Heading Diamond Creek[1] on his mule, Garces made for the romantic retreat of the Havasupais in the canyon of Cataract Creek, a tributary from the south of the Grand Canyon. He was the first white man, so far as known, to visit this place, and in reaching it he passed near the rim of the great gorge, though he did not then see it. This was the region of the Aubrey cliffs and the place in all probability where Cardenas approached the Grand Canyon, 236 years before. Garces arrived among the Havasupai or Jabesua, as he called them, by following a trail down their canyon that made his head swim, and was impassable to his mule, which was taken in by another

---

[1] This name, by the way, has no connection with the notorious "Arizona" diamond swindle of more recent years. It bore this name in Ives's time and the swindle was much later—1872. The alleged diamond field also was not in Arizona at all, but in north-western Colorado.

route. At one place a ladder was even necessary to complete the 2000 feet of descent to the settlement, where a clear creek suddenly breaks from the rocks, and, rapid and blue, sweeps

The Grand Canyon from Bright Angel Trail.
Painting by THOMAS MORAN.

away down 2000 or more feet to the Colorado, falling in its course at one point over a precipice in three cataracts aggregating 250 feet, from which it takes its name. Here are about

400 acres of arable land along the creek, on which the natives raise corn, beans, squashes, peaches, apricots, sunflowers, etc. There are now about 200 of these people, and they are of Yuman stock. Garces was well treated and rested here five days.

Soon after leaving this retreat he "halted at the sight of the most profound caxones which ever onward continue, and within these flows the Rio Colorado."

"There is seen [he continues] a very great Sierra which in the distance looks blue, and there runs from the southeast to the northwest a pass open to the very base, as if the sierra were cut artificially to give entrance to the Rio Colorado into these lands. I named this singular pass Puerto de Bucareli,[1] and though to all appearances would not seem to be great the difficulty of reaching thereunto, I considered this to be impossible in consequence of the difficult caxones which intervened. From this position said pass bore east northeast."

The padre is standing in admiration before the long line of the Kaibab seen as a great sierra from this position on the southeast, and as the land on the south rises toward the rim it probably appeared to him as if the sierra were really a continuation of the San Francisco Mountains on his right, and was cut in twain by the great gorge of the river. From his standpoint he looked up Marble Canyon, and all the directions he mentions are exactly correct. They saw smokes on the north, which his guides said were made by the Payuches (Pai Utes) living on the other side. The Kaivavitz band of Pai Utes in summer occupy their lands on the summit of the Kaibab, hunting deer and camping in the lovely open glades surrounded by splendid forest. This same day his guides pointed out some tracks of Yabipai Tejua, who go this way to see and trade with their friends, "those who live, as already said, on the other side of the Rio Colorado." It was one of the intertribal highways. Just where it crossed the canyon is hard to say. There were several old trails, and one came down from the north, reaching the river a few miles below the Little Colorado, but where it came out on the south side I do not know. There was once

[1] After the viceroy.

another trail which came from the north down the canyon of Kanab Creek and found a way across to the Coconinos or Havasupai; at least Jacob Hamblin [1] told me he was so informed by the Pai Utes. The "Hance" trail, I believe, was built on the line of an old native one, and probably this was the one the Yabipais were heading for.

The Moki Town of Mishongnuvi, Arizona.
The hill surmounted by the town lies itself on top of a mesa.
Photograph by E. O. BEAMAN.

Garces had a good understanding of the topography, for he says when he reached the Rio Jaquesila de San Pedro, as he called the Little Colorado, that it joined the main stream just above his Puerto de Bucareli. Coues thought it probable that Cardenas on his way to the Grand Canyon, followed from Moki the same trail Garces is now taking to reach that place, and that therefore the first view Cardenas had of the canyon was from near the same place as that of Garces—that is, he saw the Puerto de Bucareli. This is hardly probable, as Garces was only five days reaching Moki from here, and Cardenas travelled twenty from Tusayan to the canyon. As I pointed out on a previous page, so far as the data go, Cardenas reached the Grand Canyon opposite the east side of the Shewits plateau.

Of the Little Colorado Garces said: "The bed of this river as far as the confluence is a trough of solid rock, very profound.

[1] Jacob Hamblin, whom I knew very well, was the "Leather-stocking" of Utah—a man who knew the Amerinds of Utah and northern Arizona better than any one who ever lived.

and wide about a stone's throw." That this was an accurate statement the view on page 95 amply proves. Indeed, the accuracy of most of these early Spaniards, as to topography, direction, etc., is extraordinary. As a rule where they are apparently wrong it is ourselves who are mistaken, and if we fully understand their meaning we find them to be correct. Garces found his way down to the Little Colorado by means of a side canyon and got out again on the other side in the same way. Finally, on July 2nd, he arrived at the pueblo of Oraibi, his objective point, and when he and his tired mule had climbed up on the mesa which bears the town, the women and children lined the housetops to get a glimpse of the singular stranger.

Spaniards were something of a novelty, though by no means unheard of, just as even I was something of a novelty when I visited Oraibi one hundred years after the Padre Garces, because the Oraibis never encouraged white visitors.[1] The first missions were established among the Moki in 1629, when Benavides was custodian of the Rio Grande district, and included Zuñi and Moki in his field. Three padres were then installed at Awatuwi, one of the towns, on the mesa east of what is now called the "East" Mesa. Four were at work amongst the various towns at the time of the Pueblo uprising in 1680, and as one began his labours at Oraibi as early as 1650, a priest was not an unknown object to the older people. All the missionaries having been killed in 1680, and Awatuwi, where a fresh installation was made, having been annihilated in 1700 by the Moki, for three-quarters of a century they had seen few if any Spaniards. Therefore the women and children were full of curiosity. Padre Escalante had been here from Zuñi the year before, looking over the situation with a view to bringing all the Moki once more within the fold. At that time Escalante also tried to go on to what he called the Rio de los

---

[1] A year or two after my visit, James Stevenson, of the Bureau of Ethnology, was driven away from Oraibi. Thomas Keam and he then went there with a force of Navajos and compelled the surrender of the chiefs who had been most obnoxious. They took them to Keam's Canyon and confined them on bread and water till they apologised.

The Canyon of the Little Colorado.
Photograph by C. BARTHELMESS.

Cosninos, the Colorado, but he was unable to accomplish his purpose. Had he once had a view of the Grand Canyon it would undoubtedly have saved him a good many miles of weary travel in his northern entrada of this same year that Garces reached Oraibi.

Garces was not permitted to enter the house where his Yabipai guide intended to stop, and he therefore made his way to a corner formed by a jutting wall, and there unsaddled his faithful mule, which the Yabipai took to a sheep corral. The padre remained in his corner, gathering a few scattered cornstalks from the street, with which he made a fire and cooked a little atóle. All day long the people came in succession to stare at him. I can testify to the sullen unfriendliness of the Oraibi, and I have seen few places I have left with greater pleasure than that I felt when, in 1885, I rode away from this town. Garces was not able to make a favourable impression, and after considering the feasibility of going on to Zuñi, and deciding against it, he thought he would visit the other towns with a hope of being better received, but a few yells from some herders sent him back to his Yabipai guide and several friendly Zuñis at Oraibi, where he occupied his corner again. In the morning he perceived a multitude approaching, some bedecked with paint and feathers, and when four of these came forward and ordered him to leave he held up his crucifix and assured them of his desire to do good to them. They made wry faces and cried "No, no," so that he called for his mule and departed, smiling upon them as he went. He returned by the same route. It was the 4th of July when Garces was expelled by the Oraibis, a declaration of independence on their part which they have maintained down to the present day. That other Declaration of Independence was made on this same day on the far Atlantic coast. The Colonies were engaged in their battle for freedom, but no sound of that strife then reached New Mexico, yet its portent was great for that region where, three-quarters of a century later, the flag of the Great Republic should float triumphant over all.

Garces reached the Colorado once more on July 25th, his arduous journey absolutely fruitless so far as missionary work

was concerned. He arrived at his mission of Bac September
17, 1776.

On July 29, 1776, another even greater entrada was begun
at Santa Fé by the Fray Padre Francisco Silvestre Velez Escalante,[1] in his search for a route to Monterey, unaware that
Garces had just traversed, next to that of Oñate, the most
practicable short route to be found. Garces had written

A Court in Wolpi, Arizona.
Drawing by F. S. DELLENBAUGH.

to Escalante, ministro doctrinero of Zuñi, a letter from
Oraibi, but as the ministro had already departed for Santa Fé,
leaving Fray Mariano Rosate in charge at Zuñi, the letter
probably did not reach him till his return. The northern

[1] H. H. Bancroft gives a map of the route as he understands it, *History of
the Pacific States*, p. 35, vol. xxv., also a condensation of the diary. Philip Harry
gives a condensation in Simpson's *Report*, Appendix R., p. 489. Some river
names have been shifted since Harry wrote. What we call the Grand, upper
part, was then the Blue.

country, notwithstanding several small entradas and the considerable one of Juan Maria Ribera in 1761, who went as far as Gunnison River, was still a terra incognita, and the distance to the Pacific was also an uncertain quantity. Escalante believed a better road existed to Monterey by way of the north than by the middle route, and a further incentive to journey that

A Zuñi Home.
Photograph by J. K. Hillers, U. S. Geol. Survey.

way was probably the rumours of large towns in that direction, the same will-o'-the-wisp the Spaniards for nearly three centuries had been vainly pursuing. The authorities had urged two expeditions to Alta California, to establish communication; Garces and Captain Anza had carried out one, and now Escalante was to execute the other.

Besides the ministro Escalante, there were in the party eight persons, Padre Francisco Dominguez, Juan Pedro Cisneros, alcalde of Zuñi, Bernardo Miera y Pacheco, capitain miliciano of Sante Fé, Don Juan Lain, and four other soldiers. Lain had been with Ribera and was therefore official guide. They went from Sante Fé by way of Abiquiu and the Chama River to the San Juan about where it first meets the

The Governors of Zuñi.

Shows well the general type of the Puebloans of the Basin of the Colorado.
Photograph by J. K. HILLERS.

north line of New Mexico, and thence across the several tributaries to the head of the Dolores River, which they descended
for eleven days.   I am at a loss to exactly follow the route,
not having been able to consult either the copy or the original
of Escalante's diary.   The party made its way across Grand
River, the Book Plateau, White River, and finally to the
Green, called the San Buenaventura, which was forded, apparently near the foot of Split-Mountain Canyon.   Here they

killed one of the
bisons which were
numerous in the
valley. Following
the course of the
river down some
ten leagues, they
went up the Uinta
and finally crossed
the Wasatch, coming down the western side evidently
by way of what
is now known as
Spanish Fork, to
Utah Lake, then
called by the natives Timpanogos.
Here they heard
of a greater lake
to the north, but
instead of seeking

Upper Waters of Rio Virgen.
Photograph by J. K. HILLERS, U. S. Geol. Survey.

it they turned their course south-westerly in what they considered the direction of Monterey through the Sevier River
Valley, the Sevier being called the Santa Isabel, and kept
down along the western edge of the High Plateaus.   It
being by this time the 7th of October, Escalante concludes
that it will be impossible to reach Monterey before winter sets
in and persuades his companions that the best thing to do is to
strike for the Moki Towns.   They cast lots to determine this,

and the decision is for Moki. Evidently he thought this would be an easy road. When he was at Moki the year before, had he not failed to go to the Colorado he would have better un-

Pai Ute Girls, Southern Utah, Carrying Water.
The jugs are wicker made tight with pitch.
Photograph by J. K. HILLERS, U. S. Colo. Riv. Exp.

derstood the nature of the undertaking he now set for his expedition.

Going on southward past what is now Parowan, they came to the headwaters of a branch of the Virgen, in Cedar Valley, and this they followed down to the main stream which they left flowing south-westerly. The place where they turned from

it was probably about at Toquerville.[1]   They were now trying
to make their general course south-east.   Could I but see the
original I certainly could identify the route from here on, having been over the region so often.   As Escalante was obtaining
what information he could from the natives, it seems to me
that his first course "south-east" was to Pipe Spring along the
foot of the Vermilion Cliffs, then his "north-east" was up toward Kanab and through Nine-Mile Valley to the head of the
Kaibab, where a trail led him over to House Rock Valley, on
his "south-east" tack, skirting the Vermilion Cliffs again.   But
they lost it and struck the river at Marble Canyon, through a
misunderstanding of the course of the trail, which bore easterly
and then northerly around the base of the cliffs to what is now
Lee's Ferry, where there was an ancient crossing.   Another
trail goes (or did go) across the north end of the Paria Plateau
and divides, one branch coming down the high cliffs about
three miles up the Paria from the mouth, by a dizzy and zig-
zag path, and the other keeping on to the south-east and striking the river at the very point for which Escalante was evidently
now searching.   Perhaps the Pai Utes had told him of this
trail as well as the one he tried to follow, which would have
taken him to the Lee's Ferry crossing about thirty-five miles
below.   He seems to have reached the brink of Marble Canyon, perhaps half-way between the Paria and the Little Colorado,[2] and followed up-stream first north and then (beyond
Paria) north-east, hunting for a ford.   Twice he succeeded in
descending to the water, but both times was unable to cross.
They had now become so reduced in food that they were
obliged to eat some of their horses.   With great difficulty they
climbed over the cliffs, and at the end of twelve days from
their first arrival at the river they found the ford, which ever
since has been called El Vado de los Padres.   This was the
8th of November, 1776.   The entrance to the river from the

[1] From here to the California mission of San Gabriel would hardly have been
as difficult as the route taken, excepting perhaps the matter of water, and little if
any further than the distance to Santa Fé, but the Pai Utes could give him no information of the distance to the sea.

[2] There was an old crossing near there, also.

west, the side of their approach, is through a small canyon in the homogeneous sandstone, no more than ten feet wide. The course is then about half a mile down the middle of the river over a long bar or shoal to the opposite side, where the exit is made upon a rocky slope. It is a most difficult ford. The trail through the water at the low stage, when, only, fording is possible, is marked by piles of large stones. There is no ford at the Lee's Ferry crossing.

From this Crossing - of - the - Fathers, just above where the river enters Arizona, to the Moki Towns Escalante had a plain trail, and a much simpler topography, and had no difficulty in arriving there. The remainder of his road, from Moki to Zuñi and around to Santa Fé, was one he had travelled before, and the party soon completed the circuit of more than 1500 miles mainly through unknown country, one of the most remarkable explorations ever carried out in the West. It is sometimes stated that Escalante crossed the Grand Canyon, but, as is perfectly plain from the data, he did not; in fact, he could not have done it with horses.

Ashtishkel, a Navajo Chief.
Photograph by E. O. BEAMAN,
U. S. Colo. Riv. Exp.

Garces was not yet finished with his labours on the lower Colorado, and we will return to him. The authorities had decided to establish there two nondescript settlements, a sort of cross between mission, pueblo, and presidio. Captain Palma, the Yuma chief, whose devotions and piety had so delighted the good Father, was eager to have missions started, and constantly importuned the government to grant them. Garces, therefore, went to Yuma again in 1779 to prepare the way, and in 1780 two of the hybrid affairs were inaugurated, one at what

is now Fort Yuma, called Puerto de la Purisima Concepcion,
after the little canyon hard by, so named by Garces previously,
a canyon fifty feet deep and a thousand feet long; the other,
about eight miles down, called San Pedro y San Pablo de
Bicuner.   There were four padres; Garces and Barraneche
at the upper station, and Diaz and Moreno at the lower.   Each
place had eight or ten soldiers, a few colonists, and a few
labourers.   The Spaniards were obliged to appropriate some
of the best lands to till for the support of the missions, and
this, together with the general poverty of the establishments
when he had expected something fine, disgusted Palma and
exasperated him and the other Yumas.   In June, 1781, Captain Moncada, lieutenant-governor of Lower California, arrived
with soldiers and recruits en route for California settlements,
and encamped opposite Yuma.   After some of these people
had been sent forward or back as the plans demanded, Moncada remained at the camp with a few of his soldiers.   No one
suspected the tornado which was brewing.   All the life of the
camp, of the missions, and of the Yumas went on with the
same apparent smoothness, but it was only a delusion suddenly
and horribly dispelled on the fateful 17th of July.   Without a
sign preliminary to the execution of their wrath, Captain
Palma and all his band threw piety to the winds, and annihilated with clubs Moncada's camp and most of the men in the
two missions.   Garces and his assistant, Barraneche, were at
first spared.   Even the conscience of Palma hesitated to murder the good and amiable Garces, who had never been to him
and his people anything but a kind and generous friend, but
the rabble declared these two were the worst of all, and under
this pressure Palma yielded.   It was the last terrible scene of
this act in the life-drama we are following.   The lights were
out, the curtain down.   Military expeditions were sent to
avenge the massacre, but they might as well have chased the
stars.   The missions on the Colorado were ended.   Never
again was an attempt made to found one.   The desert relapsed
into its former complete subjection to the native tribes, and
the indifferent Colorado swept on to the conflict with the sea-
waves as if neither white man nor Amerind had ever touched

its waters. Nearly half a century passed before the face of a
white man was again seen at the mouth of the river, and all
the toil of Kino, Garces, and the rest was apparently as completely wasted as if they had tried to stop the flow of the
Colorado with a broom.

CHAPTER V

Breaking the Wilderness—Wanderings of the Trappers and Fur Traders—General
Ashley in Green River Valley, 1824—Pattie along the Grand Canyon, 1826—
Lieut. Hardy, R.N., in a Schooner on the Lower Colorado, 1826—Jedediah
Smith, Salt Lake to San Gabriel, 1826—Pattie on the Lower Colorado in
Canoes, 1827–28.

AS the "sweet Afton" of old gently flowing among its
green braes compares with the fierce Colorado, so do
those earnest padres who so faithfully tried to plant their cross
in the waste places, as sketched in the chapter just closed with
the martyrdom of Garces, compare with the new set of actors
that now appear, as the development of this drama of the
wilderness continues. The former fitted well into the strange
scenery; they became a part of it; they fraternised with the
various tribes native to the land, and all things together went
forward with pictorial harmony. They were like a few mellow
figures blended skilfully into the deep tones of an ancient canvas. But now the turbulent spirit of the raging river itself per-
vades the new-comers who march imperiously upon the mighty
stage with the heavy tread of the conqueror, out of tune with
the soft old melody; temporising with nothing; with a heed-
less stroke, like the remorseless hand of Fate, obliterating all
obstacles to their progress. Not theirs the desire to save natives from perdition; rather to annihilate them speedily as useless relics of a bygone time. They are savages among savages;
quite as interesting and delightful in their way as the older occupants of the soil. It became in reality the conflict of the old
and the new, and then was set the standard by which the native tribes have ever since been measured and dealt with.

The inevitable was simply coming to pass: one more act in the world-play of continental subjugation to the European. The United States, born in privation and blood, were growing into a nation eager for expansion, and by 1815 they had already ventured beyond the Mississippi, having purchased from France all territory north of Red River, the Arkansas, and the 42nd parallel, as far as the unsettled British boundary and the disputed region of Oregon. Naturally, then, Americans wanted to know what was to be found in this vast tract unknown to them, and when a few bold spirits pushed out to the great mountains it was discovered that fur-bearing animals existed in multitude. In the trapping of these and the trading in their pelts a huge industry sprang up. In this trade future millionaires laid their foundations.

The beaver were then the most profitable of all, and they were the most abundant. The pelts were estimated by "packs," each of which consisted of about eighty skins, weighing one hundred pounds, and worth in the mountains from three hundred to five hundred dollars. The profits were thus speedy and very great. In the search for the richest rewards the trapper continually pushed farther and farther away from the "States," encroaching at length on the territory claimed by Spain, a claim to be soon (1821) adopted by the new-born Mexican Republic. Trespassing on the tribal rights of Blackfoot, Sioux, Ute, or any other did not enter into any one's mind as something to be considered. Thus, rough-shod the trapper broke the wilderness, fathomed its secret places, traversed its trails and passes, marking them with his own blood and more vividly with that of the natives. Incidentally, by right of their discoveries and occupation of the wilderness, much of it became by the law of nations a part of the lands of the United States, though still nominally claimed by Mexico. Two years after the return of the famous Lewis-and-Clark expedition, Andrew Henry "discovered" South Pass (1808), and led his party through it into the Green River[1] Valley. His

[1] The name Green River was used as early as 1824, and was probably derived from the name of the early trapper. Till about 1835 it was usually called by the Crow name, Seedskeedee.

discovery consisted, like many others of the time, in following up the bison trails and the highways of the natives. The latter, of course, knew every foot of the whole country; each tribe its own special lands and more or less into and across those of its neighbours.

By the time the second decade of the nineteenth century was fairly begun the trappers were crossing in considerable numbers from the headwaters of the Missouri and the Platte into the valley of the Colorado and the Columbia, and as early as 1824 one of the most brilliant figures of this epoch, General Ashley,[1] having previously organised a fur-trading company in St. Louis, then the centre of all Western commerce, had established himself in Green River Valley with a large band of expert trappers which included now famous names like Henry, Bridger, Fitzpatrick, Green, Sublet, and Beckwourth. Provo (or Provost) was already encamped in Brown's Hole. One of Ashley's principal camps was what they called the "rendezvous" (there were a great many French-Canadians engaged in the fur business, and hence numerous French words were in common use among the trappers of the period), just above "The Suck," on Green River. This Suck was at the entrance to Flaming Gorge, as it has since been named. Beckwourth says of this: "The current, at a small distance from our camp, became exceedingly rapid, and drew toward the centre from each shore." The river here narrows suddenly and attacks a high ridge. Doubling around a point to the left and then as suddenly to the right, the swift water or "Suck" slackens up in the quieter reach of Flaming Gorge. In their journeys after beaver the Ashley party had been able to go into this gorge and the two following ones, Horseshoe and Kingfisher, and had doubtless trapped in them. Here were many beaver, and Ashley drew the inference that as many existed below in the deeper canyon. Though he had discovered the dangerous character of the river he decided to build boats and set forth on

---

[1] Wm. Henry Ashley, born in Virginia, 1778; went to Missouri 1802; general of militia; elected first governor 1820; went into fur trade 1822 with Andrew Henry; elected to Congress 1831; twice re-elected; continued in office till March 4, 1837.—Chittenden.

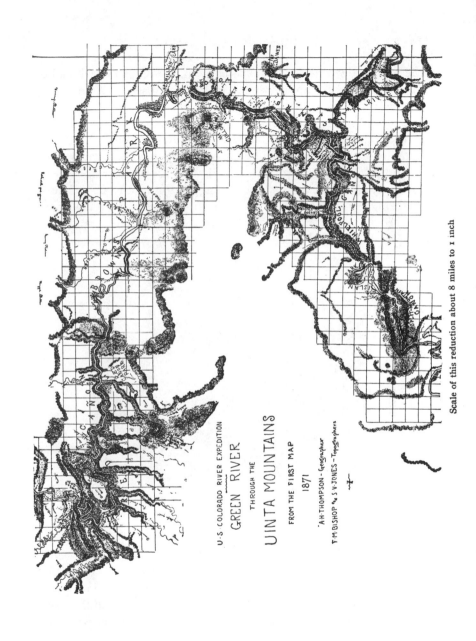

U.S. COLORADO RIVER EXPEDITION

GREEN RIVER

THROUGH THE

UINTA MOUNTAINS

FROM THE FIRST MAP

1871

A.H. THOMPSON - Geographer

F.M. BISHOP & J.V. JONES - Topographers

Scale of this reduction about 8 miles to 1 inch

the current in order to trap the canyon, the length of which he did not know and underestimated.   A purpose of reaching St. Louis by this route has been attributed to Ashley, but as Hunt and others some years before understood this to be a stream on whose lower waters Spaniards lived, Ashley doubtless had the same information, and from that he would have known that it was no practicable route to St. Louis.   Beckwourth, who relates the story of the trip,[1] makes no suggestion of any far-off destination, nor does he say they took their packs along, as they

Flaming Gorge, Green River.   Beginning of the Canyons.
Picture taken just inside the entrance.   Walls 1300 feet.
Photograph by E. O. Beaman, U. S. Colo. Riv. Exp.

would have done if going to a commercial centre.   It seems to have been purely a trapping expedition, and was probably the very first attempt to navigate Green River.   They took along few provisions, expecting to find beaver plentiful to the end of the canyon, but after a few miles the beaver were ab-

[1] *Life and Adventures of James P. Beckwourth*, edited by T. D. Bonner. Beckwourth was always called " Beckwith " in the mountains, but this was probably only a perversion of the original, though Chittenden seems to think he only assumed the former spelling on publishing his book.

sent, and, having preserved none of the meat, the party began
to suffer for food.   They were six days without eating, and, the
high precipitous walls running ever on and on, they became
disheartened, or, in Western phrase, "demoralised," and proposed to cast lots to find which should make food for the

Red Canyon at Low Water.
Length 25 miles.   Walls 1800 to 2500 feet high.   Average width of river, 250 feet.

others, a proposition which horrified Ashley, and he begged
them to hold out longer, assuring them that the walls must
soon break and enable them to escape.   They had not expected so long a gorge.   Red Canyon is twenty-five miles and,
with the three above, the unbroken canyon is about thirty-five

miles.   Under the circumstances the canyon seemed intermin-
able and the cliffs insurmountable.   The latter grow more precipitous toward the lower end, and scaling would be a difficult
feat for a man well fed and strong, though well-nigh hopeless
for any weakened by lack of proper food.   At last, however,
an opening appeared.   Here they discovered Provo encamped
with an abundance of provisions, so their troubles were
quickly over.   The opening they had arrived at was probably
Brown's Hole.   There is only one other place that might be
called an opening, and this is a small park-like break on the
right side of the river, not far above Brown's Hole, formerly
called Little Brown's Hole and also Ashley Park.   The Ashley
men would have had a hard climb to get out of this place, and
it is not probable that Provo would have climbed into it, as no
beaver existed there.   It seems positive, then, that Ashley came
to Provo in Brown's Hole.   Thus he did not "make his peril-
lous way through Brown's Hole," as one author says, because
he ended his journey with the beginning of that peaceful park.
They lost two of their boats and several guns in Red Canyon,
and Ashley left there a mark to identify the time of his passage.   He wrote his name and the date, 1825, on a large rock
above a sharp fall, which was (later, 1869,) named in his honour.
I saw this inscription in 1871 and made a careful copy of it,
which is given here.   See also the illustra-
tion of Ashley Falls on page 113.   The location of it is just west of C in the
words "Red Cañon " on the map, page 109.
In the canyon of Lodore, at the foot of
Disaster Falls, we found some wreckage in the sand, a bake-
oven, tin plates, knives, etc., which Powell first saw in 1869,
but these could not have belonged to Ashley's party, for
plainly Ashley did not enter Lodore at all.   It was evidently from some later expedition which probably started from
Brown's Park, in the days of Fort Davy Crockett.

Provo had plenty of horses, and Ashley and his men
joined him going out to Salt Lake, where Provo had come
from.

The year following Ashley's attempt to trap Green River

Ashley Falls, Red Canyon, Green River.

General Ashley wrote his name on a rock about half way up the picture, on the right, in 1825.
Photograph by E. O. BEAMAN, U. S. Colo. Riv. Exp.

was a most eventful one in the history of the Colorado. Time appeared to be ripe for great journeys. The Mexicans outside of California were more amiably inclined, and granted privileges to trappers in New Mexico. Two men who were among the first to push their way into New Mexico were James O. Pattie and his father, and the narrative of their experiences as told by the younger Pattie is one of the most thrilling and interesting books of Western adventure ever published.[1] They had trapped on the Gila, or "Helay," as they called it in 1825, and the next year they went back there with a party, trapping the Gila and its tributaries with gratifying success.[2] Working their way down the Gila, they eventually reached its junction with what they called Red River, the Great Colorado. Following up the Colorado, probably the first white men to travel here since the time of Garces, they rode through a camp of Coco-Maricopas, who ran frightened away, and the Pattie party, passing them by as if they were mere chaff, camped four miles farther on, where they were visited by about one hundred, "all painted red in token of amity." Farther up they entered the Mohave country. When they met some of the inhabitants they "marched directly through their village, the women and children screaming and hiding themselves in their huts." Three miles above, the Patties camped, and a number of the Mohaves soon came to see them. They did not like the looks of the chief, who made signs that he wanted a horse as payment for the privilege of trapping in his domain. As the trappers recognised no rights on the part of the natives, they peremptorily refused, whereat the chief drew himself erect with a stern and fierce air and sent an arrow into a tree, at the same time "raising his hand to his mouth and making their peculiar yell." The captain of the Pattie band replied by taking his gun and shooting the arrow in two. Driven out of the camp the following day, the chief

---

[1] *The Personal Narrative of James O. Pattie, of Kentucky*, etc., edited by Timothy Flint. Cincinnati, E. H. Flint, 1833. There is a copy in the Astor Library, New York.

[2] There were two classes of trappers, the free and those in the employ of some company. The Patties belonged to the former class.

The Grand Canyon from Bright Angel Trail looking East.

Point of view 1000 feet above the water.   Total depth between 5000 and 6000 feet.

Photograph by ROSE.

shot a horse as he rode past it and was himself instantly pierced with four rifle balls.

A band of his followers, armed, of course, with only bows and arrows, next day made a concerted attack, but were cut down by the rifles and fine marksmanship of the Americans. As these Mohaves had been good friends to Garces, and afterwards treated Americans well till they were instigated by the Spaniards to fight, it is probable that a somewhat more con-

Entrance to Black Canyon, first seen by James O. Pattie.
Photograph by WHEELER EXP.

ciliatory approach might have avoided the trouble this party experienced.

Farther up they reached the "Shuenas," who had apparently never before heard the report of a gun, and on the 25th of March they arrived at what we now call Bill Williams Fork. A party was sent up this stream to trap. As they did not return next day according to the plan, scouts were dispatched, who found the bodies cut to pieces and spitted before a great fire.

On the 28th of March they came to a place on the river

where "the mountains shut in so close upon its shores that we were compelled to climb a mountain and travel along the aclivity, the river still in sight, and at an immense depth beneath us." This was probably Black Canyon; they are the first white men on record to reach it. They now took a remarkable journey of fourteen days, but unfortunately little detail is given, probably because Pattie's editor considered a cut across the country of little importance. They travelled, they thought, one hundred leagues along these canyons, with the "river bluffs on the opposite shore never more than a mile" from them.[1] Thus they evidently did not see the Grand Canyon at its widest part. By April 10th they arrived "where the river emerges from these horrid mountains, which so cage it up as to deprive all human beings of the ability to descend to its banks and make use of its waters. No mortal has the power of describing the pleasure I felt when I could once more reach the banks of the river." They had suffered for food on this journey, but now they were again in a beaver country and also killed plenty of elk, the skins of which they dressed for clothing. They had made the first extended trip on record along the Grand Canyon and the other canyons of the Colorado, but whether they passed up by the north or the south I am unable to determine. My impression is that they passed by the north, as they would otherwise have met with the Havasupai in their Canyon, with the Little Colorado, and with the Moki. They would also have struck the San Juan, but the first stream mentioned as coming in is from the north, which they reached three days after arriving at the place where they could get to the water. Three days after leaving this they met a large body of Shoshones. They appear now to be somewhere on Grand River. They had a brush with the Shoshones, whom they defeated, and then compelled the women to exchange six scalps of Frenchmen whom the Shoshones had killed on the headwaters of the Platte, for scalps of members of their own party of whom the Patties had killed eight. They also took from

[1] " It is perhaps this very long and formidable range of mountains," says Pattie, " which has caused that this country of Red River has not been more explored," p. 98.

them all the stolen beaver-skins, five mules, and their dried buffalo meat.   After this interchange of civilities the trappers went on to where the river forked again, neither fork being more than twenty-five or thirty yards wide.   The right-hand-fork pursued a north-east course, and following it four days brought them (probably in Middle Park) to a large village of the "Nabahoes."   Of these they inquired as to the pass over the mountains (Continental Divide) and were informed they must follow the left-hand fork, which they accordingly did, and on the thirty-first day of May, 1826, came to the gap, which they traversed, by following the buffalo trails through the snow, in six days.   Then they descended to the Platte, and went on north to the Yellowstone, making in all a traverse of the whole Rocky Mountain region probably never since surpassed, and certainly never before approached.

A few months later a lieutenant of the British Navy, R. W. H. Hardy, travelling in Mexico, chartered in the port of Guaymas a twenty-five-ton schooner, the *Bruja* or *Sea Witch*, and sailed up the Gulf of California.   Encountering a good deal of trouble in high winds and shoals he finally reached a vein of reddish water which he surmised came from "Red River," and at two o'clock of the same day he saw an opening ahead which he took to be the mouth of the river.   An hour later all doubt was dispelled, and by half-past six he came to anchor for the night at the entrance, believing the tide to be at nearly low water.   "In the middle of the night," he says, "I was awakened by the dew and the noise of jackals.   I took this opportunity of examining the lead which had been left hanging alongside, to see what water we had.   What was my astonishment to find only a foot and a half.   The crew was sound asleep.   Not even the sentinel was able to keep his eyes open."   They got off without damage at the rise of the tide, but the next day misfortune awaited the schooner.   The helmsman neglecting his duty for a moment as they were working up the stream, the vessel lost headway, and the fierce current immediately swept her, stern foremost, into the bank and broke the rudder.   After much labour the *Bruja* was finally again placed in the stream, where they waited for slack water, expecting

The Navajo Type.
Photograph by J. K. HILLERS, U. S. Geol. Survey.

then to ship the rudder. "But in the Rio Colorado," he de-
clares with italics, *"there is no such thing as slack water.*
Before the ebb has finished running the flood commences,
boiling up full eighteen inches above the surface and roaring
like the rapids of Canada." Had he known what we now
know he might have found a simile nearer his position at the
moment. Finding he could make no further progress with the
schooner, he took a small boat and continued his voyage in it,
though not for any great distance, as he returned to the vessel
at night. Five or six thousand Yumas were seen, but they
were entirely friendly. He thought the mouth of the Gila
was below his stranded vessel, but he was mistaken in this, for
it was in reality a great many miles farther up. What he took
for the Gila was the main Colorado itself, and what he thought
was the Colorado was only a bayou or flood-water channel. It
being midsummer the river was at flood. The bayou is still
called the False or Hardy's Colorado.

After eight days of waiting they at last got their rudder
shipped, the vessel on the tide, and went back down the
stream, one of the Yuma women swimming after them till
taken on board. She was landed at the first opportunity.
The interpreter told Hardy his was the first vessel that had
ever visited the river, and that they took it for a large bird.
The lieutenant was evidently not posted on the history of the
region, and the Yuma was excusable for not having a memory
that went back eighty years.[1] Hardy gave some of the names
that still hold on that part of the river, like Howard's Reach,
where his *Bruja* was stranded, Montague and Gore Islands, etc.

The same month that Hardy sailed away from the mouth of
the Colorado, August, 1826, Jedediah Smith started from Salt
Lake (the 22d), passed south by Ashley's or Utah Lake, and,
keeping down the west side of the Wasatch and the High Plateaus, reached the Virgen River near the south-western corner of
Utah. This he called Adams River in honour of the President
of the United States. Following it south-west through the Pai
Ute country for twelve days he came to its junction with what

[1] Fernando Consag entered the river, 1746, looking for mission sites, and two
centuries before that was Alarçon.

he called the Seedskeedee, knowing it to be the same stream so called in the north. This was the Colorado. Proceeding down the Colorado to the Mohaves he was kindly received by them and remained some time recuperating his stock. It may seem strange that the Mohaves should be so perverse, killing one set of trappers and treating another like old friends, but the secret of the difference on this occasion, perhaps, lay in the difference of approach. Jedediah Smith was a sort of reincarnation of the old padres, and of all the trappers the only one

Upper Valley of the Virgen.
Photograph by C. R. SAVAGE.

apparently who allowed piety or humanitarianism to sway his will. His piety was universally known. It was not an affectation, but a genuine religion which he carried about with him into the fastnesses of the mountains. Leaving the Mohaves he crossed the desert to the Californian coast, where he afterwards had trouble with the authorities, who seemed to bear a grudge against all American trappers, and who seized every opportunity to maltreat and rob them. This, however, did not prevent Smith from returning again after a visit to the northern rendezvous. But while crossing the Colorado, the Mohaves, who had meanwhile been instigated to harass Americans by the Spaniards (so it is said), attacked the expedition, killing ten men and capturing everything. Smith escaped to be afterwards killed on the Cimarron by the Comanches.

Pattie and his father again entered the Gila country in the autumn of 1827, with permission from the governor of New Mexico to trap. After they had gone down the Gila a considerable distance the party split up, each band going in different directions, and after numerous adventures the Patties and their adherents arrived at the Colorado, where their horses were stampeded by the tribe living at the mouth of the Gila, the "Umeas." They were left without a single animal, a most serious predicament in a wild country. The elder Pattie counselled pursuit on foot to recapture the horses or die in the attempt. But the effort was fruitless. They then made their way back to their camp, devoured their last morsel of meat, placed their guns on a raft, and swam the river to annihilate the village they saw on the opposite bank. The Yumas, however, had anticipated this move, and the trappers found there only one poor old man, whom they spared. Setting fire to every hut in the village, except that of the old man, they had the small satisfaction of watching them burn. There was now no hope either of regaining the horses or of fighting the Yumas, so they devoted their attention to building canoes for the purpose of escaping by descending the Colorado. For this they possessed tools, trappers often having occasion to use a canoe in the prosecution of their work. They soon had finished eight, dugouts undoubtedly, though Pattie does not say so, and they already had one which Pattie had made on the Gila. Uniting these by platforms in pairs they embarked upon them with all their furs and traps, leaving their saddles hidden on the bank.

On the 9th of December (1827)[1] they started, probably the

---

[1] The reader may think I introduce too many year-dates but I have found most books so lacking in this regard that I prefer to err on the other side.

first navigators of this part of the river since Alarçon, 287 years
before. That night they set forty traps and were rewarded
with thirty-six beaver. Such good luck decided them to travel
slowly with the current, about four miles an hour, "and trap
the river clear." The stream was about two hundred to three
hundred yards wide, with bottoms extending back from six to

The "Navajo Church," a Freak of Erosion near Ft. Wingate, N. M.
The Basin of the Colorado is full of such architectural forms.   See
Dellenbaugh Butte, p. 269, Gunnison Butte, p. 271.
"Hole in the Wall," p. 41, etc.
Photograph by BEN WITTICK.

ten miles, giving good camp-grounds all along.   With abundance of fat beaver meat and so many pelts added to their store
they forgot their misfortunes and began to count on reaching
the Spanish settlements they thought existed near the mouth
of the river.   Sometimes their traps yielded as many as

sixty beaver in a night, and finally they were obliged to halt and make another canoe. So they went slowly down, occasionally killing a couple of hostile natives, or deer, panthers, foxes, or wild-cats. One animal is described as like an African leopard, the first they had ever seen. At length they came to a tribe much shorter of stature than the Yumas, and friendly. These were probably Cocopas. Not a patch of clothing existed in the whole band, and Pattie's men gave the women some old shirts, intimating, as well as they could, that they ought to wear some covering. These people were well formed, and many of the women had exceptionally fine figures if the judgment of the trappers can be trusted in this respect. When a gun was fired they either fell prostrate or ran away, so little did they know about firearms. The chief had a feast of young dog prepared for his guests, who partook of it with reluctance. All communication was by signs, and when the chief imitated the beating of surf and drew a cow and a sheep in the sand, pointing west, they thought they were at last nearing the longed-for Spanish settlements, and went on their way joyfully. Little did they imagine that the settlements the chief described were far off on the Californian coast.

The new year, 1828, came in and still they were going down the river, taking many beaver. As a New Year's greeting a shower of arrows from a new tribe, the Pipis, fell amongst them. The trappers killed six of them at one volley, and the rest ran away, leaving twenty-three beautiful longbows behind. The only clothing the dead men had on was snail-shells fastened to the ends of their long locks of hair. The trappers now began to seek more anxiously for the mythical settlements. "A great many times each day," says Pattie, "we bring our crafts to the shore and go out to see if we cannot discover the tracks of horses and cattle." On the 18th they thought some inundated river entering was the cause of a slackening of the current, and finally they began to rig oars, thinking they would now be obliged to work to get on down-stream, but presently, to their surprise, the current doubled its rate and they were going along at six miles an hour. None of them had ever had any experience with tides, and they therefore failed to fathom the real cause of these singular changes of speed. Suddenly, as they were descending, people of the same tribe they had fired on stood on the shore and shouted, making signs for them to land, that their boats would be capsized, but, thinking it a scheme for robbery and murder, they kept on, though they refrained from shooting. Late in the evening they landed, making their camp on a low point where the canoes with their rich cargoes were tied to some trees. Pattie's father took the first watch, and in the night, hearing a roaring noise that he thought indicated a sudden storm, he roused his companions,

Cliffs of the Rio Virgen, about 2500 Feet High.
Photograph by J. K. HILLERS, U. S. Geol. Survey.

and all was prepared for a heavy rain, when, instead, to their great consternation, the camp was inundated by "a high ridge of water over which came the sea current combing down like water over a mill-dam." The canoes were almost capsized, but this catastrophe was averted by rapid and good management. Even in the darkness, in the face of a danger unexpected and unknown, the trappers never for an instant lost their coolness and quick judgment, which was so often their salvation. Paddling the canoes under the trees, they clung to

the branches, but when the tide went out the boats were all
high and dry.   At last the day dawned bright and fair, enabling them to see what had happened, and when the tide once
more returned, they got the canoes out of the trap.

They now proceeded with the ebb tide, stopping with the
beginning of the flood, constantly on the lookout for the
Spanish settlements, and not till the 28th, when they saw before
them such a commotion of waters that their small craft would
be instantly engulfed, and wide sandy stretches, perfectly barren, all round, did they realise what a mistake they had made.

" The fierce billows," says Pattie, "shut us in from below, the river
current from above, and murderous savages on either hand on the
shore.   We had a rich cargo of furs, a little independence for each
one of us could we have disposed of them among the Spanish people
whom we expected to have found here.   There were no such settlements.   Every side on which we looked offered an array of
danger, famine, or death.   In this predicament what were furs to us."

In order to escape they worked their way back up the river as far
as they could by rowing, poling, and towing, but on February
10th they met a great rise which put a stop to progress.   They
now abandoned the canoes, buried the furs in deep pits, and
headed for the coast settlements of California.   After many vicis-
situdes, which I am unable to relate here, they finally arrived,
completely worn out, at the Spanish mission of St. Catherine.

Now they believed their troubles were over, and that after
recuperating they could go back, bring in their furs, dispose of
them handsomely, and reap the reward of all their privation
and toil.   Not so, however.   Indeed, the worst of their trials
was now to come.   Before they comprehended the intention the
Spanish official had seized their rifles and the men were locked
up with only the commonest fare to relieve their suffering.
Cruelty followed cruelty, but they believed it was the mistake
of the minor officers, and appealed to the general in charge at
San Diego, expecting an order from him for release.   Instead
of this they were marched under guard to San Diego, where
each was confined in a separate room, frustrating their plan to
recapture their arms and fight their way out.   Pattie's father

presently became ill, and no amount of entreaty was sufficient to gain permission for the son to see him even for a moment. He died in his cell. After much argument and the intercession of some of the minor officers, Pattie was permitted liberty long enough to attend the funeral. At last the men were allowed to go back for the furs, which no doubt the wily general intended to confiscate, Pattie himself being retained as a hostage. But the furs had been ruined by a rise of the river. Smallpox then began to rage on the coast, and through this fact Pattie finally gained his freedom. Having with him a quantity of vaccine virus, he was able to barter skill in vaccinating the populace for liberty, though it was tardily and grudgingly granted. He was able, at length, to get away from

The " Colob " Country, Southern Utah.
Photograph by J. K. HILLERS, U. S. Colo. Riv. Exp.

California, and returned, broken in health and penniless, by way of the City of Mexico, to his old home near Cincinnati, after six years of extraordinary travel through the wildest portions of the Rocky Mountain region and the extreme Southwest.

In the year 1826, an afterwards famous personage appeared in the valley of the Colorado, on the Gila branch, being no less than Kit Carson,[1] one of the greatest scouts and trappers of all.

[1] *Life of Kit Carson*, by Charles Burdett. There are several Lives by other biographers.

At this time he was but seventeen years old, though in sagacity, knowledge, and skill soon the equal of any trapper in the field. In 1827, Ewing Young, another noted trapper, having been driven away from the Gila by the natives, organised a company of forty men to go back and punish them, which meant to kill all they could see, innocent or guilty. Carson was one of this party. They succeeded in killing fifteen of the offenders, after which slight diversion they went on down the stream, trapping it as they went, but finally, running short of provisions, they had to eat horses. Arriving among the Mohaves, they obtained food from them, and proceeded across to San Gabriel Mission, to which place after trapping up the Sacramento Valley, they again returned, in season to assist the Spaniards to reduce the natives around the settlement to submission. This was accomplished by the simple method of killing one-third of them.

Limited space prohibits my recounting the exploits of even the smaller part of the trappers of this period, but with what follows I believe the reader will possess a sufficient picture of the life of the Rocky Mountain Trapper at this time.[1] A trail from Santa Fé to California was opened by way of what is now Gunnison Valley on Green River, and thence west by about the same route that Jedediah Smith followed, that is, down the Virgen River, by William Wolfskill who went out by this route to Los Angeles, in 1830.[2] There were trappers now in every part of the wilderness, excepting always the canyons of the Green and Colorado, which were given a wide berth as their forbidding character became better known; and as time went on the stories of those who had here and there looked into the angry depths, or had essayed a tilt with the furious rapids at one or two northern points, were enlarged upon, and, like all unknown things, the terrors became magnified.

It was in 1832 that Captain Bonneville entered Green River Valley, but as his exploits belong more properly to the valley of the Columbia, I shall not attempt to mention any of them

[1] The reader is referred for exact details to the admirable work by H. M. Chittenden, *The American Fur Trade of the Far West*.

[2] H. H. Bancroft says 1831-2.

In the Canyon of Lodore.
Walls about 2500 feet, width of river about 400 feet.

here, referring the reader to the delightful account by Washington Irving.

In May, 1839, a traveller who was a careful observer, Thomas J. Farnham, went from New Mexico across the mountains to Brown's Hole en route for Oregon, and a portion of his narrative[1] is of deep interest in this connection, because his guide, Kelly, gave him some account of the Green and Colorado, which reflects the amount of real knowledge then possessed concerning the canyon-river.

" The Grand unites with the Seedskeedee or Green River to form the Colorado of the West. From the junction of these branches the Colorado has a general course from the north-east to the south-west of seven hundred miles to the head of the Gulf of California. Four hundred of this seven hundred miles is an almost unbroken chasm of kenyon, with perpendicular sides hundreds of feet in height, at the bottom of which the waters rush over continuous cascades. This kenyon terminates thirty [should be three hundred] miles above the gulf. To this point the river is navigable. The country on each side of its whole course is a rolling desert of loose brown earth, on which the rains and the dews never fall. A few years since, two Catholic missionaries and their servants on their way from the mountains to California, attempted to descend the Colorado. They have never been seen since the morning they commenced their fatal undertaking.

"A party of trappers and others made a strong boat and manned it well with the determination of floating down the river to take beaver that they supposed lived along its banks. But they found themselves in such danger after entering the kenyon that with might and main they thrust their trembling boat ashore and succeeded in leaping upon the crags and lightening it before it was swallowed in the dashing torrent.''

They had a difficult time in getting out of the canyon, but finally, by means of ropes and by digging steps with their rifle barrels, they reached the open country and made their way back

[1] *Travels in the Great Western Prairies, the Anahuac and Rocky Mountains, and in the Oregon Territory*, by Thomas J. Farnham. There is a copy in the library of Columbia University, New York.

to the starting-point.   This was, possibly, the expedition which
was wrecked in Lodore, after Ashley's Red Canyon trip.   I
have not succeeded in finding any other account that would fit
that place.   Arriving at Fort Davy Crockett, in Brown's Park,
he describes it as

"a hollow square of one-storey log cabins, with roofs and floor of
mud.   Around these we found the conical skin lodges of the squaws
of the white trappers who were away on their fall hunt, and also the
lodges of a few Snake Indians who had preceded their tribe to this

Uinta Utes, Saiar's Home.
Photograph by J. K. HILLERS, U. S. Geol. Survey.

their winter haunt.   Here also were the lodges of Mr. Robinson, a
trader, who usually stations himself here to traffic with the Indians
and white trappers.   His skin lodge was his warehouse, and buffalo
robes spread on the ground his counter, on which he displayed his
butcher knives, hatchets, powder, lead, fish-hooks, and whiskey.   In
exchange for these articles he received beaver skins from trappers,

money from travellers, and horses from the Indians. Thus, as one would believe, Mr. Robinson drives a very snug little business. And, indeed, when all the independent trappers are driven by the appearance of winter into this delightful retreat, and the whole Snake village, two thousand or three thousand strong, impelled by the same necessity, pitch their lodges around the fort and the dances and merrymakings of a long winter are thoroughly commenced, there is no want of customers.''

With this happy picture of frontier luxury in the trapper period I will close the scene. Unwittingly, but no less thoroughly, the trappers had accomplished a mission: they had opened the gates of the wilderness.

Two-thirds of these intrepid spirits had left their bones on the field, but theirs had been the privilege of seeing the priscan glory of the wilderness.

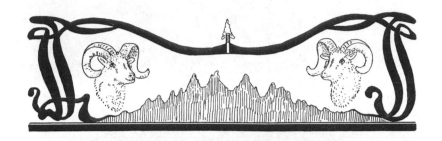

CHAPTER VI

Frémont, the Pathfinder—Ownership of the Colorado—The Road of the Gold
Seekers—First United States Military Post, 1849—Steam Navigation—
Captain Johnson Goes to the Head of Black Canyon.

THE great Western wilderness was now no longer "unknown" to white men.   By the year 1840 the American
had traversed it throughout, excepting the canyons of the
Colorado, which yet remained, at least below the mouth of
Grand River, almost as much of a problem as before the fur
trade was born.   Like some antediluvian monster the wild
torrent stretched a foaming barrier miles on miles from the
mountains of the north to the seas of the south, fortified in a
rock-bound lair, roaring defiance at conquistadore, padre, and
trapper alike.

Till now the trappers and fur companies had been the chief
travellers through this strange, weird land, but as the fourth
decade of the century fairly opens, a new kind of pioneer appears suddenly on the field; a pioneer with motives totally
different from those of the preceding explorers.   Proselyting
or profit had been heretofore the main spurs to ambition, but
the commanding figure which we now observe scanning, from
the majestic heights of the Wind River range, the labyrinthian
maze of unlocated, unrecorded mountains, valleys, rivers, and
canyons, rolling far and away to the surf of the Pacific, is imbued with a broader purpose.   His mission is to know.   The
immediately previous elements drifted across the scene like
rifle-smoke on the morning breeze, making no more impression

on the world's knowledge.   They recorded little, and, so far as information was concerned, they might almost as well never have set foot in the wilderness.   But the new man records everything: the wind, the cold, the clouds, the trees, the

Kaibab Pai Ute Boys Playing a Game of Wolf and Deer.
Photograph by J. K. HILLERS, U. S. Colo. Riv. Exp.

grass, the mice, the men, the worms, the birds, etc., to the end of his time and his ability.   He is the real explorer, the advance guard of those many expeditions which followed and whose labours form the fourth division of our subject.   Frémont is the name, since that time called "Pathfinder," though, of course, the paths he followed had often before been travelled by the redoubtable trapper, whose knowledge, like that of the native, was personal only. Indeed, he was guided in his journeys by several men now quite as famous as himself—Kit Carson, Fitzpatrick, Walker, and Godey. But the field was still new to the world and to science. Quite appropriately, one of the highest peaks from which the Colorado draws its first waters, is now distinguished by the name of the earliest scientific observer to enter its basin. Frémont came up the North Platte and the Sweetwater branch, crossing (1842) from that stream by the South Pass thirty-four years after Andrew Henry had first traversed it, over to the headwaters of the Colorado. The ascent to South Pass is very gradual, and there is no gorge or defile. The total width is about twenty miles. A day or two later Frémont climbed out of the valley on the flank of the Wind River Mountains. "We had reached a very elevated point," he says; "and in the valley below and among the hills were a number of lakes at different levels; some two or three hundred feet above others, with which they communicated by foaming torrents. Even to our great height the roar of the cataracts came up, and we could see them leaping down in lines of snowy foam." Thus are the rills and the rivulets from the summits collected in these beautiful alpine lakes to give birth to the Colorado in white cascades, typical, at the very fountainhead, of the turbulence of the waters which have rent for themselves a trough of rock to the gulf.[1] Springing from these clear pools and seething falls, shadowed by sombre pines and granite crags, its course is run through plunging rapids to the final assault on the sea, where wide sand-barrens and desolation prevail. Frémont understood this from his guides and says: "Lower down, from Brown's Hole to the southward, the river runs through lofty chasms, walled in by precipices of red rock." The descent

" of the Colorado is but little known, and that little derived from vague report. Three hundred miles of its lower part, as it ap-

[1] These mountains, as the glacial accumulations began to permanently diminish, must have annually sent a long-continued huge flood of water down the rivers heading there.

proaches the Gulf of California, is reported to be smooth and tranquil; but its upper part is manifestly broken into many falls and rapids. From many descriptions of trappers it is probable that in its foaming course among its lofty precipices, it presents many

Canyon of Lodore, Green River, Looking up the Canyon.
Walls 2000 to 2500 feet high. "Wheatstack" in distance.
Photograph by E. O. BEAMAN, U. S. Colo. Riv. Exp.

scenes of wild grandeur; and though offering many temptations, and often discussed, no trappers have yet been found bold enough to undertake a voyage which has so certain a prospect of fatal termination."

He was mistaken about the trappers, not having ventured, for, as we have seen, there are traces of at least three parties: that of Ashley, that of the missionaries mentioned by Farnham, the trappers also mentioned by him, and the one indicated by the wreckage discovered in Lodore by Powell's expeditions, though the latter and that mentioned by Farnham are possibly the same.

The fur trade, which up to about 1835 was principally in beaver skins, had now somewhat changed, and buffalo robes

Las Vegas, Southern Nevada, on the Old Spanish Trail.
Oil sketch by F. S. Dellenbaugh.

were the chief article of traffic. But the buffalo were also beginning to diminish. They were no longer found on the western slope of the mountains, and no wonder, as the fur companies *annually* gathered in about ninety thousand marketable skins during the ten years ending with 1842, yet it was only those animals killed in the cold months whose pelts were suitable for the fur business. The largest number of buffalo were killed in the summer months for other purposes; therefore one is not surprised that they were soon exterminated in the Colorado River Valley, where they never were as numerous as on the plains, and apparently never went west of the mouth of White River.

Frémont went over to the California region, returning through Nevada by way of the Spanish Trail, past Las Vegas (see cut, page 137), and up the Virgen, which he called the most dreary river he had ever seen, till he reached the point where Escalante had turned east. From here he followed Escalante's trail back to Utah Lake, passing through Mountain Meadows (1844), afterward the scene of the terrible massacre of emigrants by a body of Mormons under John D. Lee.[1] His route was full of interesting adventures, but it is not possible to give details here. Passing over the Wasatch by way of Spanish Fork, he again entered the valley of the Colorado on the headwaters of the Uinta, pausing briefly at Roubidoux's Fort on Duchesne Fork. Soon after he left, the fort and its occupants were annihilated by the Utes. Crossing Ashley Fork he climbed on the trail high up the mountain, where he had "a view of the river below shut up amongst rugged mountains;" Whirlpool Canyon and the Canyon of Lodore. Descending then to Brown's Hole, he crossed the river in a skin boat, and camped just above Vermilion Creek, opposite the remains of an "old fort," which was doubtless Fort Davy Crockett. "Here the river enters between lofty precipices of red rock" (now the Gate of Lodore), "and the country below is said to assume a very rugged character; the river and its affluents passing through cañons which forbid all access to the water." After some journeying about, along the headwaters of Grand River, Frémont returned east, and later came out (1845) to cross the Green again about in the same latitude, on his way to California.

By this time the relations between the United States and Mexico were at the point of rupture, and in 1846 Kearny's forces moved on New Mexico and California, the Mormon Battalion marking out a waggon-road down the Gila. Frémont, being in California, took an active part (1846) in the capture of

---

[1] For an account of this unfortunate affair see *The Rocky Mountain Saints*, chapter xliii., by T. B. H. Stenhouse. I knew Lee. Personally he was an agreeable man, and to me he disclaimed responsibility in this matter.

the region, but the story of that episode does not belong here, and may be found in any history of California. The same year in which the formal treaty of peace was signed (1848) another event occurred which was destined to have a vast influence on the whole country and lead streams of emigrants to the new Dorado across the broad wastes of the Colorado Valley; gold in enormous quantities was discovered on Sutter's California ranch. There were three chief routes from the "States" across the wilderness of the Colorado River basin: one down the Gila to the Yuma country, another by South Pass and so on around Salt Lake and down the Humboldt, and the third also by South Pass and Salt Lake and thence south, by Mountain Meadows and west by the Old Spanish

A Canyon in the Cliffs, Southern Nevada.
Pencil sketch by F. S. DELLENBAUGH.

Trail. On the northern road Jim Bridger had, in 1843, established a trading post on Ham's Fork of Black's Fork of Green River, and this now was a welcome stopping-place for many of the emigrants,[1] while on the southern trail a

[1] Brigham Young and his followers crossed to the Salt Lake Valley in 1847.

temporary ferry was established at the mouth of the Gila by Lieut. Cave J. Coutts, who had arrived in September, 1849, commanding an escort for some boundary surveyors under Lieutenant Whipple. For a couple of months he rendered great assistance to the stream of weary emigrants, who had reached this point on their long journey to the Golden Country of their dreams. A flatboat, built on the shore of Lake Michigan, and there fitted with wheels so that it could be used as a waggon on land, was launched on the Gila at the Pima villages and came safely down to the Colorado, bearing its owners. Coutts is said to have purchased this boat and used it till he left, which was not long after. The junction now began to be a busy place. The United States troops came and went, occupying the site of Coutt's Camp Calhoun, which Major Heintzelman, November, 1850, called Camp Independence. In March, 1851, he re-established his command on the spot where the futile Spanish mission of Garces's time had stood, and this was named Fort Yuma. It was abandoned again in the autumn of the year, as had been done with the camps of the previous seasons, but when Heintzelman returned in the spring of 1852 he made it a permanent military post.

Meanwhile a gang of freebooters, who left Texas in 1849, found their way to this point and acquired or established a ferry two or three miles below the old mission site. Their settlement was called Fort Defiance in contempt for the Yumas. They were led by one Doctor Craig. They robbed the Yumas of their wives and dominated the region as they pleased. Captain Hobbs,[1] a mountaineer who was at Yuma in 1851, says:

" The attack which wiped out this miserable band was planned by two young Mexicans, who had attempted to cross the ferry with their wives, and had them taken from them and detained by the Texans. The Mexicans went down the river and the desperadoes supposed they had gone their way and left their wives in their hands. But they only went far enough to find the chief of the tribe who had suffered so horribly at the hands of this gang, and arrange for an attack on their common enemy."

[1] *Wild Life in the Far West*, by Captain James Hobbs.

By this plan twenty-three out of the twenty-five whites, including the master scoundrel himself, Dr. Craig, were destroyed
with little loss to the attacking party.   Hobbs calls this the
best thing the Yumas ever did.   It took place only a month
before Hobbs reached the ferry, and only two or three days
before one of the periodical returns of United States troops,

Crossing the Lower Colorado.
Width 400 to 500 yards.
Photograph by DELANCY GILL.

this time a company of dragoons under Captain Hooper, probably belonging to Heintzelman's command.   To him the two
escaped desperadoes came with a complaint against the Yumas,
but the captain was posted and he put the men in irons to be
transported to California for trial.   The Yumas now established
a ferry by using an old army-waggon box which they made
water-tight, as the Craig Ferry had suffered the fate of its

owners.   Hobbs employed the Yumas to take his party over, the horses swimming, and the arrangement seems to have worked very well.

According to Hobbs, the first steamboat came up the river while he was there, frightening the Yumas so that they ran for their lives, exclaiming the devil was coming, blowing fire and smoke out of his nose, and kicking back with his feet in the water.   It was the stern-wheel steamboat *Yuma*, and this is the only mention of it I can find.   It had supplies for the troops, but what became of it afterward I do not know.   This was evidently before the coming of the *Uncle Sam*, usually credited with being the first steamboat on the Colorado, which did not arrive till a year after the reconnaissance of the river mouth by Lieutenant Derby of the Topographical Engineers, for the War Department, seeking a route for the water transportation of supplies to Fort Yuma, now ordered to be a permanent military establishment.   He came up the river a considerable distance, in the topsail schooner *Invincible* and made a further advance in his small boats.   The only guide he had to the navigation of the river was Hardy's book, referred to in a previous chapter, which assisted him a good deal.   He arrived at the mouth December 23, 1850.   "The land," he says, "was plainly discernible on both coasts of the gulf, on the California side bold and mountainous, but on the Mexican low and sandy."   There could, therefore, never have been any doubt in the minds of any of those who had previously reached this point as to the character of Lower California.   The *Invincible* sailed daily up the river with the flood tide, anchoring during the ebb, and they got on very well till the night of January 1, 1851, when the vessel grounded at the ebb,

"swung round on her heel, and, thumping violently, was carried by the tide (dragging her anchor) some two or three miles, grounding finally upon the shoal of Gull Island.   At flood tide sail was made on her as soon as she floated, and we succeeded in getting her back into the channel.   As the vessel grounded at every ebb tide and on the return of the water was violently swung around, thumping on her bottom and swinging on her anchor, I began to see that it would be neither prudent, or in fact possible, to ascend the river much higher, and we accordingly commenced making preparations for a boating expedition." [1]

The ebb tide ran at the rate of five and a half miles an hour, and the next day they saw, as it was running out, the "bore," or tidal wave, booming in to meet and overwhelm it.

"A bank of water some four feet in height, extending clear across the river, was seen approaching us with equal velocity; this huge comber wave came steadily onward, occasionally breaking as it rushed over shoals of Gull and Pelican islands; passing the vessel, which it swung around on its course, it continued up the river. The phenomenon was of daily occurrence until about the time of neap tides."

At Howard's Point the vessel was anchored while the party continued the exploration in the small boat. The Cocopas whom they met were entirely friendly. These people wore no clothing beyond the breechcloth, and were plastered from head to foot with mud. The width of the river varied from two hundred yards to half a mile. At one place they passed a Cocopa village, near which lay an old scow made from waggon-boxes which had floated down from the ferry at Yuma. On the 13th they met Major Heintzelman coming down-stream, and as he had taken field notes Derby considered it unnecessary for him to proceed, and they went back in company to the ship, arriving there the same afternoon. The vessel was then worked three miles farther up, where her cargo was discharged to be taken by teams to the fort. Heintzelman was accompanied by a Dr. Ogden and a Mr. Henchelwood, "proprietors of the ferry." The Craig gang had been destroyed earlier this year, and these men had probably established a new ferry. While lying at this berth, the vessel was roughly tumbled about by the tidal wave, till she broke from her anchor and drifted rapidly up-stream. This was the highest and most powerful spring tide, and the situation was full of peril. The

[1] *Reconnaissance of the Gulf of California and the Colorado River made in 1850–51*, by Lieut. G. H. Derby. *Ex. Doc.* 81, 32nd Congress, 1st Session, Senate.

captain, Wilcox, calmly took the helm himself, steered toward
the bank and ordered his men to leap to the ground from the
jib-boom, carrying the kedge anchor.   By this means the mad
rush of the vessel was stopped, and by the use of logs and
cables she was kept a safe distance from the bank.   When the

A Cocopa Dwelling, near Mouth of the Colorado.
Photograph by DELANCY GILL

stores were finally landed they turned gratefully but apprehen-
sively toward the sea, which they happily reached again without serious mishap.

A little later this same year (1851) George A. Johnson came
to the mouth of the river on the schooner *Sierra Nevada* with
further supplies for the fort, including lumber for the construction of flatboats with which to go up to the post.   Johnson
afterwards ran steamers on the river for a number of years, and

if Hobbs is not mistaken about the first steamboat being on the river in 1851, it was probably brought by him at this time.

Many of the emigrants, dreaming of ease and prosperity as they trudged their long course across the desolation of the South-west, never lived to touch the golden sands of wonderful California, but expired by the way, often at the hands of the

On the Yuma Desert.
Photograph by DELANCY GILL.

Apache or of some other cutthroat tribe. One of the saddest cases was that of Royse Oatman, who, en route with his large family, was massacred (1851) on the spot now known as Oatman's Flat, not far below the great bend of the Gila. His son, left for dead, revived and escaped. Two daughters were carried off and afterwards sold to the Mohaves, among whom one died and the other was restored by purchase to freedom (1856) by Henry Grinnell, and was sent to her brother's home in Los Angeles.[1] Another characteristic example is related by Hobbs. In the desert beyond Yuma,

"we came upon the remains of an emigrant train, which a month previous had attempted to cross this desert in going from the United States to California. While passing over the desert they had been met by a sand-storm and lost the road by the sand blowing over it, and had wandered off into the hills. They had finally got back into the road; but by that time they were worn out, and they perished of fatigue and thirst."

They had passed the watering-place, a small pool, and as they had already been two or three days without water, the mistake was fatal. They had lightened their loads by casting off goods, but it was useless. A squad of soldiers was sent out from Fort Yuma to bury the bodies, of which eight were women and children and nine were men. The desert has no compassion on the human intruder, and he who ventures there must count only on his own resources.

The crossing of Green River was also difficult, except at low water, on account of the depth and force of the current. Sometimes the emigrants utilised a waggon-box as a boat, and the Mormons, who passed in 1847, established a ferry. Later others operated ferries, and the valley vied with Yuma in the matter of human activity. Fort Bridger was a place for rest and repairs, for there was a primitive blacksmith forge and carpenter shop. Here lived Bridger with his dark-skinned wife, chosen from a native tribe, and Vasquez, also a famous hunter. The fort was simply a few log cabins arranged in a hollow square protected by palisades, through which was a gateway closed by timber doors. Simple though it was, its value to the emigrant so far away from any settlement can hardly be appreciated by any who have never journeyed through such a wilderness as still existed beyond the Missouri. Could we pause here and observe the caravans bound toward the sunset, we could hardly find anywhere a more interesting study. There were the Californian

---

[1] For the full story see *Capture of the Oatman Girls*, by R. B. Stratton.

emigrant, and the Mormon with his wives and their push-carts, there were the trapper and the trader, and there were the bands of natives sometimes friendly, sometimes hovering about a caravan like a pack of hungry wolves. There is now barely an echo of this hard period, and that echo smothered by the rush

A Uinta Ute.
Photograph by J. K. HILLERS, U. S. Geol. Survey.

of the express train as it dashes in an hour or two so heedlessly across the stretches that occupied the forgotten emigrant days or weeks. In the search for a route for the railway much exploration was accomplished, and these expeditions, together with those in connection with the Mexican boundary survey, added greatly to the accumulating knowledge of the desolation enveloping the Colorado and its branches.

The treaty of 1848 made the Gila the southern boundary, but the Gadsden Purchase placed it farther south, as now marked. A number of expeditions concerned in this and railway surveys traversed Arizona in the early fifties under Whipple, Sitgreaves, Emory, and others, and the country began to be scientifically known outside of the canyons and their surroundings. John R. Bartlett was appointed Boundary Commissioner, and he spent considerable time along the Gila and southwards and on the lower Colorado in 1852 to 1854.[1] A few weeks before he arrived at Fort Yuma eight of the soldiers there had a battle with the Yumas and the eight were all killed. After this Heintzelman fought them with so much vigour that they finally came in, begging for peace. Bartlett's first view of the Colorado was in the early morning at a point twelve miles below the fort. "It was much swollen, and rushed by with great velocity, washing away the banks and carrying with it numberless snags and trees." Never is the Colorado tranquil. As they followed up the stream they suddenly found the road washed away, and were obliged to cut a new path through the underbrush. This proved a long task, so with the pack-mules he pushed on, leaving the waggons to come later. Antoine Leroux was the guide. When they reached the place he had selected for a camp and had unpacked the mules, it was found that the water could not be approached because of the abruptness of the washed-out bank, so they were compelled to saddle again and go on toward the fort, though they had been riding since one o'clock in the morning.

They were finally stopped altogether by a bayou and had to wait for a boat from the fort with which to cross it. When they came finally to the crossing of the river itself to the Arizona side they had a slow and difficult time of it. Sometimes the scow they used failed to reach the landing-place on the other side and the strong current would then sweep it two or three miles down the river before the men could get it to the shore. The next operation would be to tow it back to some low place, where the animals on it could be put ashore. This is a sample of the difficulties always encountered in crossing

[1] *Personal Narrative of Exploration*, by John Russell Bartlett.

when the river was at flood. From Yuma looking northward the river can be traced for about fifteen miles before it is lost in the mountains. See cut on page 26. Bartlett desired to explore scientifically down to the mouth, but the government failed to grant him the privilege. He and Major Emory were not on good terms and there was a great deal of friction about

" Judy," a Navajo.
From a photograph by J. K. HILLERS.

all the boundary work, arising chiefly from the appointment of a civilian commissioner. Bartlett mentions Leroux's "late journey down the Colorado," on which occasion he met with some Cosninos, but just where he started from is not stated, though it was certainly no higher up than the mouth of the Grand Wash.

In 1852 the steamer *Uncle Sam* was brought out on a schooner from San Francisco and put together at the mouth of the river, but after a few months she struck a snag and went to the bottom, while her owner, Turnbull, was on the way from San Francisco with new machinery for her. Turnbull came in the schooner *General Patterson*, which was bearing stores for the fort. When the *Patterson* arrived at the mouth of the Colorado, she was able to sail easily up the river for thirty-three miles because Turnbull was met by some of his men who had been left here to take soundings, and for the

One of the Parks on the Kaibab.
Photograph by T. MITCHELL PRUDDEN.

first time a vessel was sailing with some knowledge of the channel.   The river, however, was unusually high, which was an advantage.   The wide flatlands on both sides were inundated to a distance of fifteen miles.   The current ran at a seven- or eight-mile rate and was loaded with floating snags and tree-trunks to repel the invader.   In proceeding in a small boat to the fort, Turnbull, in a distance of 120 miles, found but two dry spots on the bank where he could camp.

A new steamer was soon afloat on this fickle and impetuous tide, the *General Jesup*, owned by Captain Johnson, who had now had three or four years' experience in this navigation and had been awarded the contract for transporting the supplies from the mouth to the fort. His new boat, however, exploded seven months later, and it seemed as if the Fates had joined with the treacherous river to prevent successful steam navigation here. But Johnson would not give up. Before twelve months had passed he was stemming the turbulent flood with another steamer, the *Colorado*, a stern-wheeler, 120 feet long. As if propitiated by the compliment of having its name bestowed on this craft, the river treated it fairly well, and it seems to have survived to a good old age.

The northern part of Arizona was crossed by Captain Sitgreaves, in 1851, about on the trail of Garces, reaching the Colorado in the Mohave Valley, and following the river down to Fort Yuma. In 1854, another government expedition under Lieutenant Whipple, with Lieutenant Ives as chief assistant, explored along the 35th parallel for a railway route, and when they arrived on the Colorado at the mouth of Bill Williams Fork, they followed up the river, through the beautiful Mohave Valley to a point some eight miles above the present railway (A. & P.) bridge, where they crossed. Their experience was interesting. Lieutenant Ives directed the operations, using for a ferry-boat a singular combination: an old rubber pontoon, with the box from a spring waggon attached to the top of it for a receptacle for the goods. This was arranged at night. In the morning the pontoon was found in a state of collapse and the waggon-box filled with water, but the concern was resuscitated by the skill of Ives, and soon all was ready for crossing. Swimmers carried a long rope to an island midway, while another was retained on the shore. By means of these the boat was pulled back and forth. The first trip was entirely successful, but on the second attempt the affair was, by the weight of the ropes, upset in midstream.

"During the excitement attending this misfortune, we were advised by an Indian messenger that another great chief was about to pay us a visit. Turning around, we beheld quite an interesting spectacle. Approaching was the dignitary referred to, lance in hand, and apparelled in official robes. The latter consisted of a blanket thrown gracefully around him, and a magnificent head-dress of black plumage covering his head and shoulders, and hanging down his back in a streamer, nearly to the ground. His pace was slow, his eyes cast downward, and his whole demeanour expressive of formal solemnity. Upon his right hand was the interpreter, upon his left a boy acting as page, and following was a long procession of his warriors, attended by a crowd of men, women, and children.''

Compliments and presents were exchanged and all was well. Meanwhile the men who had been capsized with the boat were struggling to disentangle themselves from the waggon-box, and when freed they gained support on the rope till the entire combination was pulled back to the shore. The whole party were finally on the island and then used the same tactics in crossing the other deeper channel. Here they upset the ferry three times and two persons came near being drowned. The Mohaves, who are good swimmers, rendered prompt and efficient assistance in saving the floating wreckage. They were also supplied with their kind of raft, made of bundles of rushes tied together with willow twigs (see cut on page 30), which they handled dexterously. Such rafts were and are in use all the way from here to the gulf. By night the expedition was safe on the western bank, the mules having swum over, and the flock of sheep being ferried in the boat. Several sheep were drowned, and these, with two live ones and a couple of blankets, were conferred on those Mohaves who had helped in the crossing. The landing-place was a field of young wheat, which was much damaged. The lieutenant willingly paid the moderate charge the owner made for this, and there was no trouble; all the intercourse was perfectly amicable. But had he been imbued with the trapper spirit he would probably have answered the request for payment with a fatal bullet, and then would have followed a stampede of the stock, ambush, and all the rest which embroiders the history of the trappers with such violently romantic colour.

Two or three years after the Whipple expedition, a waggon-road was surveyed (1857) along the 35th parallel by E. F. Beale. He returned to the Colorado January 23, 1858, about

The Ruins in Canyon de Chelly, Arizona, called "Casa Blanca."
These were once connected.
Photograph by J. K. Hillers, U. S. Geol Survey.

153

twelve miles north of Whipple's Crossing.   One peculiarity about Beale's expedition was the use of camels instead of mules for transportation of the supplies.   A steamer had come up the river from Yuma to ferry him across; gladly its services were now utilised, as he desired to go east by his own road.   This steamer is said to have been the *General Jesup*, though the *Jesup* had exploded, according to report, in August, 1854. This voyage, according to Beale, was Captain Johnson's individual enterprise. Lieut. White and fifteen soldiers were on board. On December 1, 1857, Lieutenant Ives, commissioned to explore the Colorado to the head of navigation, arrived at Robinson's Landing, at the mouth of the river, in the schooner *Monterey*, bringing an iron steamer in sections. Johnson was sent down from the fort to transport the garrison - supplies the schooner brought, and he reached the landing with two steamers on December 17th.   He was, therefore, acquainted with the design of the expedition, and when he went up to Beale's intended crossing to ferry him over, he did not stop at that point, but hurried on up as far as he could, pushing with his powerful boat clear through Black Canyon to the highest point attainable by steamers,

The Queen.

Pinnacle 200 feet high on Vermilion Creek.

Photograph by E. O. BEAMAN, U. S. Colo. Riv. Exp.

expressly to anticipate the expedition of Lieutenant Ives. As he was descending he passed Ives on his *Explorer*, a smaller boat, going up.[1]

[1] I have no details of this trip of Johnson's. He related the incident to Robert Brewster Stanton, who told me the main facts. Johnson said his desire was " to get ahead of Ives."

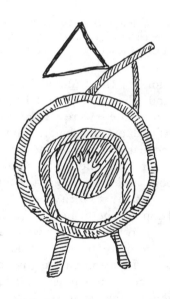

CHAPTER VII

Lieutenant Ives Explores to Fortification Rock—By Trail to Diamond Creek, Havasupai Canyon, and the Moki Towns—Macomb Fails in an Attempt to Reach the Mouth of Grand River—James White's Masterful Fabrication.

STEAM navigation on the Colorado was now successfully established, and when Lieutenant Ives was planning the exploration of the river there were already upon it two powerful steamers exactly adapted, through experience of previous disasters, to the peculiar dangers of these waters, while Johnson, the chief owner and pilot, had become an expert in handling a steamboat amid the unusual conditions. He had succeeded in making a truce with the dragon. And he had secured the friendship of the tribes of Amerinds living along the banks; his men and his property were safe anywhere; his steamers often carried jolly bands of Cocopas or of Yumas from place to place. In arranging a government expedition to explore to the farthest point practicable for steamboats, the sensible course would have been to advise with Johnson and to charter his staunch steamer *Colorado*, together with himself, thus gaining at the very outset an immense double advantage: a boat perfectly modelled for the demands to be made upon it, and a guide entirely familiar with the tricks of the perfidious waters. Especially important would this have been because Lieutenant Ives, who was instructed to direct this work, was ordered to accomplish it at the lowest and worst stage of the

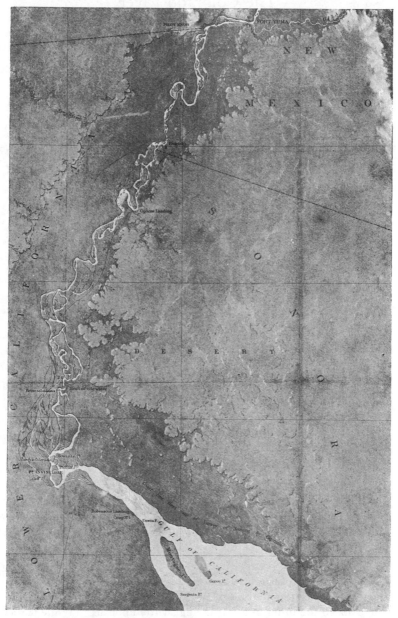

157   **Part of Map No. 1, by Lieut. J. C. Ives, 1858.**

From the Gulf to the mouth of the Gila.

Scale of this reduction is about 12 miles to 1 inch.

stream. Ives had been Whipple's chief assistant in 1853-54, and therefore well understood the situation. But he states that the company was "unable to spare a boat except for a compensation beyond the limits of the appropriation." As a boat was spared, however, for the less important matter of going far up the river to ferry Beale across, it would appear that either the negotiations were not conducted in a proper spirit, or that Ives rather preferred a boat of his own. The cost of building in Philadelphia the boat he used, and sending her in sections to San Francisco, and thence to the Colorado, must have been very great. The steamer was ordered June 1, 1857, and had to be at the mouth of the Colorado by December 1st of the same year. After a trial on the Delaware, a mill-pond compared with the Colorado, she was hastily shipped, with all her defects, by way of Panama, there being no time to make any changes. The chief trouble discovered was radical, being a structural weakness of the hull. To, in a measure, off-set this, timbers and bolts were obtained in San Francisco, the timbers to be attached to the *outside* of the hull on putting the sections together, there being no room within. It requires little understanding of naval architecture to perceive that a great handicap was thus imposed on the little vessel. Yet Lieutenant Ives says, on the trial trip she was "found satisfactory"! By November 1st, the party was on board the schooner *Monterey*, bound for the head of the Gulf. Though the vessel was loaded down with supplies for Fort Yuma, room was made for the Ives expedition and they arrived, passing through a heavy gale in the gulf, at Robinson's Landing on November 30th. The schooner was anchored over a shoal, and was soon aground, as the fierce tide ran out, a circumstance that enabled her to stay there and stem the torrent. A deep booming sound was presently heard, growing louder and nearer, and

"in half an hour a great wave several feet in height, could be distinctly seen flashing and sparkling in the moonlight, extending from one bank to the other and advancing swiftly upon us. While it was only a few hundred yards distant, the ebb tide continued to flow by at the rate of three miles an hour. A point of land and an exposed bar close under our lee broke the wave into several long swells, and as these met the ebb the broad sheet around us boiled up and foamed like the surface of a cauldron, and then, with scarcely a moment of slack water, the whole went whirling by in the opposite direction. In a few moments the low rollers had passed the islands and united again in a single bank of water, which swept up the narrowing channel with the thunder of a cataract.''

This was the great tidal bore once more, which, at the occurrence of the spring tides, makes the entrance of the river ex-

Robinson's Landing.
Mouth of the Colorado River.   Starting-point of Lieut. Ives's Exploration.
Photograph by Lieut. Ives.   Redrawn by J. J. Young.

tremely dangerous.   It is due to the narrowing of the Gulf of California forcing the tides into close quarters, and its violence is augmented by collision with the equally furious current of the Colorado.   The battle between this tidal wave and the Colorado continues for many miles, till at last the sea tide gradually loses its power and succumbs to the flood of the river.[1]   The latter falls at the mouth, according to Ives, about

[1] The tide ascends thirty-seven miles.   Lowest stage of water about three feet, average six feet, and highest about twenty feet.

thirty feet in a few hours after the ebb begins.   The shallower the water as the tide rushes in against the ebb, the angrier the wave becomes, sometimes reaching a height of ten or twelve feet.

At Robinson's Landing, a mere mud flat, a camp was established and preparations made for the voyage to the extreme limit of navigation.   The parts of the steamer were put ashore and a suitable spot selected whereon to set her up. The high tides were over for a month, and the mud began to dry, enabling the party to pitch their tents.   It was an uncomfortable spot for expedition headquarters, but the best that could be had, as the *Monterey* was not permitted by her owners to venture farther up the river.   But this delay, discomfort, and difficulty, to say nothing of expense, might have been avoided could a contract have been made with the existing steamboat company.   As the bank on which the boat was to be reconstructed was not likely to be overflowed more than a foot by the next high tide, a month later, an excavation was made wherein to build the steamer that she might certainly come afloat at the desired time.   Sixty holes had to be made in the iron plates so that the four stiffening timbers could be attached to the bottom to prevent the craft from breaking in two under the extra-heavy boiler.   Inside, cross timbers were also added to resist the strain.   On December 17th, two steamers appeared from the fort, in command, respectively, of Johnson and Wilcox, to transport the army supplies to their destination.   Robinson, after whom the landing was called because he had a cabin there, was with the steamboats, and, as he knew the river, especially as far as Yuma, Ives engaged him for pilot.

By the end of the month, the *Explorer*, as the Ives boat was named, was ready for the expected high tide.   She was fifty-four feet long over all, not quite half the length of Johnson's *Colorado*.   Amidships she was open, but the bow was decked, and at the stern was a cabin, seven by eight feet, the top of which formed an outlook.   For armament, she was supplied on the bow with a four-pound howitzer, though this weapon was not likely to be of much service.   When the anticipated flood arrived on the night of December 30th, steam was turned on at the critical moment, the engines worked the stern-wheel, and Lieutenant Ives had the satisfaction of seeing the *Explorer*, under the bright moonlight, slowly back out of the pit which had been her cradle into the swirling, seething current. As the tide continued to rise, Ives feared the whole flat would soon be inundated, so everything belonging to the expedition was stowed on board till the *Explorer's* gunwales were no more than six inches above the surface.   Through this circumstance,

The Steamer " Explorer " in which Lieut. Ives in 1857 Ascended the Colorado to Foot of Black Canyon.

Sketch by H. B. MOLLHAUSEN.

the expedition came near a disastrous end the next night, when the steamer proceeded up the river on the flood tide. A squall was met and the boat shipped water alarmingly, but fortunately the wind died away as quickly as it had come up. The *Explorer* was saved, and the journey was continued over the swiftly gliding torrent.

As they went on after this in daylight, some Cocopas they met grinned rather contemptuously, and called this the "chiquito steamboat."   A considerable amount of stores was left on the bank in their care, to be picked up by Captain Wilcox, who, going down on one of the fort steamers, had passed the *Explorer*, and offered to take these extra stores to the fort on his return.   They were placed with the Cocopas by his direction, an arrangement that better describes the relations of the steamboat people and the natives than anything that could be said about them.   The fuel used was wood, of which there was great abundance along the shore, the hard, fine-grained mesquite making a particularly hot fire.   The routine of advance was to place a man with a sounding-pole at the bow, while Robinson, the pilot, had his post on the deck of the cabin, but the sounding was more for record purposes than to assist Robinson, who was usually able to predict exactly when the water would shoal or deepen.   Later, Ives says: "If the ascent of the river is accomplished, it will be due to his skill and good management."   Besides the ordinary shifting of the sands by the restless current, there was another factor occasionally to guard against.   This was earthquakes.   Sometimes they might change the depth of water on the lower river in the twinkling of an eye.   On one occasion, a schooner lying in a deep part was found suddenly aground in three feet of water, with no other warning than a rumble and a shock.   Heintzelman, in one of his reconnoissances, discovered the adjacent land full of cracks, through which oozed streams of sulphurous water, mud, and sand, and Diaz, in 1540, came to banks of "hot ashes" which it was impossible to cross, the whole ground trembling beneath his feet.   At low water, even in the lower reaches of the river, a boat is liable to run aground often, and has to be backed off to try her fortune in another place. The bottom, however, is soft, the current strong, so no harm is done and the rush of water helps to cut the boat loose.   One does not easily comprehend how sensitive a pilot becomes to every tremor of the hull in this sort of navigation.   The quality of the boat's vibration speaks to his nerves in a distinct language, and the suck of the wheel emphasises the communication.

The *Explorer* at length arrived at Yuma.   Here the remainder of the party, including Dr. Newberry, having come

Looking down the Grand Canyon from the Mouth of the Kanab.

Depth about 4000 feet.
Oil sketch by F. S. DELLENBAUGH.

163

across country, joined the expedition, and further preparations were made for the more difficult task above. The craft was lightened as far as possible, but at the best she still drew two and one-half feet, while the timbers bolted to the bottom were a great detriment, catching on snags and ploughing into the mud of the shoals. There were twenty-four men to be carried, besides all the baggage that must be taken, even though a pack-train was to leave, after the departure of the boat, to transport extra supplies to the end of the voyage, wherever that might be. It is not easy to understand why so large a party was necessary. Some few miles above Yuma they came to the first range of mountains that closes in on the water, suddenly entering a narrow pass several hundred feet deep. Seven miles farther on, they went through a small canyon where another range is severed. This was called Purple Hill Pass, while the first one was named Explorer's Pass, after the steamer. The first approach to a real canyon was encountered a short distance above. Emerging from this, called Canebrake, from some canes growing along the sides, the *Explorer* ran aground, resting there for two hours. They had now passed through the Chocolate Mountains, the same range that Alarçon mentions, and as he records no other he probably went no farther up than the basin Ives is now entering, the Great Colorado Valley. Alarçon doubtless proceeded to the upper part of this valley, about to latitude thirty-four, where he raised the cross to mark the spot. Two miles above the head of the canyon, the power of the *Explorer* was matched against a stiff current that came swirling around the base of a perpendicular rock one hundred feet high. With the steam pressure then on, she was not equal to the encounter and made no advance, whereupon she was headed for a steep bank to allow the men to leap ashore with a line and tow her beyond the opposition. Above, the current was milder, but the river spread out to such an extent that progress was exceedingly difficult, and Ives expresses a fear that this might prove the head of navigation, yet he must then have been aware (and certainly was when he published his report) that Johnson at that very moment was far beyond this with a steamer larger than the one he was on. It was now January 17, 1858, and it was on January 23d that Johnson was at the point where Beale intended to cross. The steamer accomplishing its errand, he left on this day for Yuma. He seems then to have gone to the head of navigation before meeting Beale. Ives and Johnson must now pass each other before the end of this month of December, and the meeting of the two steamers took place somewhere in this Colorado Valley, for, under date of January 31st, Ives says: "Lieutenant Tipton took advantage of an opportunity afforded a few days ago, by our meeting Captain Johnson, with Lieutenant White and party returning to the fort, and went back with them in order to bring up the pack-train." He does not mention, however, that Johnson was piloting a steamboat larger than the *Explorer*. Indeed, I have been told that he failed to reply to Johnson's salute. Slowly they worked their way up, and on up, toward their final goal, though the water was exceptionally low. At last reaching Bill Williams Fork, Ives, who had seen it at the time he was with Whipple about four years earlier, could not at first find it, though, on the former occasion, in the same season, it had been a stream thirty feet wide. It was now a feeble rivulet, the old mouth being filled up and overgrown with willows. Approaching Mohave Canyon, a rapid was encountered, necessitating the carrying forward of an anchor, from which a line was brought to the bow, and this being kept taut, with the boat under full steam the obstruction was surmounted without damage. This was the common method of procedure at rapids. This canyon, Ives, says was a "scene of such imposing grandeur as he had never before witnessed," yet it is only a harbinger of the greater sublimity extending along the water above for a thousand miles. Mohave Canyon and The Needles soon were left behind, and they were steaming through the beautiful Mohave Valley, where the patient footsteps of the padres and the restless tramp of the trappers had so long ago passed and been forgotten. Probably not one of that party remembered that Pattie on horseback had covered this same field over thirty years before, or that rare old Garces guided his tired mule along these very banks a full half century

ahead of Pattie.   To-day, the comfortable traveller on the railway, crossing the river near The Needles, has also forgotten
these things and Lieutenant Ives as well.

Many Cocopas, Yumas, Mohaves, and Chemehuevis were
met with since the trip began, but there had been no trouble
with any of them.   Ives now began to inquire for a former
guide of Whipple's, whom he pleasantly remembered and
whose name was Ireteba.   Fortunately, he soon came across
him and engaged his services.   Ireteba was a Mohave, but

Black Canyon — Looking Down.
Photograph by WHEELER EXP.

possessed one of those fine natures found in every clime and
colour.   He was always true and intelligent, and of great
service to the expedition.   The *Explorer* pushed on, encountering many difficulties, some due to the unfortunate
timbers on the bottom, which often became wedged in rocks,
besides increasing the draught by about six inches, a serious
matter at this extremely low stage of water.   "It is probable,"
says Ives, "that there is not one season in ten when even the
Explorer would encounter one fourth of the difficulty that she
has during the unprecedentedly low stage of water."   At one
rapid, after the boat by hard labour had been brought to the

crest, the line broke and she at once fell back, bumping over the rocks and finally lodging amidst a mass so firmly that it required half the next day to pull her out. The second attempt to surmount the rapid was successful, and they were then rewarded by a fierce gale from the north, detaining them twenty-four hours, filling everything with sand, and dragging the steamboat from her moorings to cast her again upon the rocks. When, at last, they could go on they came after a short time to a canyon deeper and grander than any they had yet seen, called Black Canyon, because it is cut through the Black Mountains. Ives was uncertain, at the moment, whether this was the entrance to what was called Big Canyon (Grand Canyon) or not. The *Explorer* by this time had passed through a number of rapids and the crew were growing expert at this sort of work, so that another rapid a hundred yards below the mouth of the canyon was easily conquered. The current becoming slack, the steamer went gaily on toward the narrow gateway, where, "flanked by walls many hundreds of feet in height, rising perpendicularly out of the water, the Colorado emerged from the bowels of the range." Suddenly the boat stopped with a crash. The bow had squarely met a sunken rock. The men forward were knocked completely overboard, those on the after-deck were thrown below, the boiler was jammed out of place, the steampipe was doubled up, the wheelhouse torn away, and numerous minor damages were sustained. The *Explorer* had discovered *her* head of navigation! They thought she was about to sink, but luckily she had struck in such a way that no hole was made and they were able by means of lines and the skiff to tow her to a sandbank for repairs. Here the engineer, Carroll, and Captain Robinson devoted themselves to making her again serviceable, while, with the skiff, Ives and two companions continued on up the deep gorge. Though this was the end of the upward journey, so far as the *Explorer* was concerned, Johnson with his steamboat had managed to go clear through this canyon.

Rations were at a low stage, consisting entirely, for the past three weeks, of corn and beans, purchased from the natives, but even on this diet without salt the skiff party worked its way steadily upward over many rapids through the superb chasm. "No description," says Ives, "can convey an idea of the varied and majestic grandeur of this peerless waterway. Wherever the river makes a turn, the entire panorama changes, and one startling novelty after another appears and disappears with bewildering rapidity." I commend these pages of Lieutenant Ives, and, in fact, his whole report, to all who delight in word-painting of natural scenery, for the lieutenant certainly handled his pen as well as he did his sword.[1] Emerging

Fortification Rock.
Castellated Gravels at the foot. Near the head of Black Canyon.
Photograph by WHEELER EXP.

from the solemn depths of Black Canyon (twenty-five miles long) he and his small party passed Fortification Rock and continued on two miles up the river to an insignificant little stream coming in from the north, which he surmised might be the Virgen, though he hardly thought it could be, and it was not. It was Vegas Wash. This was his highest point. Turning about, he descended to the steamboat camp and called that place the head of navigation, not that he did not believe a

[1] It may be of interest to state that Lieutenant Ives became an officer in the Confederate Army, and was killed in one of the battles of the Civil War.

steamer might ascend, light, through Black Canyon, but he considered it impracticable. Running now down-stream in the *Explorer*, the expected pack-train was encountered at the foot of Pyramid Canyon, and a welcome addition was made to the supplies.

The steamboat was now sent back to the fort and Ives prepared for a land journey, which led him eastward over much

The Canyon of Diamond Creek.
Photograph by W. H. JACKSON.

the same route that Garces had traversed so long ago on his march to Oraibi. Ireteba was his guide. They went to the mouth of Diamond Creek, where they had their first view of the Grand Canyon, or Big Canyon, as they called it, of which Ireteba had before given them some description. The illustrations given in Ives's report of both Black and Grand Canyons are a libel on these magnificent wonder-places, and in no way compare with the lieutenant's admirable pen-pictures. Crossing the Colorado Plateau (which another explorer ten or twelve years later claims the honour of naming, forgetting that Ives uses the name in his report), they visited the Havasupai in their deep canyon home, just as Garces had done, and then proceeded to the towns of the Moki. Ives was deeply impressed by the repellant nature of the great canyon and the surroundings, and remarks: "It seems intended by nature that the Colorado River, along the greater portion of its lonely and majestic way, shall be forever unvisited and undisturbed."

Late in the same year that Lieutenant Ives made his interesting and valuable exploration, another military post was established on the Colorado, and called Fort Mohave, just about where the California line intersects the stream. Lower down, Colorado City had been laid out several years before (1854) under amusing circumstances. The Yuma ferry at that time was operated by a German, thrifty after his kind, and on the lookout for a "good thing." A party of indigent prospectors, returning from the survey of a mine in Mexico, reached the Arizona bank with no money to pay for the crossing, and hit upon the ingenious plan of surveying a town site here and trading lots to the German for a passage. Boldly commencing operations, the sight of the work going on soon brought the ferryman over to investigate, and when he saw the map under construction he fell headlong into the scheme, which would, as they assured him, necessitate a steam ferry.[1] The result was the immediate sale of a portion of the town to him and the exchange of a lot for the necessary transportation to the opposite bank. Afterwards, these parties did what they could to establish the reality of the project, but up to date it has not been noted as a metropolis, and the floods of 1861–2 undermined its feeble strength. Another name for it was Arizona City.

The year following the Ives expedition, Captain Macomb (1859) was sent to examine the junction of the Green and Grand rivers. For a considerable distance he followed, from Santa Fé, almost the same trail that Escalante had travelled

[1] *Across America and Asia*, by Raphael Pumpelly, p. 60. The portion of this admirable work relating to the vicinity of the Colorado River will be found of great interest in this connection.

eighty-three years previously. Dr. Newberry, the eminent geologist who had been with Ives, was one of this party, and he has given an interesting account of the journey. The region lying immediately around the place they had set out for is one of the most formidable in all the valley of the Colorado. Looking about one there, from the summit of the

Fort Yuma and the Old Railway Bridge of the Southern Pacific.
Photograph by C. R. Savage.

canyon walls, it seems an impossibility for anything without the power of flight to approach the spot, except by way of the river channels. Macomb and Newberry succeeded in forcing their way to within about six miles of the junction, there to be completely baffled and turned back. Arriving finally at the brink of the canyon of Grand River, Newberry says:

" On every side we were surrounded by columns, pinnacles, and castles of fantastic shapes, which limited our view, and by impassable cañons, which restricted our movements.   South of us, about a mile distant, rose one of the castle-like buttes, which I have mentioned, and to which, though with difficulty, we made our way. This butte was composed of alternate layers of chocolate-colored sandstone and shale about one thousand feet in height; its sides nearly perpendicular, but most curiously ornamented with columns and pilasters, porticos and colonnades, cornices and battlements, flanked here and there with tall outstanding towers, and crowned

At the Junction of the Green and Grand on the Surface.
Photograph by E. O. BEAMAN, U. S. Colo. Riv. Exp.

with spires so slender that it seemed as though a breath of air would suffice to topple them from their foundations.   To accomplish the object for which we had come so far, it seemed necessary that we should ascend this butte.   The day was perfectly clear and intensely hot, the mercury standing at 92° in the shade, and the red sandstone, out of which the landscape was carved, glowed in the heat of the burning sunshine.   Stripping off nearly all our clothing, we made the attempt, and, after two hours of most arduous labor, succeeded in reaching the summit.   The view which there burst upon us was such as amply repaid us for all our toil.   It baffles description.''

He goes on to say that, while the great canyon, meaning the Grand Canyon, with its gigantic cliffs, presents grander scenes, they have less variety and beauty of detail than this. They were here able to see over an area of some fifty miles diameter, where, hemmed in by lines of lofty step-like mesas, a great basin lay before them as on a map. There was no vegetation, "nothing but bare and barren rocks of rich and varied colours shimmering in the sunlight. Scattered over the plain were thousands of the fantastically formed buttes to which I have re-ferred . . . pyramids, domes, towers, columns, spires of every conceivable form and size." There were also multitudes of canyons, ramifying in every direction, "deep, dark, and ragged, impassable to everything but the winged bird." At the nearest point was the canyon of the Grand, while four miles to the south another great gorge was discerned joining it, which their Amerind guides pronounced to be that of Green River. Find-ing it utterly impossible for them to reach this place, they returned.

Thus, after all these years of endeavour, the mighty Colorado foamed away amidst this terrible environment as if no human element yet existed in the world. And as it con-tinued to baffle all attempts to probe its deeper mysteries, the dread of it and the fear of it grew and grew, till he who sug-gested that a man might pass through the bewildering chasms and live, was regarded as light-headed. Then came the awful war of the Rebellion, and for several years little thought was bestowed on the problem.[1]

Some few prospectors for mineral veins began investigations in the neighbourhood of the lower part of the Grand Canyon, and the gorge was entered from below, about 1864, by O. D. Gass and three other men. I met Gass at his home at Las Vegas (see cut, page 137) in 1875, but I did not then know he had been in the canyon and did not hear his story.

It was not till 1866 that any one tried again to navigate the river above Mohave. In that year Captain Rodgers, who for

---

[1] The troops that were so foolishly and feebly sent against the Mormons in 1857 had some experience in Green River Valley, but it was not directly con-nected with this story and I will not introduce an account of it here.

four years had been on the lower Colorado, took the steamboat *Esmeralda*, ninety-seven feet long and drawing three and
one-half feet of water, up as far as Callville, near the mouth
of the Virgen, which was several miles beyond the highest
point attained by Ives in his skiff, but little, if any, farther
than Johnson had gone with his steamboat. He ascended the
most difficult place, Roaring Rapids in Black Canyon, in seven
minutes, and was of the opinion that it could as easily be surmounted at any stage of water, except perhaps during the
spring rise. It does
not matter much now,
for it is not likely that
any steam craft will
soon again have occa-
sion to traverse that
canyon. The comple-
tion of the railways
was a death blow to
steam navigation on the
Colorado, yet, in the
future, when the fertile
bottoms are brought
under cultivation, small
steamboats will proba-
bly be utilised for local
transportation.

The Barrel Cactus Compared with the Height
of a Man.

Photograph by C. R. SAVAGE.

The journey of the
Esmeralda added noth-
ing to what was al-
ready known. The
following year, 1867, a man was picked up at Callville, in
an exhausted and famishing condition, by a frontiersman
named Hardy. When he had been revived he told his
story. It was that he had come on a raft through the
Grand Canyon above, and all the canyons antecedent to that
back to a point on Grand River. The story was apparently
straightforward, and it was fully accepted. At last, it was
thought, a human being has passed through this Valley of the

Shadow of Death and lived to tell of its terrors. Hardy took him down to Fort Mohave, where he met Dr. Parry,[1] who recorded his whole story, drawn out by many questions, and believed it. This was not surprising; for, no man ever yet having accomplished what White claimed to have done, there was no way of checking the points of his tale. "Now, at last," remarks Dr. Parry, "we have a perfectly authentic account, from an intelligent source, from a man who actually traversed its formidable depths, and who, fortunately for science, still lives to detail his trustworthy observations of this remarkable voyage." The doctor was too confiding. Had I the space I would give here the whole of White's story, for it is one of the best bits of fiction I have ever read. He had obtained somehow a general smattering of the character of the river, but as there were trappers still living, Kit Carson, for example, who possessed a great deal of information about it, this was not a difficult matter. But that he had no exact knowledge of any part of the river above the lower end of the Grand Canyon, is apparent to one who is familiar with the ground, and the many discrepancies brand the whole story as a fabrication. In the language of the frontier, he "pitched a yarn," and it took beautifully. Hardy, whom I met in Arizona a good many years ago, told me he believed the man told the truth, but his belief was apparently based only on the condition White was in when rescued. That he was nearly dead is true, but that is about all of his yarn that is. White was thirty-two years old, and from Kenosha, Wisconsin. He said that, with two others, he was prospecting in Southwestern Colorado in the summer of that year, 1867, when, on Grand River, they were attacked by the Utes. Baker, the leader, fell mortally wounded. Of course, White and the other man, Strole, stood by their leader, in the teeth of the enemy's fire, till he expired. What would the story have been without this example of devotion and fortitude? Then, holding the pursuers in check, they slowly retreated down the side canyon they were in to

---

[1] Parry's full record of White's story is given in William A. Bell's *New Tracks in North America*. Dr. C. C. Parry was assistant geologist of the U. P. Railway Survey, and wrote in 1868.

the main gorge, where they discovered an abundance of drift-wood, and decided to make a raft with which to escape.   This raft consisted of three sticks of cottonwood about ten feet long and eight inches diameter, tied together with lariats.   They had abandoned their horses above, bringing only their arms, ammunition, and some food.   Waiting for midnight to come so that their pursuers might not discover their intention, they seized their poles and, under the waning moon, cast off and were soon on the tempestuous tide, rushing through the yawn-ing chasm.   "Through the long night they clung to the raft as it dashed against half-concealed rocks, or whirled about like a plaything in some eddy."   When daylight came they landed, as they had a smoother current and less rugged banks, though the canyon walls appeared to have increased in height.   They strengthened their raft and went on.   In the afternoon, after having floated about thirty miles from the starting point they reached the junction of the Grand and Green.   So far all is well, but here he makes his first break, as he had no conception of the actual character of the rivers at the junction.   He says the canyon now far surpassed that of either of the forming streams, which is not so.   For five or six miles below the junction there is little change, yet he describes the walls as being four thousand feet high, an altitude never attained in Cataract Canyon at all, the highest being somewhat under three thousand, while at the junction they are only thirteen hundred.   Then he goes on to say that detached pinnacles appeared to rise "one above the other," for one thousand feet more, giving an altitude here of five thousand feet, clearly an impression in his mind of the lower end of the Grand Canyon, which he had doubtless become somewhat familiar with in some prospecting trip.   He fancied the "Great Canyon" be-gan at the junction of the Grand and Green, and he did not ap-preciate the distance that intervened between Callville and that point.   They tied up at night and travelled in the day.   No mention is made of the terrific rapids which roar in Cataract Canyon, but he speaks of the "grey sandstone walls" the lower portion smooth from the action of floods.   There exist some greyish walls; but most are red except in the granite

177 Canyon of San Juan River Looking West at Honiket Trail, Utah.
2000 feet deep
Photograph by CHARLES GOODMAN

gorges of the Grand Canyon, where, for a thousand feet, they are black. Below the junction, forty miles, they came to the mouth of the San Juan! Yet Cataract Canyon and Narrow together, the first canyons of the Colorado proper, are fifty

A Glen of Glen Canyon.
These are numerous hence the name.

miles long and the San Juan comes in at least seventy-five miles below their end. The walls of the San Juan he describes as being as high as those of the Colorado, which he has just been talking about, that is, five thousand feet, yet for these seventy-five miles he would have actually been passing be-

tween walls of about one thousand feet. He says he could not
escape here because the waters of the San Juan were so violent they filled its canyon from bank to bank. In reality, he
could have made his way out of the canyon (Glen Canyon) in
a great many places in the long distance between the foot of
Narrow Canyon and the San Juan. There is nothing difficult
about it. But not knowing this, and nobody else knowing it
at that time, the yarn went very well. Also, below the San
Juan, as far as Lee's Ferry, there are numerous opportunities
to leave the canyon; and there are a great many attractive
bottoms all the way through sunny Glen Canyon, where landings could have been made in a *bona fide* journey, and birds
snared; anything rather than to go drifting along day after day
toward dangers unknown. "At every bend of the river it
seemed as if they were descending deeper into the earth, and
that the walls were coming closer together above them, shut-
ting out the narrow belt of sky, thickening the black shadows,
and redoubling the echoes that went up from the foaming
waters," all of which is nonsense. They were not yet, even
taking their own, or rather his own, calculations, near the
Grand Canyon, and the whole one hundred and forty-nine
miles of Glen Canyon are simply charming; altogether delightful. One can paddle along in any sort of craft, can leave the
river in many places, and in general enjoy himself. I have
been over the stretch twice, once at low water and again at
high, so I speak from abundant experience. Naïvely he remarks, "as yet they had seen no natural bridge spanning the
chasm above them, nor had fall or cataract prevented their safe
advance!" Yet they are supposed to have passed through
the forty-one miles of Cataract Canyon's turmoil, which I venture to say no man could ever forget. They had been only
four days getting to a point below the San Juan, simply drifting; that is about two hundred miles, or some fifty miles a
daylight day. Around three o'clock on the fourth day they
heard the deep roar as of a waterfall in front of them.

"They felt the raft agitated, then whirled along with frightful
rapidity towards a wall that seemed to bar all further progress. As

they approached the cliff the river made a sharp bend, around which
the raft swept, disclosing to them, in a long vista, the water lashed
into foam, as it poured through a narrow precipitous gorge, caused
by huge masses of rock detached from the main walls.   There was

Cataract Canyon Rapid at Low Water.
Photograph by E. O BEAMAN, U. S. Colo. Riv. Exp

no time to think.   The logs strained as if they would break their
fastenings.   The waves dashed around the men, and the raft was
buried in the seething waters.   White clung to the logs with the grip
of death.   His comrade stood up for an instant with the pole in his
hands, as if to guide the raft from the rocks against which it was

plunging; but he had scarcely straightened before the raft seemed to leap down a chasm and, amid the deafening roar of waters, White heard a shriek that thrilled him to the heart, and, looking around, saw, through the mist and spray, the form of his comrade tossed for an instant on the water, then sinking out of sight in a whirlpool.''

On the fifth day White lashed himself to the raft. He then describes a succession of rapids, passing which with great difficulty he reached a stream that he afterward learned was the Little Colorado. He said the canyon was like that of the San Juan, but they are totally different. The current of this stream swept across that of the Colorado, ''causing in a black chasm on the opposite bank a large and dangerous whirlpool.'' He could not avoid this and was swept by the cross current into this awful place, which, to relieve the reader's anxiety, I hasten to add, does not exist. There is no whirlpool whatever at the mouth of the Little Colorado, nor any other danger. But White now felt that further exertion was useless, and amidst the ''gurgling'' waters closed his eyes for some minutes, when, feeling a strange swinging sensation, he opened them and found that he was circling round the whirlpool, sometimes close to the terrible vortex, etc. He thought he fainted. He was nothing if not dramatic. When he recovered it was night. Then for the first time he thought of prayer. ''I spoke as if from my very soul, and said: 'Oh, God, if there is a way out of this fearful place, show it to me, take me to it.' '' His narrator says White's voice here became husky and his features quivered. ''I was still looking up with my hands clasped when I felt a different movement of the raft and turning to look at the whirlpool it was some distance behind (he could see it in the night!), and I was floating on the smoothest current I had yet seen in the canyon.'' The current was now very slow and he found that the rapids were past. The terrible mythical whirlpool at the innocent mouth of the Little Colorado was the end of the turmoil, though he said the canyon went on, the course of the river being exceedingly crooked, and shut in by precipices of white sand rock! There is no white ''sand-rock'' in the Grand Canyon. All through this terrific gorge

Looking up the Grand Canyon from Mouth of Kanab Canyon.
Pencil sketch by F. S. DELLENBAUGH.

wherein the river falls some eighteen hundred feet, White found a slow current and his troubles from rapids were over! For 217 miles of the worst piece of river in the world, he found no difficulty. The gloom and lack of food alone oppressed him, and he thought of plunging from the raft, but lacked the courage. Had he really entered the Grand Canyon his raft would have been speedily reduced to toothpicks and he would not have had the choice of remaining upon it. Finally, he reached a bank upon which some mesquite bushes grew, and he devoured the green pods. Then sailing on in a sort of stupor he was roused by voices and saw some Yampais, who gave him meat and roasted mesquite beans. Proceeding, he heard voices again and a dash of oars. It was Hardy and at last White was saved!

We have seen various actors passing before us in this drama, but I doubt if any of them have been more picturesque than this champion prevaricator. But he had related a splendid yarn. What it was intended to obscure would probably be quite as interesting as what he told. Just where he entered upon the river is of course impossible to decide, but that he never came through the Grand Canyon is as certain as anything can be. His story reveals an absolute ignorance of the river and its walls throughout the whole course he pretended to have traversed.

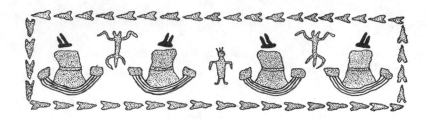

CHAPTER VIII

The One-armed Knight—A Bold Attack on the Canyons—Powell and His Men
—The Wonderful Voyage—Mighty Walls and Roaring Rapids—Capsizes and
Catastrophes.

WHEN the Civil War was finally over, the wilds of the Far West again called in seductive voice to the adventurous and the scientific. The fur-trade as an absorbing industry was dead, but mining, prospecting, ranching, and scientific exploring took its place. Among the naturalists who crossed the Rocky Mountains for purposes of investigation, fascinated by the broad, inviting field, was a one-armed soldier, a former officer of volunteers in the Union Army. His right forearm had remained on the battlefield of Shiloh, but when a strong head is on the shoulders a missing arm makes little difference, and so it was with Major Powell. In the summer of 1867, when he was examining Middle Park, Colorado, with a small party, he happened to explore a moderate canyon on Grand River just below what was known as Middle Park Hot Springs, and became enthused with a desire to fathom the Great Mystery. Consequently, he returned the next year, made his way to the banks of White River, about 120 miles above its mouth, and there erected cabins, with the intention of remaining through the snow season till the following spring should once again unlock the frost-gates of the range. There being now no bison trails hard-beaten into the snow, it was a more difficult undertaking to cross, except in summer. Mrs. Powell was with the party.

During this winter of 1868–69, Powell made several im-

John Wesley Powell.

Explorer of the Canyons of the Colorado, Founder and, till his death, Director of the Bureau of American Ethnology, and long Director of the U. S. Geological Survey. As he looked during the decade following his two descents of the Colorado. Taken about 1876 in Washington   Major Powell died September 23d, 1902.

portant journeys in connection with his purpose of exploring
the great walled river; one was down toward the south as far
as Grand River; a second followed White River to its junction
with the Green, and a third went northward around the eastern
base of the Uinta Mountains, skirting the gorges afterward
named Lodore, Whirlpool, Red Canyon, etc.   In these travels
he formed his plans for an attempt to fully explore, by means
of a boat voyage, the remarkable string of chasms which for
more than three centuries had defied examination.   He decided that the starting point must be where the Union Pacific
Railway had just been thrown across Green River, and that
the only chance for success was to continue on the torrential
flood till either he should arrive at the end of the great canyons near the mouth of the Rio Virgen or should himself be
vanquished in the endeavour.   It was to be a match of human
skill and muscle against rocks and cataracts, shut in from the
outer world, always face to face with the Shadow of Death.
It was to be a duel to the finish between the mysterious torrent on the one side and a little group of valiant men on the
other.   Never had plumed knight of old a more dreadful an-
tagonist.   Like the Sleeping Beauty, this strange Problem lay
in the midst of an enchanted land guarded by the wizard
Aridity and those wonderful water-gods Erosion and Corrasion,
waiting for the knight-errant brave, who should break the
spell and vanquish the demon in his lair.   No ordinary man
was equal to this difficult task, which demanded not alone
courage of the highest order, but combined with this courage
a master-mind and the strategic skill of a general.   But there
comes a time for everything.   The moment for shattering this
mystery had apparently arrived and the mortal who was to
achieve this wonderful feat enters upon the scene with the
quiet nerve and perfect confidence of a master.   He realised the
gravity of the proposition and therein rested his strength.   He
knew no ordinary boat could hope to live in the turmoil of waters
that lashed themselves to fury among the rocks and against the
towering and continuous cliffs; and he knew the party must
be self-supporting in every sense of the term, depending on
nothing but their own powers and what they could carry along.

Character of Green River Valley in the Vicinity of the Crossing of the U. P. Railway.
Photograph by E. O. Beaman.   U. S. Colo. Riv. Exp.

187

The universal dread of the Colorado and its gorges had by this time considerably augmented. The public imagination pictured the roaring flood ploughing its dismal channel through dark subterranean galleries where human life would not be worth a single drop of tossing spray; or leaping at a bound over precipices beside which the seething plunge of Niagara was but a toy. No one could deny these weird tales. No one

Part of a Rapid.
Photograph by J. K. Hillers.   U. S. Colo. Riv. Exp.

knew. But Powell was fortified by Science, and he surmised that nowhere would he encounter any obstruction which his ingenuity could not surmount.

I remember one morning, on the second voyage, when we had made an early start and the night-gloom still lingered in the depths of Marble Canyon as we bore down on a particularly narrow place where the river turned a sharp bend to disappear between walls vertical at the water, into a deep blue haze, it seemed to me that *anything* might be found there, and looking up from my seat in the bow of our boat into the gallant explorer's face, I said: "Major, what would you have done on the first trip if just beyond that bend you had come upon a fall like Niagara?" He regarded me a moment with his penetrating gaze, and then answered: "I don't know." Perhaps he thought that what we now would find there was enough for the moment.

Captain Mansfield, reporting to the Secretary of War, wrote in his letter of December 10, 1867: "Above Callville for several hundred miles the river is entirely unknown." He recommended Callville as the starting-place for exploration, and a small steamer for the work, with skiffs and canvass boats for continuing beyond the steam-navigation limit; but Captain Rodgers, who had gone with the steamboat *Esmeralda* up through Black Canyon, thought the great canyon should be entered above Callville after the fall of water in the spring, and his was more nearly a correct idea. The War Department continued, however, to butt against the wrong end, even after the success of the other way had been demonstrated. Some Mormons, who did not know, reported the two hundred miles above Callville to be better than the one hundred below. The two hundred miles above contain some of the most dangerous portions of the river. Colonel Williamson stated in March, 1868, that he could obtain no information of importance with regard to the "Big" canyon except that contained in Dr. Parry's account of White's alleged journey, which journey, as I have pointed out, was a myth.

"If that report be reliable," he says, "it is evident that in the high or middle stage of the river a strongly built boat can come down the cañon with safety. Before reading that report I had an idea that it would be a very dangerous experiment to attempt to go down this cañon in a boat of any kind, because I feared there were falls, in going down, in which a boat might be upset or even dashed to pieces. As it is, now I believe there are no falls, and I am inclined to think the best way is to start above and descend."

During these efforts of the regular army officers to secure information as to the possibility of exploring the great canyons, Powell approached the problem from an entirely different direction, and his quick and accurate perception told him that to go down with the tide was the one and only way. He was not a rich man; and expeditions require funds, but this was no more of a bar to his purpose than the lack of an arm. His father was a Methodist clergyman of good old stock, vigorous of mind and body, clear-sighted, and never daunted. My immediate impression in meeting the father, even in his old age, was of immense mental and moral strength, resolution, and fortitude. These qualities he bequeathed to his children, and it was a fine inheritance. Major Powell, therefore, had his ancestry largely to thank for the intellect and the courage with which he approached this difficult problem.

Funds for the proposed expedition were furnished by the State Institutions of Illinois and the Chicago Academy of Science; none by the general Government, so that this was in no way a Government matter, except that Congress passed a joint-resolution authorising him to draw rations for twelve men from western army posts. Early in the spring of 1869, after returning from the rambles along Green River of the previous winter, Powell went to Chicago and engaged a competent builder to construct four strong boats after his suggestions. Three of these were of oak, twenty-one feet long, and one of light pine, sixteen feet long, the latter intended as an advance boat, to be quickly handled in the face of sudden danger. At the bow and stern of each was a water-tight compartment, in which supplies and instruments could be packed, and they would yet give buoyancy to the boats when they would be filled with water by the breaking waves of the rapids. Amidships the boats were open, and here also goods, guns, etc., were stowed away. Each had a long rope, to use in lowering past the most dangerous places. Unlike all the explorations on the lower course of the river, this expedition would require no lines for towing. These four little craft, which were to be the main reliance of the daring men composing the party, were transported free of charge, together with the men

who were from the country east of the mountains, to Green
River Station, Wyoming, by the courtesy of the officials of the
Chicago, Burlington, and Quincy, and the Union Pacific railways, who took a deep interest in the proposed descent. The
names given to the boats were, for the small one, *Emma Dean*,
the pilot boat (after Mrs. Powell), *Kitty Clyde's Sister*, *Maid*

Canyon of Lodore—The Wheatstack.
Photograph by E. O. BEAMAN. U. S. Colo. Riv. Exp.

of the Canyon, and *No-Name*. The members of the party,
together with their disposition in the boats at starting, were as
follows: John Wesley Powell, John C. Sumner, William H.
Dunn—the *Emma Dean ;* Walter H. Powell, G. Y. Bradley—
Kitty Clyde's Sister ; O. G. Howland, Seneca Howland, Frank
Goodman—the *No-Name ;* William R. Hawkins, Andrew Hall
—*Maid of the Canyon.*

Powell, as noted, had been a volunteer officer in the Civil War. After that he was connected with the Wesleyan University at Bloomington, Illinois, and with the Normal University at Normal, in the same state. Sumner, generally known as Jack Sumner, had also been a soldier in the late war. He was fair-haired and delicate-looking, but with a strong constitution. Dunn had been a hunter and trapper. Walter Powell was Major Powell's youngest brother. He had been in the late war and had there suffered cruelly by capture and imprisonment. Bradley was an orderly sergeant of regulars, had served in the late war, and resigned from the army to join this party. O. G. Howland had been a printer. Seneca Howland was his younger brother. Goodman was a young Englishman. Hawkins had been a soldier in the late war, and Andrew Hall was a Scotch boy nineteen years old.

The spring was chosen for the beginning of the voyage because the Green then is at flood and there would be less trouble about floating the boats through the shoal places and amongst the rocks. The river in some respects is safer at a lower stage of water, but the work is harder. This, however, was not known then, and Powell had to take his chances at the flood. On May 24, 1869, the boats were manned and soon were carried out of sight of the haphazard group of houses which at that time constituted this frontier settlement of Green River. They were heavily laden, for ten months' rations were carried, as Powell expected when winter came to be obliged to halt and make a permanent camp till spring. He calculated the river might be filled with ice. It has since been ascertained, however, that the Colorado proper rarely has any ice in it. I remember once hearing that a great many years ago it was frozen over in the neighbourhood of Lee's Ferry, where for a little distance the current is not rapid. Powell was providing for every contingency he could think of, and trouble with ice was a possible one. But even without ice the water in winter is so cold that, as men who make the descent must continually be saturated by the breaking waves and by the necessity of frequently jumping overboard in avoiding rocks, the danger of pneumonia is really greater than that from wreck. They had an abundance of warm clothing for winter, plenty of ammunition, two or three dozen traps, tools of various kinds, nails, screws, etc. In the line of scientific instruments there were two sextants, four chronometers, a number of barometers, thermometers, compasses, etc. With the exception of the *Emma Dean*, which had on board only instruments and clothing, the boats were loaded in such a way that if one should be lost the expedition would still possess a variety of articles and food.

The first day they met with the usual number of minor accidents, such as a starting expedition of this kind is seldom

Green River above Flaming Gorge.
Photograph by E. O. BEAMAN.   U. S. Colo. Riv. Exp.

free from, like breaking an oar, running on a shoal, and so on, but all went very well, and when the evening came an early camp was made, and Powell climbed up and away from the river to survey the situation.

"Standing on a high point," he says, "I can look off in every direction over a vast landscape with salient rocks and cliffs glittering in the evening sun. Dark shadows are settling in the valleys and gulches, and the heights are made higher, and the depths deeper by the glamour and witchery of light and shade. Away to the south, the Uinta mountains stretch in a long line; high peaks thrust into the sky, and snow-fields glittering like lakes of molten silver; and pine forests in sombre green; and rosy clouds playing around the borders of huge black masses; and heights and clouds and mountains and snow-fields and forests and rock-lands are blended into one grand view."

This was the country before him. The Uinta Mountains, stretching their picturesque and mighty barrier across the determined course of the river, produce the first series of superb canyons on the threshold of which Powell and his daring band were now setting foot. On the third day they were at Henry's Fork, in the neighbourhood of that first camp in this locality made by Ashley in 1825, and of his start in the experiment in canyon running which so nearly terminated his brilliant career. The "Suck," noted for its danger among the early trappers, was easily passed and Powell makes no mention of it. So far as I can ascertain there were two records kept on this expedition, one by Powell on strips of brown paper, and the other by Jack Sumner on foolscap. The latter, comprised in some six or eight pages, was the more complete, I believe, and is now in Washington. I have not seen it since 1871, when we were in the habit of daily reading its thrilling pages to find out what we might next expect in our descent. If any other diary or journal was kept by the men of this expedition I have not heard of it.

The first rapid is in Horseshoe Canyon, and it was no obstacle, being small and docile, but when they had gone through the next canyon, named Kingfisher, they found themselves at the beginning of a new and closer, deeper gorge, Red Canyon, where the waters first begin to exhibit their grim intention. Here they encountered real rapids, the boats often dashing along at railroad speed, the waves fiercely breaking over them, and bailing becoming an imperative accomplishment. The attempt of a Ute to run through this canyon was described in picturesque terms by one of the tribe. "Rocks, heap, heap, high," he said; "water go hoowoogh, hoowoogh; water-pony heap buck; water catch um; no see um Injun any more! no see um squaw any more! no see um papoose any more!'' and thus begins and ends the only history of native navigation on this upper river I ever heard of.

After considerable hard work the party reached a particularly sharp, though not very high, fall, announced before arrival by

Red Canyon—Green River. Upper Portion. Looking up Stream.
Photograph by E. O. BEAMAN. U. S. Colo. Riv. Exp.

a loud and angry roar. Here a portage was deemed wise, and the goods were carried up over the huge broken rocks and so on down to a point well below the foot of the drop, where the cargoes were again restored to the boats, which meanwhile had been lowered by lines. It was here that the name of Ashley and a year date were found inscribed on a rock. Of this I made a careful copy in 1871, which is given on page 112. The second figure could, of course, be only an 8, and the fourth was plainly a 5. The third, however, was obscure, and Powell was uncertain whether it was a 3 or a 5. It could have been nothing but a 2, because, as we have seen, it was in the twenties of the last century that Ashley operated in this region; and it was in 1825 that he made the Red Canyon journey. At the date which a 3 would make he was a Congressman, and he was never in the Far West again. Running on through Red Canyon with exhilarating velocity, but without any serious drawback, the party came out into the tranquil Brown's Hole, henceforth called Brown's Park. At the foot of this, without any preliminaries, they were literally swept into the heart of the mountains, for it is here that the river so suddenly rends the massive formations in twain and speeds away toward the sea between wonderful precipices of red sandstone, churning itself to ivory in the headlong rush. This was named the Canyon of Lodore at the suggestion of one of the men. The work of safely proceeding down the torrent now grew far more difficult. Rapids were numerous and the descent in most of them very great. The boats had to be handled with extra caution. The method of travelling was for Powell to go ahead in the *Emma Dean* to examine the nature of each rapid before the other boats should come down to it. If he saw a clear chute he ran through and signalled "come on," but if he thought it too risky he signalled "land," and the place was examined as well as he was able from the shore. If this investigation showed a great many dangerous rocks, or any other dangerous element, a portage was made, or the boats were let down along the edge by lines without taking out the cargoes. In this careful way they were getting along very well, when one day they came to a particularly threatening place. Powell immediately perceived the danger, and, landing, signalled the other boats to do likewise. Unfortunately, the warning came too late for the *No-Name*, which was drawn into a sag, a sort of hollow lying just above the rapid, to clutch the unwary and drive them over the fall to certain destruction. Powell for a moment had given his attention to the last boat, and as he

The Canyon of Lodore—Upper Part of Disaster Falls.
Where Powell lost the *No-Name* in 1869.
Photograph by E. O. BEAMAN.   U. S. Colo. Riv. Exp.

turned again and hurried along to discover the fortune of the
No-Name, which was plunging down, without hope of escape,
toward the frightful descent, he was just in time to see her
strike a rock and, rebounding, career so that the open compartment filled with water. Sweeping on down now with railway

The Canyon of Brush Creek—Looking Up.
This stream enters the Green not far below foot of Split-Mountain Canyon.
Photograph by J. K. HILLERS.   U. S. Colo. Riv. Exp.

speed, broadside on, she again struck a few yards below and
was broken completely in two, the three men being tossed into
the foaming flood. They were able to gain some support by
clinging to the main part of the boat, which still held together.
Drifting on swiftly over a few hundred yards more to a second
rapid full of large boulders, the doomed craft struck a third

time and was entirely demolished, the men and the fragments
being carried then out of sight.   Powell climbed as rapidly as
possible over the huge fallen rocks, which here lie along the
shore he was on, and presently he was able to get a view of his
men.   Goodman was in a whirlpool below a great rock; reaching this he clung to it.   Howland had been washed upon a low
rocky island, which at this stage of water was some feet above
the current, and Seneca Howland also had gained this place.
Howland extended a long pole to Goodman and by means of
it pulled him to the island, where all were safe for the time
being.   Several hundred yards farther down, the river took another and more violent fall, rendering the situation exceedingly
hazardous.   A boat allowed to get a trifle too far towards this
descent would be treated as the *No-Name* had been served
higher up, and the expedition could not afford to lose a second
boat with its contents.   The water in these rapids beats furiously against the foot of the opposite vertical cliff, and if a
boat in either place should by chance get too far over towards
this right-hand wall it would be dashed to pieces there, even
could it escape the rocks of the main channel.   The problem
was how to rescue the men from the island and not destroy
another boat in doing it.   Finally, the *Emma Dean* was
brought down, and Jack Sumner undertook to reach the island
in her.   Keeping well up stream, as near the first fall as he
could, a few bold strokes enabled him to land near the lower
end.   Then, all together, they pulled the boat to the very head
of the island and beyond that as far as they could stand up in
the water.   Here one man sat on a rock and held the boat
steady till the others were in perfect readiness to pull with all
their power, when he gave a shove and, clinging on, climbed
in while the oarsmen put their muscle to the test.   The shore
was safely attained, and Powell writes: "We are as glad to
shake hands with them as though they had been on a voyage
around the world, and wrecked on a distant coast."   This disaster was most serious, even though the men were saved, for,
besides the loss of the craft itself, all the barometers by some
miscalculation were on the *No-Name*.   They were able to make
camp on the shore and survey the situation.   "No sleep comes

to me in all those dark hours," writes Powell. To meet with such a reverse at so early a stage was very discouraging, but Powell had counted on disaster, and, as he was never given to repining, as soon as breakfast was eaten the next morning he cast about for a way to rescue the barometers which were in a part of the wreck that had lodged among some rocks a half mile below. Sumner and Dunn volunteered to try to reach the place with the small boat, and they succeeded. When they returned, a loud cheer went up from those on shore, and Powell was much impressed with this exhibition of deep interest in the safety of the scientific instruments, but he soon discovered that the cheer was in celebration of the rescue of a three-gallon keg of whiskey that had been smuggled along without his knowledge and happened to be on the ill-fated *No-Name*.

It required a good deal of work to complete the portage around the double fall so that night again compelled them to camp near its spray, this time on a sand bank at the foot of the lower descent. Here, half buried in the gravel of the beach, some objects were discovered which revealed the fact that some other party had suffered a similar disastrous experience. These were an iron bake-oven, several tin plates, fragments of a boat, and other indications of a wreck at this place long years before. In his report, Powell ascribes this wreck to Ashley, but this is a mistake, for Ashley seems never to have entered this canyon, ending his voyage, as I have previously stated, when he reached Brown's Park. This wreckage then was from some other and later party. Powell also states that Ashley and one other survivor succeeded in reaching Salt Lake, where they were fed and clothed by the Mormons and employed on the Temple foundation until they had earned enough to enable them to leave the country. These men could not have been Ashley and a companion, for several reasons: one cited above; another that the Mormons had not yet settled at Salt Lake in Ashley's day; and a third, that Ashley was a wealthy and distinguished man, and would not have required pecuniary help. The disaster recorded by the bake-oven, etc., must then have occurred after 1847, the year the Mormons went into the Salt Lake Valley. Possibly it may have been the party mentioned by Farnham in 1839, though this would not be true if the men found Mormons at Salt Lake. An old mountaineer, named Baker, once told Powell of a party of men starting down the river and named Ashley as one, and this story, which referred

The Canyon of Lodore.
Looking down at Triplet Falls. Depth about 2500 feet.
Photograph by E. O. BEAMAN. U. S. Geol. Survey

undoubtedly to the real Ashley party, became confused with some other wherein the survivors probably did strike for Salt Lake and were helped by the Mormons.[1] At any rate, the

[1] Should any reader have knowledge of the men who were wrecked in Lodore between the time of Ashley and Powell, the author would be glad to hear of it.

rapids which had wrecked the earlier party and swallowed up the *No-Name* were appropriately called Disaster Falls.

The river descends throughout Lodore with great rapidity and every day brought with it hard work and narrow escapes. Sometimes the danger was of a novel and unexpected character, as on June 16th, when the dry willows around camp caught fire. Powell had started for a climb of investigation and looking down on the camp he perceived a sudden tremendous activity without being able for some moments to discover the cause. So rapidly did the fire spread that there was no escape except by the boats. Some had their clothing burned and their hair singed, while Bradley even had his ears scorched. The cook in his haste stumbled with his arms full of culinary utensils, and the load disappeared beneath the waters, ever on the alert to swallow up man, boat, or beast. Just below the camp was a rapid and, casting off, they were forced to run this without stopping to examine it. No harm was done to the boats, and they landed at the first opportunity. When the fire had burned out they went back along the rocks to pick up what had been left behind and was unconsumed. On the same day, as the men were in the act of lowering a boat by lines, she broke away and started on an independent run. Fortunately, she soon became entangled in an eddy, where she halted long enough to permit them to hurry down the small boat and recapture her. Sometimes the channel was beset with innumerable great rocks, amidst which the river seethed and boiled in a manner sufficient to terrify any boatmen, but, luckily, they were able to work their way cautiously along, and without further disaster they came, on the 17th of June, to a place where the walls broke away and they emerged into a beautiful park-like widening of the canyon with bounding cliffs only about 600 feet high near the river. After the continuous cliffs of from 2000 to 2500 feet this place seemed like open country. Once more they camped in a quiet place at the mouth of a river entering through a deep canyon on the left or east side. It was the Yampa, sometimes called Bear River. After a side trip of several hours up this canyon they started again on the descent and, skirting the smooth perpendicular wall which forms the west side of Echo Park, they turned a corner and found themselves in a new gorge, which, on account of many whirlpools existing at that stage of water, was called Whirlpool Canyon. The run through this was ac-

Echo Rock on Right, from which Echo Park Takes its Name.
To one sitting in a boat near foreground a sentence of ten words is repeated.
Photograph by E. O. Beaman.

complished with great rapidity, as there were no serious obstacles, and in two days the expedition emerged into another expansion of the walls, where the tired men had a brief respite before they perceived the rocks again closing in on the water.

Here a deer was brought in by one of the men, and, as they killed a mountain sheep farther up, they had not suffered for fresh meat. The entrance to the next canyon was very abrupt, and they were soon whirling along on a swift current. Though there were many rapids, landings were easy, and there was plenty of standing room everywhere, so that in two days they had the pleasure of pulling out of this Split Mountain Canyon into the Wonsits Valley, the longest opening in the whole line of canyons. Thus far, no Amerinds had been seen, not even signs of them, but here they found some tipi poles and the dead embers of a camp-fire, showing that other human beings besides themselves had traversed the lands now about them. Pushing ahead over the sluggish waters of the river in this valley, they were not long in arriving at the mouth of the Uinta River, where Powell and two others walked out to the Ute Agency, about forty miles distant up the Uinta. One of the crew of the wrecked *No-Name*, Frank Goodman, here decided that he had seen all the canyons his education required and took his departure. This was not unwelcome to Powell, for the boats were still heavily loaded and the three men who had composed the crew of the wrecked boat were no longer actually required. Starting again, they arrived, not far below the mouth of the Uinta, at an island where a small crop had been planted by a "squaw-man," [1] who had visited Powell's camp the previous winter. On that occasion he had disclosed his intention of tilling this place and invited Powell to help himself when he passed there in his boats. The man was not at the farm, and nothing was ripe, but Hall suggested that potato-tops make good "greens." A quantity was therefore secured, and, at the noon stop, cooked and eaten, with the obvious result that all were violently sick. Luckily, the sickness was brief, and they were able to proceed by the middle of the afternoon. Often, the longing, by men living on bacon and beans, for something fresh in the vegetable line, leads to foolish experiments.

This Wonsits Valley soon came to an end and once more the rocks closed in, forming a canyon lacking the vegetation

[1] A white man married to a squaw, and living with the tribe.

that had accompanied the cliffs along the river above. Because of this general barren appearance the gorge was called the Canyon of Desolation. On July 11th, they approached a rapid which seemed at first glance no more difficult to run than many they had successfully dashed through. The leading boat by Powell's direction pulled into it, but this move was no sooner made than he perceived that at the bottom the river turned

The Canyon of Desolation—Sumner's Amphitheatre.
Walls about 1200 feet.
Photograph by E. O. Beaman.   U. S. Colo. Riv. Exp.

sharply to the left and the waters were piled against the foot of the cliff in an alarming manner. An effort was made to land, but as they had shortly before broken one oar and lost another, the two remaining were not sufficient to propel the boat with force enough to reach the desired point. At the same time, a huge wave striking the boat turned it instantly upside down and cast Powell some distance away. He suc-

The Canyon of Desolation—Low Water.

Cliffs about 2700 feet.   Note boat with men on rocks, middle distance, making a let-down.
Photograph by E. O. BEAMAN.   U. S. Colo. Riv. Exp.

ceeded in reaching her side, and there found Sumner and Dunn clinging. When quiet water was again entered they attempted to right the craft, and in doing this Dunn lost his hold and went under, though at the critical moment, as he came up, Sumner succeeded in grasping him and drawing him to the boat. By this time, they had drifted a long way down and saw another rapid approaching. By swimming desperately, they avoided being carried into this in their awkward plight, and, towing the boat after them, landed none too soon on a pile of driftwood on the bank. A gun, some barometers, and other articles that were in the open compartment, were lost, though one roll of blankets had been caught and saved by Powell as it drifted by. Building a large fire on the shore, they dried their clothing, while out of one of the logs they manufactured much-needed oars.

Fortified by these, they ran several bad rapids the following day. In one, Bradley was knocked overboard, but, his foot catching under the seat, he was dragged head down through the water till the worst of the fall was passed, when one of the other men managed to haul him in. Just below this, they emerged again into an expansion of the walls, leaving the ninety-seven miles of Desolation behind. But another mile brought the rocks back once more, and the thirty-six miles of Gray Canyon must be passed before they came to Gunnison Valley. Beyond this, walls of sandstone about one thousand feet high hemmed the river in for some sixty miles, but the stream was not dangerous and the party moved on quickly, though the absence of rapids and swift water made rowing obligatory. At the foot of this gorge, called from its wind-ing character, Labyrinth Canyon, there was a brief expansion before the next walls closed upon them. These were closer than any seen above, but the river, though swift, had no dan-gerous element, so that progress was safe and easy, and in a trifle over forty miles they came to the mouth of a river almost as large as the Green, flowing in a canyon of similar depth and character. This was Grand River. At last they had reached the place where these two streams unite, thirteen hundred feet below the surrounding country; the mysterious Junction which, so far as the records go, Macomb and all white men before had failed to find. Therefore when Powell and his band floated down till the waters of the Green mingled with those of the Grand they were perhaps the first white men ever to arrive at the spot. The Colorado proper was now before them. It was the mystery of mysteries.

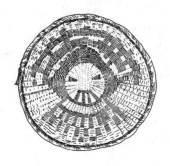

CHAPTER IX

A Canyon of Cataracts — The Imperial Chasm — Short Rations — A Split in the Party — Separation — Fate of the Howlands and Dunn — The Monster Vanquished.

POWELL'S winter of investigation had probably given him a good idea of what kind of rapids might be expected in the formations composing the canyons as far as the mouth of Grand River, but he now had confronting him water which for aught he could tell might indulge in plunges of a hundred feet or more at one time, between absolutely vertical walls. And the aspect of the surroundings at the junction of the Green and the Grand is not reassuring. It is a barren and dismal place, with no footing but a few sand-banks that are being constantly cut away and reformed by the whirling current, except on their higher levels where a few scrawny hackberry trees and weeds find room to continue a precarious existence. To get out of or into this locality either by climbing the cliffs or by navigating the rivers is a difficult feat, and to trust oneself to the current blindly rushing down toward the sea is even worse, more especially so on the occasion of this first descent when all beyond was a complete blank. But the party faced the future bravely and cheerfully. They climbed out at two points on tours of inspection of the country above, while some took the opportunity to overhaul the supply of rations, which, having been so often wet, was seriously damaged. The flour was musty and full of hard lumps. To eliminate the lumps, therefore, they screened it with a piece of mosquito netting for a sieve; at the same time they eliminated more than two hundred pounds of the precious freight and threw this away, a foolish proceeding, for by proper cooking it might have been utilised for food.   Together with the losses by the wreck of the *No-Name* and other mishaps, and with what had been consumed, their food-supply was now reduced from the original

Junction of the Grand and Green.
On the surface; bare rock.   Photograph by E. O. BEAMAN,
U. S. Colo. Riv. Exp.

ten-months' amount to a two-months' quantity, though they had not yet been on the way quite sixty days; that is, they had used up eight months' supplies in two months, including a mountain sheep and a deer the hunters had brought down, and they were barely more than half-way to the end of the journey.   At this alarming rate they would be starving long before they saw the walls of the Grand Canyon break away.

Nevertheless no thought of pursuing any course but the one planned occurred to them, and on July 21st they cast off from

In Cataract Canyon.
Highest walls in this canyon 2700 feet.
Photograph by E. O. BEAMAN, U. S. Colo. Riv. Exp.

the sand-banks and were carried rapidly down on the swift torrent of the Great Colorado. They had not gone far before plenty of hard work was furnished, in the shape of two portages that were necessary to pass particularly dangerous places, and

numerous bad rapids to run. In the afternoon the *Emma
Dean*, in attempting to navigate one of the more favourable-
looking foaming descents, was swamped, pitching Powell and
the others headlong into the roaring flood. They were fortunately able to cling to the boat till they floated into more
tranquil waters, where they managed to climb on board, sig-
nalling the other boats to land before the plunge. This they
could do, and the boats were brought down by a portage,
which took all the rest of the day. The approach of darkness
compelled a halt for the night on some rocks where they
had barely room enough to lie down. Three much-needed
oars had been lost with the capsize of the *Dean*. These were
sadly missed in the rough water that surrounded them the
following day, so at the first large pile of driftwood they made
a landing and secured a cottonwood log for oar-timber. While
the oars were making, Powell and his brother climbed up to
where some pinyon trees were seen growing, and collected a
quantity of gum with which to calk the leaky boats. They
needed all the preparation possible, for the rapids now came
ever thicker, ever faster, and more violent. The walls also
grew in altitude from the thirteen hundred feet of the Junction
to fifteen hundred feet, then to eighteen hundred feet, nearly
vertical in places.

An examination of the barometric record was now made to
see how much they had by this time descended toward sea-
level, and, by comparison, about what might be expected in the
river below. The conclusion was that though great descents
were still ahead, if the fall should be distributed in rapids
and short drops, as it had been above, and not concentrated
in great plunges, they would meet with success. But there
always remained the possibility of arriving on the brink of
some high fall where no footing on either side could be obtained, and where a fierce current would prohibit a return. In
such a case the exploration would have ended then and there.
The newspapers before this time had printed a story of the
expedition's collapse. The outer world supposed that Powell
and all his men but one had been destroyed, though A. H.
Thompson wrote to the *Chicago Inter-Ocean*, which first pub-

lished it, showing its absurdity. Mrs. Powell heard the story at her father's home in Detroit and she pronounced it a fabrication, for she had received a letter subsequent to the date given for the destruction of the party. She also had faith in her husband's judgment, caution, and good sense, so she refused to accept the tale at all, which was circulated by a man who had started from Green River Station, and who, by "pitching" this picturesque yarn, secured the sympathy and the purses of the passengers on an east-bound Union Pacific train. He told how Powell and all the men but himself had been suddenly swallowed up in an awful place, dark and gloomy and full of fearful whirlpools, called Brown's Hole. From the shore, where he alone had remained, he had despairingly witnessed the party disappear in a mighty whirlpool never to rise again. But he made a mistake, so far as Mrs. Powell was concerned, in naming the spot. She knew very well that there was no danger whatever in Brown's Hole, and that the river in this pretty park was the quietest on the whole course. But for its inventor the yarn had fulfilled its purpose, and he found himself east of the Mississippi, where he wanted to be, with a pocket full of dollars. A week or two after the story appeared letters were received from Powell via the Uinta Agency. These positively proved the falsity of the tale.

On the fourth day in Cataract Canyon three portages were compulsory at the very outset to pass safely over a stretch where the waters tumbled seventy-five feet in three quarters of a mile, and at the end of this three quarters of a mile they camped again, worn out by the severe toil. Rapids now came with even greater frequency, between walls more than two thousand feet high and often nearly vertical from the water. On the 27th a flock of mountain sheep was discovered on the rocks not more than one hundred feet above their heads. The game did not see the hunters, who landed quickly in a convenient cove, and two fat sheep were added to the rapidly diminishing larder. On the next day they were startled by the sudden closing in of the walls, till the canyon, now nearly three thousand feet deep, became very narrow, with the river filling the chasm from one blank cliff to the other. The water

was also swift and the canyon winding, so that it was not possible to see ahead.   Powell was much disturbed lest they
should run upon some impassable fall, but luckily in about a
mile and a half they emerged again into a more broken gorge

The Crags at Millecrag Bend, foot of Cataract Canyon.
Photograph by E. O. BEAMAN, U. S. Colo. Riv. Exp.

without having had the least difficulty.   He justly remarks
that after it was done it seemed a simple thing to run through
such a place, but the first doing of it was fraught with keen
anxiety.   In the late afternoon of this same day, they came
to the end of the forty-one miles of Cataract Canyon, marked

by a deep canyon-valley entering from the left at a sharp bend where millions of crags, pinnacles, and towers studded the summit of the right-hand wall, now again thirteen hundred feet high. It was called Millecrag Bend, either then, or on the second expedition. A new canyon immediately formed; a narrow, straight canyon, with walls terraced above and vertical below. The thirteen hundred feet of altitude speedily diminished and in nine miles the voyagers were at the end. Low walls again began, forming the head of the next canyon of the series. Presently they arrived at the mouth of a river flowing in from the right, or west. The pilot boat ran up into this stream, and as the water of the Colorado had been particu-

The Music Temple Alcove, Glen Canyon.

So called because the men of Powell's first expedition sang in the place. On entering one finds a huge cavern. Here the men who were later killed by the Shewits carved their names.

Photograph by E. O. BEAMAN, U. S.Colo. Riv. Exp.

larly muddy, the men were eager to discover clear, sparkling affluents and springs. One behind shouted, "How is she, Jack?" and Jack sententiously replied, "Oh, she 's a dirty devil!" and by this title the river was long called, and probably is still so known in that region, though on the maps it was afterwards changed by Powell to Frémont River, in honour of the Pathfinder.

They were now in the beginning of what has since been called Glen Canyon. Powell at first gave the name of Mound to the upper half, and Monument to the lower, but after 1871 Glen was substituted for the whole. On July 31st they passed the mouth of the San Juan, which enters through a canyon similar to that of the main river, about a thousand feet deep. They tried to climb out near this point, but failed to accomplish it. The next day they made camp in one of the peculiar alcoves or glens from which the canyon is named, worn by the waters into the homogeneous sandstone composing the walls. This particular glen is a beautiful spot. The wide entrance contains a number of cottonwood trees, and passing these one finds himself in a huge cavern some five hundred feet wide and two hundred feet high, with a narrow slit leading up to the sky, and extending back far beyond the limits of the glen. The men found this a delightful place. They sang songs, and their voices sounded so well that they bestowed upon the cavern the name of Music Temple. It now holds a special interest because three of them, O. G. Howland, Seneca Howland, and William Dunn, carved their names on a smooth face of rock, and it forms their eternal monument, for these three never saw civilisation again.

For 149 miles the easy waters of Glen Canyon bore them along, and by August 4th they had passed the Crossing of the Fathers, or Ute Ford, as it was called in that country before its identification as the point where Escalante crossed, and were at the mouth of the Paria, since 1873 better known as Lee's Ferry. They had now before them the grandest of all the gorges, though only two hundred feet deep at the beginning; but they had not proceeded far into it before the walls ran rapidly up while the river ran rapidly down. Numerous falls appeared, one following another in quick succession, necessitating portages and much hard work. When Powell managed to climb out on the 7th, the walls had grown to twenty-three hundred feet. They soon increased to about thirty-five

217   **The Depths of the Grand Canyon at Sunset.**

Studio painting by F. S. DELLENBAUGH, in the possession of Prof. A. H. Thompson, who considers it the best representation of the canyon from below that he has seen, "the truest—far better than any photograph because more comprehensive."

hundred feet, often vertical on one or the other side at the water, and even in the upper portions extremely precipitous. By the 10th they had reached the mouth of the Little Colorado, where White's imagination had pictured the greatest terror of the whole river, and the end of all the dangerous part. The walls of this tributary are, as is usually the case, the same as those of the main gorge, but the stream itself was small, muddy, and saline. Powell walked up it three or four miles, having no trouble in crossing it by wading when desirable. He called the new gorge now before him, really only a continuation of the one ending with the canyon of the Little Colorado, the "Great Unknown," and a party some twenty years later, emulating the early Spaniards in the art of forgetting, called it the same, but it was the Great Unknown only once, and that was when Powell on this occasion first faced the sublime, unfathomed depths that here lay in his course. Only one month's rations remained as a reliance in this terrible passage. Powell says: "We have an unknown distance yet to run; an unknown river yet to explore. What falls there are we know not; what rocks beset the channel, we know not; what walls rise over the river, we know not. . . . The men talk as cheerfully as ever; jests are bandied about freely this morning; but to me the cheer is sombre and the jests are ghastly." With anxiety and much misgiving they drifted on between mile-high cliffs, rising terrace on terrace to the very sky itself. Even now, when the dangers are known and tested, no man lives who can enter the great chasm for a voyage to the other end without feeling anxiety as to the result, and the more anxiety he feels, the more probability there is that he will pass the barriers safely. Running rapids and passing falls by portages and let-downs, they met no formidable obstacle till August 14th, when they ran into a granite formation, the "First Granite Gorge." While the gorge was wide above, it grew narrower as the river level was approached, till the walls were closer than anywhere farther up; and they were ragged and serrated. They had noticed that hard rocks had produced bad river, and soft rocks smooth water; now they were in a series of rocks harder than any

The Grand Canyon. The " Sockdologer " Rapid.
Fall of about eighty feet in one third of a mile.
Photograph by J. K. HILLERS, U. S. Colo. Riv. Exp.

before encountered. There was absolutely no way of telling what the waters might do in such a formation, which ran up till a thousand feet of it stood above their heads, supporting more than four thousand feet more of sedimentary rocks, making a grand total of between five thousand and six thousand feet. The same day on which they entered the granite they arrived, after running, and portaging around, several bad rapids, at a terrific fall, announced by a loud roar like the steady boom of Niagara, reverberating back and forth from wall to wall, and filling the whole gorge with its ominous note. The river was beaten to a solid sheet of reeling foam for a third of a mile. There was but one choice, but one path for the boats, and that lay through the midst of it, for on each side the waves pounded violently against the jagged cliffs which so closely hemmed them in. Men might climb up to the top of the granite and find their way around the obstruction, one thousand feet above it, descending again a mile or two down, but they could not take the boats over such a road. They must, therefore, run the place, a fall of about eighty feet in the third of a mile, or give up the descent. So they got into their boats and started on the smooth waters, so soon shattered into raging billows. Though filled with water, the boats all rode successfully and came out below crowned with success.

Often a rapid is greatly augmented by enormous boulders which have been washed into the river from some side canyon, and, acting like a dam, block the water up and cause it to roar and fret tenfold more. Black and dismal is this granite gorge; sharp and terrible the rapids, whose sheeted foam becomes fairly iridescent by contrast. The method of working around some of the worst places is illustrated well by the following extract:

"We land and stop for an hour or two to examine the fall. It seems possible to let down with lines, at least part of the way, from point to point, along the right-hand wall. So we make a portage over the first rocks, and find footing on some boulders below. Then we let down one of the boats to the end of her line, when she reaches a corner of the projecting rock, to which one of the men clings and steadies her, while I examine an eddy below. I think we can pass the other boats down by us, and catch them in the eddy. This is soon done and the men in the boats in the eddy pull us to their side. On the shore of this little eddy there is about two feet of gravel beach above water. Standing on this beach, some of the men take a line of the little boat and let it drift down against another projecting angle. Here is a little shelf on which a man from my boat climbs, and a shorter line is passed to him, and he fastens the boat to the side of the cliff. Then the second one is let down, bringing the line of the third. When the second boat is tied up, the two men standing on the beach above spring into the last boat, which is pulled up alongside ours. Then we let down the boats, for twenty-five or thirty yards, by walking along the shelf, landing them again in the mouth of a side canyon. Just below this there is another pile of boulders, over which we make another portage. From the foot of these rocks we can climb to another shelf, forty or fifty feet above the water. On this bench we camp for the night. We find a few sticks, which have lodged in the rocks. It is raining hard, and we have no shelter, but kindle a fire and have our supper. We sit on the rocks all night, wrapped in our ponchos, getting what sleep we can.''

At this season of the year there is a good deal of cloudy and rainy weather in the Grand Canyon region, and this makes the gorge decidedly gloomy when one is .compelled to stay in it and descend the river. The next morning with two hours of similar manœuvring the rapid was passed. The same day they found a stretch where the river was so swift the boats were tossed from side to side like feathers, entirely unmanageable. Here they met with another rapid and two of the boats were in such a position they could not escape running it. But they went through without damage. Then the third crew tried to reach land, and succeeded, only to find that there was no foothold. They pushed out again, to be overwhelmed by a powerful wave which filled the boat full. She drifted helpless through several breakers and one of these capsized her. The men hung to the side, the only thing to do in the Colorado unless one has on a life preserver (and even then it is advisable), as she drifted down to the other boats, where she was caught and

righted.   It has always seemed strange to me that Powell on
this crucial expedition did not provide himself and his men
with cork life-jackets, a precaution that suggests itself immediately in such an undertaking.   No one ought ever to attempt
a descent without them.

The next day they reached a clear little stream coming in
through a deep canyon on the right, and because they had
honoured the devil by conferring his name on a river higher
up, Powell concluded to honour the good spirits by calling this
Bright Angel River.   In its narrow valley ruined foundations

Bottom of the Grand Canyon.
Looking down from foot of Bright Angel Trail.
Photograph by T. MITCHELL PRUDDEN.

of houses and fragments of pottery were discovered.   There
were also indications of old trails by which the builders had
made their way about.   By the 17th of August, the rations
were reduced to musty flour enough for ten days, a few dried
apples, and plenty of coffee.   The bacon had spoiled and was
thrown away.   Now the problem of food was a paramount
consideration.   Should they be detained by many bad places
they might be forced by the food question to abandon the
river, if possible, and strike for the Mormon settlements lying
to the north.   The barometers were rendered useless, so that
they could not determine the altitude to see what proportion

In the Midst of a Grand Canyon Rapid.
Studio painting by F. S. DELLENBAUGH.

223

of descent still remained ahead.   They hoped, however, that
the worst was behind.   They now carefully divided evenly
among the boats the little stock of flour, so that, in case of
disaster, all of it should not be lost at once.   Notwithstanding
all the difficulties and the dark outlook, Powell never failed in
his wonderful poise of mind and balance of nerve.   But he
was anxious, and he sang sometimes as they sailed along till
the men, he once told me, he believed thought he had gone
crazy.   Of course the singing was more or less a mask for his
real feelings.

On the 19th the pioneer boat, running some distance ahead
of the others, was again upset by a wave.   As usual the men
succeeded in clinging to the upturned craft, the closed compartments always keeping the boat afloat, and were carried
down through another rapid.   The companion boats were detained by whirlpools and could not quickly go to the rescue,
but when they finally did reach the *Dean*, she was bailed out, the
men climbed on board of her again, and they all went on without even trying to land.   The next day, in one hour, they
ran on a wild dashing river ten miles without stopping, and,
what was to them most important, they ran out of the granite.
The bright colours of the sedimentary rocks put new cheer
into them.   On they ran, down the narrow canyon, now about
three thousand feet deep, always on swift water, but for a
time there were no bad rapids.   On August 25th they reached
a fall where the river was once dammed up for a great height
by an overflow of lava from craters on and near the brink.
One of the craters was plainly visible from below.   The canyon
appeared to have been once filled by the lava to the depth of
fifteen hundred feet.   They named the descent Lava Falls and
made a portage.   Not far below this they found a garden
which had been planted by the Shewits Pai Utes living on the
plateau above.   The corn was not ripe, though some squashes
were, and helping themselves to a few of these they ran on to
a comfortable place and had a feast.

So well did they now get on, running rapids and making fine
time, that they began to look forward with great hope to a
speedy termination of the canyon.   When therefore the river

took an unexpected turn towards the south and the lower formations once more began to appear, till the black granite, dreaded and feared, closed again threateningly about them, they were considerably disheartened.   At the very beginning

The Grand Canyon-Granite Buttresses.
Photograph by J. K. HILLERS, U. S. Colo. Riv. Exp.

they were compelled to make a portage.   Then they reached a place which appeared worse than anything they had yet seen. This was partly due to the condition of the men and it was partly a fact.   They could discover no way to portage or to let down, and Powell believed running it meant certain destruction.

They climbed up and along on the granite for a mile or two, but there appeared no hope for success. In trying to secure an advantageous position from which to view the fall Powell worked himself into a position where he could neither advance nor retreat. His situation was most precarious. The men were obliged to bring oars from the boats four hundred feet below, to brace into the rocks in order to get him safely back. The absence of his right arm made climbing sometimes very difficult for him. This was on the side opposite their first landing. Descending, they recrossed the river and spent the whole afternoon trying to decide on a plan. At last Powell reached a decision. It was to lower the boats over the first portion, a fall of eighteen or twenty feet, then hug the right cliff to a point just above the second drop, where they could enter a little chute, and having passed this point they were to pull directly across the stream to avoid a dangerous rock below. He told the men his intention of running the rapid the next morning, and they all crossed the river once more to a landing where it was possible to camp.

New and serious trouble now developed. The elder Howland remonstrated with Powell against proceeding farther by the river and advised the abandonment of the enterprise altogether. At any rate, he and his brother and William Dunn would not go on in the boats. Powell sat up that night plotting out his course and concluded from it that the mouth of the Virgen could not be more than forty-five miles away in a straight line. Calculating eighty or ninety miles by the river, and allowing for the open country he knew existed below the end of the Grand Canyon, he concluded that they must soon reach the mouth and be able to find the Mormon settlements about twenty miles up the Virgen River. Then he awoke Howland and explained the situation, and they talked it over. The substance of this talk is not stated, but Howland went to sleep again while Powell paced the sand till dawn, pondering on the best course to take. The immediate danger of the rapid he thought could be overcome with safety, but what was below? To climb out here, even were it possible, was to reach the edge of a desert with the nearest Mormon town not less than seventy-five miles distant, across an unknown country. So heavily did this situation weigh upon him that he almost concluded to abandon the river and try the chance on the top, but then he says: "For years I have been contemplating this trip. To leave the exploration unfinished, to say that there is a part of the canyon which I cannot explore, having already almost accomplished it, is more than I am willing to acknowledge, and I determine to go on." So he awoke Walter Powell and explained to him Howland's decision. Walter agreed to stand by him, and so did Sumner, Hawkins, Bradley, and Hall. The younger Howland wished to remain, but would not desert his brother. O. G. Howland was determined to leave the river, and Dunn was with him.

I have never met any of the men of this party except Powell and his brother Walter, so I have no other account of the affair than the one just stated, which is from Powell's Report, and is the same that he gave me orally before that Report was printed. Walter Powell never mentioned the subject, or in any way suggested to me that there was anything behind the version of Powell. But others have. They have said that the real cause of the break was an incompatibility between Powell and the elder Howland. It is quite possible that Powell may have discovered Howland *persona non grata*, but had this been as serious as some have said, Howland would not have waited. it seems to me, till they came to a particularly bad-looking place to take his departure. At any rate, that was a long night for Powell, and whatever the main cause of Howland's leaving was, it was a trying ordeal for the leader. Howland's obligation certainly was to go on as if he were an enlisted soldier, and he evidently failed in this duty. When daylight finally came a solemn breakfast was prepared and eaten. No one had much heart. The river was then crossed again to the north side. The decision of the three men to leave rendered one boat useless, and the poorest, the *Dean*, which was a pine boat, was left behind. Two rifles and a shotgun were given to the men who were leaving, but their share of the rations they refused to take, being sure they could secure all the game they required. Their calculations were correct enough, and they would have arrived at the settlements had not an unforeseen circumstance prevented. When the river party were ready to start the three deserters helped lift the two boats over a high rock and down past the first fall. Then they parted. Powell wrote a letter to his wife which Howland took, Sumner gave him his watch with directions that it be sent to his sister in the event of the river party being annihilated, and the duplicate records of the trip were separated, one set being given to Howland, who at the last begged them not to go on down the river, assuring them that a few miles more of such river as that now ahead of them would consume the last of the scant rations and then it would be too late to try to escape. In fact each party thought the other was taking the more desperate chance. By a mistake the duplicate records were wrongly divided, each party having portions of both sets. This afterwards made gaps in the river data below the Paria as far as Catastrophe Rapid. Powell entered the *Maid of the Canyon* and pulled away while the departing men stood on an overhanging crag looking on. Both boats succeeded in going through without accident, and it was then apparent that the place was not so bad as it looked and that they had run many that were worse. Down below it they waited for a couple of hours hoping the men would change their minds, take the *Dean*, and come on. But they were never seen again by white men. They climbed up the mighty cliffs to the summit of the Shewits Plateau, about fifty-five hundred feet, and that it is a hard climb I can testify, for I climbed down and back not far above this point. At length they were out of the canyon, and they must have rejoiced at leaving those gloomy depths behind. Northward they went, to a large water-pocket, a favourite camping-ground of the Shewits, a basin in the rocky channel of an intermittent stream, discharging into the Colorado. The only story of their fate was obtained from these Utes. Jacob Hamblin of Kanab learned it from some other Utes and afterwards got the story from them. They received the men at their camp and gave them food. During the night some of the band came in from the north and reported certain outrages by miners in that country. It was at once concluded that these whites were the culprits and that they never came down the Colorado as they claimed. In the morning, therefore, a number secreted themselves near the

The Basket Maker.
Old woman of the Kaibab Pai Utes. Behind is the typical Pai Ute dwelling of boughs and brush. The dwellings of the Shewits are similar.
Photograph by J. K. Hillers, U. S. Colo. Riv. Exp.

edge of the water-pocket. The trail to the water leads down under a basaltic cliff perhaps thirty or forty feet high, as I remember the spot, which I visited about six years later. As the unfortunate men turned to come up from filling their

canteens, they were shot down from ambush.   In consequence
I have called this the Ambush Water-pocket.   The guns,
clothing, etc., were appropriated by the Shewits, and I believe
it was through one of the watches that the facts first leaked
out.   I have always had a lurking suspicion that the Shewits
were glad of an excuse (if they had one at the time) for killing
the men.   When I was there they were in an ugly mood and
the night before I got to the camp my guide, a Uinkaret, and
a good fellow, warned me to be constantly on my guard or
they would steal all we had.   There were three of us, and
probably we were among the first whites to go there.   Powell
the autumn after the men were killed went to the Uinkaret
Mountains, but did not continue over to the Shewits Plateau.
Thompson went there in 1872.

Meanwhile the boat party dashed safely on through a succession of rapids till noon, when they arrived at another very
bad place.   In working through this by means of lines, Bradley was let down in one of the boats to fend her off the rocks,
and finding himself in a serious predicament started to cut the
line, when the stem of the boat pulled away and he shot down
alone.   He was a powerful man, and snatching up the steering oar, with several strong strokes he put her head down
stream and immediately boat and all disappeared amidst the
foaming breakers.   But he came out unharmed, and in time to
render service to Powell's boat, which was badly shaken up in
the passage.   The other men of Bradley's boat, left behind,
were obliged to make a long and difficult climb before they
were able to rejoin their craft.   By night they had run entirely
out of the granite, and at noon the next day, without encountering any more serious trouble, they emerged at last from the
depths of the giant chasm.   They were at the mouth of the
Grand Wash.   The Dragon of Waters was vanquished.   Not
that the Dragon would not fight again just as before, but
those who attacked him in future would understand his temper.

Below this point Powell was guided by a manuscript journal which Jacob Hamblin and two other Mormons, Miller and
Crosby, had kept on a boat journey a few years earlier from
the Grand Wash to Callville.   Ives and others having been up

to Callville, the exploration of the Colorado was now complete. There was no part of it unknown; and Powell's feat in descending through the long series of difficult canyons stands unrivalled in the annals of exploration on this continent. "The relief from danger and the joy of success are great," he writes. "Ever before us has been an unknown danger, heavier

Brother Belder's — Virgen City.
A typical frontier Mormon home.
Photograph by U. S. Geol. Survey.

than immediate peril. Every waking hour passed in the Grand Canyon has been one of toil." His chief concern now was the fate of the men who had deserted him, but this was not revealed till the next year. Had they remained with the others, they probably would have gone safely through, but had they died, it would have been properly and gloriously, in the battle with the fierce river.   In the history of expeditions, it is usually those who depart from the original plan who suffer most, for this plan is generally well considered beforehand, whereas any subsequent change is mainly based on error or fear.   Running on through a couple of small canyons, they discovered on the bank some Pai Utes, who ran away, but a little farther down they came to another camp where several did not run.   Nothing could be learned from them about the whites, yet a short distance below this they came upon three white men and a native hauling a seine.   They had reached the goal!   It was the mouth of the Virgen River!   The men in the boat had heard that the whole party was lost and were on the lookout for wreckage.   They were a father and his sons, named Asa, Mormons from a town about twenty miles up the Virgen.   The total stock of food left the explorers was ten pounds of flour, fifteen of dried apples, and about seventy of coffee.   Powell and his brother here said farewell to their companions of the long and perilous journey.   They went to the Mormon settlements, while the others continued down the river in the boats to Camp Mohave.

This expedition, by hard labour, with good boats had, accomplished in about thirty working days the distance from the mouth of Grand River down, while White claimed to have done it on a clumsy raft in eleven!   And where White professed to find smooth sailing in his imaginary voyage, Powell had discovered the most dangerous river of all.

Of his companions on this extraordinary journey, Powell says "I was a maimed man, my right arm was gone; and these brave men, these good men, never forgot it.   In every danger my safety was their first care, and in every waking hour some kind service was rendered me, and they transfigured my misfortune into a boon."

CHAPTER X

Powell's Second Attack on the Colorado—Green River City—Red Canyon and a
Capsize—The Grave of Hook—The Gate of Lodore—Cliff of the Harp—
Triplet Falls and Hell's Half-Mile—A Rest in Echo Park.

THOUGH Powell had demonstrated the possibility of passing alive through the thousand-mile stretch of canyons
on the Green and Colorado, the scientific results of his hazardous voyage were not what he had desired. Owing to the
numerous disasters many of the instruments had been lost,
and he had been prevented by this, as well as by other circumstances, from fully accomplishing his intention. On this account he concluded to continue his labours in this direction,
and determined to make another descent if he could secure
the pecuniary aid of the Government. His application was
favourably considered, as it certainly deserved to be, and Congress appropriated a sum for a second expedition that should
also examine the adjacent country for a distance of twelve
miles on each side of the river. To insure certainty of food
supplies for the continuance of the work, Powell visited the
region in 1870 for the purpose of examining the feasibility of
having rations taken in by pack-trains at several points. He
concluded this could be done at the mouth of the Uinta River,
at the mouth of the Dirty Devil, at the Ute Ford or Crossing
of the Fathers, and at the mouth of the Paria, where he expected to retire from the river for the winter, to conduct
explorations in the surrounding mountains. It was on this
occasion that he went to the Uinkaret Mountains (September,
1870) and investigated the cause of the disappearance of the

233

Howlands and Dunn. Returning then to Kanab, at that time
the farthest frontier settlement of the Mormons, he visited
the Moki Towns, across the Colorado, and went back to the
East to finish his preparations. In the winter of 1871–72
Congress made an additional appropriation for this expedition. The supervision was vested in that noble character,
Joseph Henry, then Secretary of the Smithsonian Institution.

Green River Station, U. P. Ry., Wyoming, 1871.
Starting point of the two Powell expeditions.

Professor Henry was entirely favourable and sympathetic, and
his approval was of the highest value. He secured some instruments for the work and lent his aid in every possible manner. A privilege of drawing rations at the Western army posts
was also again granted, and this saved a great deal of expense.

Through a friend who was an old army acquaintance of
Powell's I secured an interview in Chicago, whither I went for

the purpose. Its character was a good illustration of the explorer's quick decision. As I advanced towards him he rose to his feet, surveyed me with a lightning glance, and said heartily, "Well, Fred, you 'll do." These words constituted me a member of his party, and I began my preparations forth-

Thompson, Hattan, Jones, Steward, W. C. Powell, Richardson, Dellenbaugh, Bishop.

Our First Camp, Green River, Wyoming.

U. S. Colorado River Expedition, 1871.

The borrowed table was, of course, left behind. Photograph by E. O. BEAMAN.

with. Dozens of men applied to join the expedition, but no more were taken, the party being now full.

The boats for this trip were modelled on those used on the former descent, with such changes and improvements as experience had suggested. They were honestly and thoroughly constructed by a builder named Bagley, who had a yard where he turned out small craft, at the north end of the old Clark Street bridge, and we often felt a sense of gratitude to him for doing his work so well. They were three in number, of well-seasoned, clear-grained, half-inch oak, smooth-built, double-ribbed fore and aft, square-sterned, and all practically the same, the former trip having shown the needlessness of taking any smaller or frailer boat for piloting purposes. These were each twenty-two feet long over all, and about twenty on the keel. They were rather narrow for their length, but quite deep for boats of their size, drawing, if I remember correctly, when fully laden, some fourteen or sixteen inches of water. This depth made it possible to carry a heavy load, which was necessary, and at the same time which acted as ballast to keep them right side up amidst the counter-currents and tumbling waters. A rudder being entirely out of place in the kind of navigation found in the canyons, a heavy rowlock was placed at the stern to hold a strong, eighteen-foot steering oar. The boats were entirely decked over on a level with the gunwales, excepting two open spaces left for the rowers. These open spaces, or standing-rooms, were separated from the decked portions by bulkheads, thus forming under the decks three water-tight compartments or cabins, that would not only protect the cargoes and prevent loss in the event of capsize, but would also serve to keep the boats afloat when loaded and full of water in the open parts. The rowlocks were of iron, of the pattern that comes close together at the top, so that an oar must either be slipped through from the handle end or drawn up toward the thin part above the blade to get it out. By attaching near the handle a rim of hard leather, there was no way for the oar to come out accidentally, and so well did this arrangement work that in a capsize the oars remained in the rowlocks. To any one wishing to try the descent of the Colorado, I commend these boats as being perhaps as well adapted to the work as any that can be devised; though perhaps a pointed stern would be an improvement. Iron construction is not advisable, as it is difficult to repair.

When I went the first time to look at the boats lying on

Bagley's wharf, their ominous porpoise-like appearance gave me a peculiar sensation.   I had expected rough-water, but this was the first understanding I had that the journey was to be more or less amphibian.   On a day when the waves on Lake Michigan were running high we took them out for trial.   The crews were filled out by Bagley's men, our party not all being present, and with some reporters and a cargo of champagne and cigars our course was laid for the open sea.   The action of the boats was all that could be desired, and, in the great billows it was so constant that our reportorial friends found

The Boats of Powell's Second Expedition on the Beach at Green River, Wyoming.
Photograph by E. O. Beaman, U. S. Colo. Riv. Exp.

some difficulty in obtaining their share of the refreshments. We were satisfied that the boats could ride any sea, and they were accordingly placed on a car and sent by way of the Chicago, Burlington, and Quincy and the Union Pacific railways to Green River Station.   These companies charged nothing for this service and also transported all the men and baggage on the same terms.   On the 29th of April we alighted at Green River and found the boats already there.   This place, when the railway was building, had been for a considerable time the terminus, and a town of respectable proportions had grown up, but with the completion of the road through this region, the terminus had moved on, and now all that was to be seen of those golden days was a group of adobe walls, roofless and forlorn. The present "city" consisted of about thirteen houses, and some of these were of such complex construction that one hesitates whether to describe them as houses with canvas roofs, or tents with board sides. The population consisted of a few whites, a number of Chinese railway labourers, an occasional straggling miner, native, or cattleman, and last but not least, at the small railway-station eating-house, honoured by the patronage of emigrant-trains, his highness Ah Chug, the

Ruins of Green River Terminus
Photograph by E O BEAMAN, U S Colo Riv Exp

cook, whose dried-apple pies, at twenty-five cents apiece, I have never ceased to enjoy, for they were the ladder by which I was able to descend from a home table to the camp fare of bacon and beans. I then despised these ruder viands, but now I desire to pay my tribute to them by saying that as a basis for campaigning they are the very best. In hot weather you eat more beans and less bacon, and when the weather is cold your diet is easily arranged in the reverse order.

The boats were speedily launched upon the swift current at the bridge and steered down to a little cove on the left, a few hundred yards below, where they were hauled out on a beach to give them the finishing touches of preparation, like attaching canvas covers to the cabins, and so forth. Nearby, amongst the willows, we established our first camp—a place of real luxury, for Mr. Field, who had an outfitting house here, lent us a table and two benches. Andy set up some crotches and a cross-bar, to hang his kettles on, and with a cast-iron bake oven—one of the kind like a flat, iron pot, in which, after it is stood upon a bed of hot coals, the bread is placed, and then the cast-iron cover is put on, and laden with hot coals—began his experiments in cookery, for it was a new art to him. In the beginning he was rather too liberal with his salaratus, but the product gave us the pleasant delusion of having reached a land of gold nuggets. Andy soon improved, and we learned to appreciate his rare skill to such an extent that the moment he took his old hat and with it lifted the coffee-pot off the fire, and then placed beside it the bread and bacon with the pleasing remark: "Well, now, go fur it, boys!" we lost not a moment in accepting the invitation. As bread must be made for every meal, Andy's was no easy berth, for his work on the river was the same as that of the rest of us. It was only when we were engaged in a portage near dinner or supper time that he was permitted to devote his entire attention to the preparation of our elaborate meals. Bean soup, such as Andy made, is one of the most delicious things in the world; and Delmonico could not hold a candle to his coffee.

Our three boats bore the names *Emma Dean*, after Mrs. Powell, *Nellie Powell*, after Major Powell's sister, Mrs. Thompson, and *Cañonita*. The men and their assignment to the boats were these: J. W. Powell, S. V. Jones, J. K. Hillers, F. S. Dellenbaugh—the *Emma Dean*; A. H. Thompson, J. F. Steward, F. M. Bishop, F. C. A. Richardson—the *Nellie Powell*; E. O. Beaman, W. C. Powell, A. J. Hattan—the *Cañonita*.

Jones had been a teacher in Illinois. He went as a topographer. Hillers was a soldier in the Civil War, and was at first not specially assigned, but later, when the photographer gave out, he was directed to assist in that branch, and eventually became head photographer, a position he afterwards held with the Geological Survey for many years. A large number of the photographs from which this volume is illustrated were taken by him and they speak for themselves. Thompson was from Illinois. He also had been a soldier in the war, and on this expedition was Powell's colleague, as well as the geographer. To his foresight, rare good judgment, ability to think out a plan to the last minute detail, fine nerve and absolute lack of any kind of foolishness, together with a wide knowledge and intelligence, this expedition, and indeed the scientific work so admirably carried on by the United States Survey of the Rocky Mountain region and the Geological Survey for three decades in the Far West, largely owe success. Steward was an old soldier, was from Illinois, and went with us as geologist, assisting Powell himself in this line. Bishop had been a captain in the war, had been shot through and through the left lung, and was an enthusiast in Western exploration. He was one of the topographers. Richardson was from Chicago and was general assistant to the geologists and topographers. Beaman was from New York. He was photographer; and W. C. Powell, from Illinois, and a nephew of Major Powell, was his assistant. Hattan was a Virginian, but had lived long in Illinois. He had been a soldier in the war, and went with us as cook, because he wanted the trip, and there was no other post open to him. I hailed from Buffalo, was the youngest of the party, and served as artist to the geologists, and later was placed on the topographical work. Mrs. Powell and Mrs. Thompson spent several days at Green River and rendered much assistance, the latter presenting each boat with a handsome flag made by her own hands.

An arm-chair obtained from Field was arranged so that it could be strapped on the deck of the middle cabin of our boat, as a seat for Powell, to enable him to be comfortable and at the same time see well ahead. This had a tendency to make the *Dean* slightly top-heavy, but only once did serious consequences apparently result from it, and I am not sure that the absence of the high load would have made any difference. Though Powell had descended before, he could not remember every detail and kept a sharp lookout always. The provisions—

Almon Harris Thompson.

Powell's colleague in the second descent of the Colorado and subsequent work. For over thirty years prominently connected with United States survey work in the basin of the Colorado and adjacent country, and in the Eastern States.

Recent photograph by CLINEDINST.

everything, in fact, except the bacon, which was too greasy—
were put in rubber sacks that, when closed, were absolutely
water-tight.   These bags were encased in cotton sacks and
gunny bags to protect the rubber.   Each man was allowed one
hundred pounds of baggage, including his blankets, and was
given two rubber bags to stow it in.   When the time came to
load up we found we had a formidable pile of things that must
go.   The photographic apparatus was particularly bulky, for
neither the dry-plate nor film had yet been invented.   The

Ready for the Start, U. S. Colorado River Expedition, Green River,
Wyoming, 1871.
Photograph by E. O BEAMAN

scientific instruments were also bulky, being in wooden, canvas-
covered cases; and there were eleven hundred pounds of flour
in twenty-two rubber sacks.

On the 22d of May, 1871, all being ready, and the boats
finally packed, we prepared to push off.   To save time, breakfast was taken at Field's place, which, owing to the kindness
of himself and his charming family, had seemed very much like
home to us.   Then the populace to the number of about fifteen
—the Chinamen refusing to countenance any outfit harbouring
such a terrible engine of the devil as a photographic apparatus

The Men of the Colorado River Expedition of 1871

W. C. Powell • John F. Steward • F. M. Bishop

J. W. Powell • A. H. Thompson

J. K. Hillers • F. S. Dellenbaugh • S. V. Jones

Portraits of All but Two Members of the Boat Party of the U. S. Colorado River Expedition of 1871.

The others were E. O. Beaman and Andrew J. Hattan. In 1871 Messrs. Bishop, Steward, and Beaman were obliged to leave on account of ill health, and did not enter the Grand Canyon. These portraits were taken within a year or two after the expedition, that of Mr. Hillers on a hasty visit to Salt Lake.

—assembled on the beach to give us God-speed. The cheerful conception of this service on the part of a deaf-mute was to fill the air with violent gestures to indicate—and it was vivid enough—that we could not possibly escape destruction. One of his series represented with uncomfortable clearness a drowning man vainly striving to climb up a vertical wall. This pantomime was the last thing I saw from my position at the oars as we turned a bend and left the "city" behind.

We were much better provided for than the first party. We had a guide, our boats were superior, our plan for supplies was immeasurably better, both as to caring for what we took along and what we were to receive at the several indicated places—mouth of the Uinta, mouth of the Dirty Devil, Crossing of the Fathers, and the Paria. We also had rubber life-preservers to inflate at the more dangerous points. Mine did me little good, as I soon found it was in my way and I never wore it; nor did Hillers wear his. As we handled the oars of our boat we concluded it would be safer to do it in the best manner possible, and not be encumbered by these sausages under our elbows, but we always placed them behind us at bad places, ready for use; all the others, however, wore theirs and seemed to find no objection to them in the way of interference. A cork jacket could be worn easier when rowing, and I would recommend it, but the thing of first importance is to have the *right kind* of boats, and know how to handle them. An humble spirit is also a great safeguard. After starting, the usual number of slight accidents occurred, but there was nothing to interfere with our steady progress into the silent, lonely land, where the great Dragon, whose tail we were now just touching, tore the air to tatters with his writhings. Our light oars were snapped like reeds, but luckily we had plenty of extras, and some ten-foot ones were cut down to eight, and these proved to be strong enough. On the morning of the 23d we were treated to a snow-storm and the air was very cold. It soon cleared, however; and the sun shone again bright and warm, and we went on rejoicing. The next day we reached the mouth of Black's Fork, and after this the river was deeper and we were less troubled by grounding, the boats being only three inches out of water at the gun-wales. The area between Black's Fork and the Green was strewn with beautiful moss-agates. I longed to secure a quantity, but this was out of the question. Geese and ducks floated on the water around us, but with our rifles it was difficult to get any. There was not a shot-gun in the party. We soon came in sight of the superb snow-covered Uinta range, extending east and west across the land, and apparently an effectual barrier to any progress of the river in that direction, but every day we drew nearer to it. Some of our men shot

Green River Valley.   Camp at Tilted Ledge near Henry's Fork.
Photograph by E. O. Beaman, U. S. Colo. Riv. Exp.

three deer, and we had fresh meat for a day or two, "jerking" all we could not consume in that time. There was plenty of game along the river here and for a long distance down, but we were not skilled hunters, nor did we have time to follow game or manœuvre for it, so our diet was mainly confined to what Andy could produce by his manipulation of the supplies we carried. The day following the one that gave us the deer, the river became very winding, and a fearful gale blew across it, carrying sand into our eyes and some water into our boats. In the late afternoon we bore down on a ridge, about one thousand feet high, which extended far in both directions athwart our course.   It was the edge of the Uinta Mountains. At its very foot the river seemed to stop.   It could be seen neither to right nor to left, nor could any opening be detected in the mountain, except high up where Powell pointed out to us a bare patch of brilliant red rocks saying it was the top of Flaming Gorge, the beginning of the canyon series.   Passing the mouth of Henry's Fork on the right, the river doubled suddenly to the left between two low cliffs, where there was a small whirlpool, which I take to be the "Green River Suck" of Ashley and the early trappers.   Around another point we swept and found ourselves floating on the tranquil waters of Flaming Gorge.   A fine grove of deep green cottonwoods stood out on the left in contrast to the rough red rocks. There were moored the other boats, which on this occasion had preceded us, and the ever-faithful Andy was engaged in preparing dinner.   The next and first real canyon was the one called Horseshoe, a short and beautiful gorge some sixteen hundred feet in depth, and containing rapid "Number One," a very mild affair, but particularly noticeable because it is the first of the six hundred, great and small, we had the satisfaction of vanquishing in our war against the falling waters.   We had already descended something over one hundred and fifty of the five thousand feet we expected to go down, but there had been only swift water at that stage of flood; nothing that, on the Colorado, would be considered a serious rapid.

Every morning the cabins of the boats were packed like so many trunks.   The blankets were rolled up and put in their rubber cases, all bags of supplies were securely tied and stowed away, in short, every article was placed in the cabins and the hatches firmly buttoned in place, with the canvas cover drawn snugly over the deck.   Only a grand smash-up could injure these things.   Nothing was left out but such instruments as were hourly needed, the guns, life-preservers, and a camp-kettle in each boat for bailing purposes.   On each of two boats there was a topographer, whose duty was to sight the direction of every bend of the river and estimate the length of the stretch.   Thompson, on his boat, also kept a similar record.

Head of Kingfisher Canyon, Green River.
Photograph by E. O. BEAMAN, U. S. Colo. Riv. Exp.

The sighting was done with a prismatic compass, and one of these was rendered more interesting by bearing on the leather case the name of George B. McClellan, written by the future general when he was a lieutenant of engineers. There was seldom much discrepancy between the different estimates made during the day, as men grow very accurate in such matters, but a check on all estimates was obtained by frequent observations for latitude and longitude.

The third canyon is also a short one, the three aggregating less than ten miles. Because of the many kingfishers flying about it was called Kingfisher Canyon, and a point where they were especially numerous was named Bee-hive. At the foot of this third short canyon the rocks ran together in a forbidding manner, and out of the depths beyond came a roar; just as one outside of the jungle might hear the lion's note within. On a bright Friday morning we were ready to try our fortune, and with all made snug, pulled in between the cliffs where in a moment we beheld a wild sea of descending foam. Rapid quickly followed rapid and immediately we had some exciting work. Our boat was swept so near the right-hand cliff that one of the after rowlocks was torn off, and at about the same time the *Nellie Powell*, following but signalled to keep to to the left, was seen to strike rocks near the opposite side and capsize. The next instant we were borne out of sight. Hillers, with only one rowlock, could not use his oars, so the work devolved entirely on me. The boat was heavy for one pair of oars, and we were being carried down stream at a terrific pace. On the left was a little beach where we might land, and I pulled for this with all my power. At length to my great relief I felt the keel touch bottom. We were still about fifteen feet from the beach, but the water was not any deeper than the grating of the keel indicated, so we were overboard in a moment and pulled her to the bank. At the same instant the *Cañonita* ran in, dashing up like a horse finishing a race. The crew reported the other boat upside down, but they were unable to stop to help her. They thought the crew were safe, and we hoped with all our hearts they were. There was nothing we could do but wait for some sign from above, and in about three quarters of an hour the boat came rushing down with all hands safe and exceedingly happy over claiming the distinction of the first capsize.   Now many rapids fell to our lot, and we were kept busy every moment.   On the 4th of June we passed the wrecks of some boats half-buried in the sand, and on landing we discovered a grave on a little knoll some distance back from the water, with a pine board stuck up at its head bearing the name of Hook.   The rapid that had apparently caused the disaster told by these objects we easily ran.   The unfortunates had attempted the descent in flat-bottomed boats, that shipped much water and toppled over with the slightest provocation. They had followed Powell on his former trip, declaring that if he could go down the river so could they, but they learned their mistake and paid dearly for the experience.   The leader, whose bones lie in these splendid depths of Red Canyon, was said to have been the first mayor of Cheyenne.   Many more rapids we ran with a current of from six to twelve or fifteen miles per hour, and we made many "let-downs," which means working a boat along the edge of a rapid by the aid of lines, without removing the cargo.   We called this process, when we removed the cargo, a "line portage," as distinguished from a complete portage where the boats were taken out of the water.

Shortly after dinner one day we heard a deep roaring, which implied that we were approaching a violent fall, and hugging the left-hand bank, we drifted slowly down to within a rod or two of the drop and easily landed.   It was Ashley Falls.   In the centre of the river protruded an immense rock, twenty-five feet square, and the river rushed by on each side making a sudden descent of about eight feet.   It would have been nothing to run had it been free from rocks; but it was in reality the rocks which formed it.   They had fallen from the left-hand wall within some comparatively recent time, and acted as a dam.   Many more were piled up against the left-hand cliff.   The river, averaging about two hundred and fifty feet wide, had been narrowed by about one-third and a rapid had thus been changed into a fall.   We made a portage here with the first and third boats.   The second we allowed to run through with lines attached, but as she got several severe knocks we deemed it unsafe to risk the other. Our camp was on a small level place among some pine trees, almost over the fall, and I think I never saw a more romantic spot. The moon shone down into the canyon with surpassing brilliancy, and this, in contrast to our lavish camp-fire and extremely comfortable surroundings, made a combination ever to be remembered. See pages 113 and 112.

It was on one of the huge rocks above the river on the left that Ashley wrote his name. This was in black letters, sheltered by a slight projection of the rock which acted as a cornice. Thus it had remained distinct, except one figure of the date, for forty-six years, having been done in 1825. The portage around Ashley Falls was laborious as we were obliged to climb with everything about fifty feet above the river, but labour is better than disaster, and it was on such points as these that Powell and Thompson always exhibited good sense. Smaller men would have been unable to resist the temptation to run everything, for there comes an exhilaration in this work that is subtle and dangerous. Below this the declivity was very great, but as there were few rocks our boats were able to go down flying. The walls were two thousand to twenty-five hundred feet high, but not vertical. Suddenly we ran out into a beautiful little valley on the right known to trappers as Little Brown's Hole, and renamed by our party Red Canyon Park. Here we camped for a day and then went on between high walls over a number of rapids, to emerge into Brown's Park. This place, I take it, was the end of Ashley's journey down the river. Sailing along on a quiet current in a valley six miles wide, we ran upon a camp of cattle herders, where Richardson left us, as Powell decided that he was not able to stand the work. He regretfully went back with some of the cattlemen to Green River Station.

The temperature was now often 99° F. in the shade, and rowing on the slow current was irksome, so we lashed the boats together and drifted along while the Major in his arm-chair read aloud selections from Scott, Emerson, and others, whose condensed poetical works and a couple of Bibles were all the literature to be found in the party, as books are heavy and weight was to be avoided. At times some of the men amused themselves by diving under the boats, swimming around and ahead of them, or surprised a coyote on the bank with a rifle-shot, and otherwise enjoyed the relaxation we had well earned by our toil in Red Canyon. The river was smooth and deep and about six hundred to eight hundred feet wide. At the very foot of the valley we made a camp under the shadow of that magnificent and unrivalled portal, the Gate of Lodore, which had been visible to us for many miles; the

The Heart of Lodore.
Photograph by E. O. BEAMAN, U. S. Colo. Riv. Exp.

dark cleft two thousand feet high, through which the river cuts into the heart of the mountains, appearing as solemn and mysterious as the pathway to another world. From an eminence we could peer into its depths for some distance, and there was no sign of a rapid, but we were not deceived, having posted ourselves by extracts from Jack Sumner's diary, whose description of "how the waters come down at Lodore" was contained in the frequent repetition of the words, "a hell of foam." Lodore, indeed, is almost one continuous rapid for the whole twenty miles of its length, and the passage through it will tax the endurance of any man. The declivity is the greatest of the whole river with the exception of the First Granite Gorge of the Grand Canyon and a portion of Cataract Canyon. A diagram of it is given on page 57. I have space only to describe one or two characteristic incidents. The

The Canyon of Lodore.   Looking down Stream.
Photograph by E. O. BEAMAN, U. S. Colo. Riv. Exp.
River here was extremely swift.   Fall at left distance.   Second expedition landed with
difficulty on right at foot of tall pines.   The dark lines at water's edge are the boats.

current of the river was extraordinarily swift; it must have been in some places nearly twenty miles an hour. The stream averaged about three hundred feet wide. The boats in a rapid fairly flew along amidst the foam, plunging and rearing in the "tails" of waves which always terminate rapids of this class. One day about noon we came shooting down over one of these places, having just run a rather bad rapid, when we saw only a few hundred yards below an ugly looking fall. The left wall came down very straight into the water and threw a deep shadow over it so that we could not tell exactly what was there. Opposite was a rocky wooded point, and between the two the river bodily fell away. Altogether it was a beautiful, though a startling picture. The whole set of the current was towards this drop with headlong fury. There were no eddies, no slack water of any kind. But we could not do such a foolhardy thing as to go into it without knowing what it was and therefore a landing was imperative. Accordingly we headed for the right bank, and laid to our oars till they bent like straws. We almost reached the shore. It was only a few feet away, but the relentless current was hurling us, broadside on, toward the dark rocks where the smooth water was broken and torn and churned to shreds of snowy foam. There was only one thing for us to do, if we did not want to run upon the rocks, and that was to leap overboard, and trust to bringing the boat to a stop by holding on to the bottom, here not so far down. This was done, and the depth turned out to be about to our waists; but for a little time the boat sped on as before. Planting our shoes firmly against the boulders of the bottom as we slid along, we finally gained the upper hand, and then it was an easy matter to reach the shore. Hardly had we done this when the *Nell* came tearing down in the same fashion. We rushed into the water as far as we dared, and they pulled with a will till they came to us, when they all jumped into the water and we tugged the boat ashore, just in time to plunge in again and help the *Cañonita* in the same way. Dinner over, the rapid was examined and it was discovered that by pulling straight out into it clear of the rocks, we could easily get through. This was accordingly done and one after the other the boats sped down as if towed by an express train. Then we ran a number of smaller ones with no trouble, and toward evening arrived at a place where the entire river dropped into a sag, before falling over some very bad rapids. We avoided the sag by keeping close to the left bank, and rounded a little point into a broad eddy, across which we

could sail with impunity.   Then we landed on a rocky point at
the head of the first bad plunge, the beginning of Disaster
Falls, where the *No-Name* was wrecked two years before.   At
this place we camped for the night.   The descent altogether

The Canyon of Lodore.   Looking across a Rapid.
Photograph by E. O. Beaman, U. S. Colo. Riv. Exp.

here is about fifty feet.   In the morning all the cargoes were
taken over the rocks to the foot of the first fall, and the boats
were cautiously worked down along the edge, to where the
cargoes were, where they were reloaded and lowered to the
head of the next descent, several hundred yards.   Here

the cargoes were again taken out and carried over the rocks down to a quiet bay. This took till very late and every one was tired out, but the boats were carried and pushed on skids up over the rocks for twenty or thirty yards, past the worst of the fall, and then lowered into the water to be let down the rest of the way by lines. Two had to be left there till the following day. We had found a one hundred pound sack of flour lying on a high rock, where it had been placed at the time of the wreck of the *No-Name*, and Andy that day made our dinner biscuits out of it. Though it was two years old the bread tasted perfectly good; and this is a tribute to the climate, as well as to the preservative qualities of a coating of wet flour. This coating was about half an inch thick, and outside were a cotton flour-sack and a gunny bag. The flour was left on the rock and may be there yet. Not far below this we came to Lower Disaster Falls, which a short portage enabled us to circumnavigate and go on our way. The current was so swift all the time that objects on shore flitted past as they do when one looks from a window of a railway train. Just opposite our camp on this night the cliff was almost perpendicular from the water's edge to the height of about twenty-five hundred feet. The walls seemed very close together, only a narrow strip of sky being visible. As we sat after supper peering aloft at this ribbon of the heavens, the stars in the clear sky came slowly out like some wonderful transformation scene, and just on the edge of the opposite wall, resembling an exquisite and brilliant jewel, appeared the constellation of the Harp. Immediately the name "Cliff of the Harp" suggested itself and from that moment it was so called. Here and there we discovered evidences of the former journey, but nothing to indicate that human beings had ever before that been below Disaster Falls. There we saw the same indications of an early disaster which Powell had noticed on the first trip, a rusty bake-oven, some knives and forks and tin plates, in the sand at the foot of the second fall. The day after the Cliff of the Harp camp we began by making a line-portage around a very ugly place, which took the whole morning. In the afternoon there was another similar task, so that by night we had made only three or four miles, and camped at the beginning of a decidedly forbidding stretch. Just below us were three sharp rapids which received the name of Triplet Falls. A great deal of work was required to pass these, and then we ran three or four in good style, which brought us, in the late afternoon, to where the whole river spread out amongst innumerable rocks and for more than half a mile the water was a solid sheet of milky foam, sending up the usual wild roar, which echoed and echoed again and again amongst the cliffs around and above us. Some one proposed the name of "Hell's Half-Mile" for this terrible place and the idea was at once adopted, so appropriate did it seem. The turmoil of the dashing waters was almost deafening, and, even when separated by only a few feet, we could only communicate with each other by shouting at the top of our lungs. It was a difficult task to get our little ships safely below this half-mile, but it was finally accomplished, and on we went in search of the next dragon's claw. At our camp the fire in some way got into a pine grove and soon was crackling enough to rival the noise of the rapid. The lower region seemed now to be sending its flames up through the bottom of the gorge and the black smoke rolled into the sky far above the top of the walls. Many and varied were our experiences in this magnificent canyon, which for picturesqueness and beauty rivals even the Grand Canyon, though not on such a giant scale. Its passage would probably be far easier at low water. At last, one evening, as the soft twilight was settling into the chasm, a strange, though agreeable silence, that seemed almost oppressive, fell around us. The angry waters ceased their roaring. We slid along on a smooth, even river, and suddenly emerged into a pretty little park, a mile long, bounded by cliffs only some six hundred feet high. Running our boats up into the mouth of a quiet river entering from the left we tied them up and were quickly established in the most comfortable camp since Brown's Park. We were at the mouth of Yampa River. From a wonderful echo which repeated a sentence of ten words, we called the place Echo Park. Such an echo in Europe would be worth a fortune. The Echo Rock is shown on page 203.

Canyon ot Lodore at Triplet Falls.

Cliffs about 2500 feet high   River about 300 feet wide.
Photograph by E. O. BEAMAN, U. S. Colo. Riv. Exp.

Here a stop was made for several days, and one evening some of us took a boat and went up the Yampa a little distance. The walls were vertical and high, and the shadows thrown by the cliffs as we floated along their base were fairly luminous, so bright was the moon. A song burst from the rowers and was echoed from wall to wall till lost in the silence of the night-enveloped wilderness. Nothing could have been more beautiful, and the tranquillity was a joy to us after the days of turmoil in Lodore.

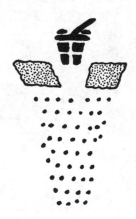

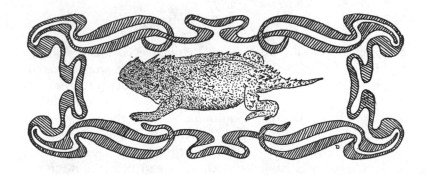

CHAPTER XI

An Island Park and a Split Mountain—The White River Runaways—Powell
Goes to Salt Lake—Failure to Get Rations to the Dirty Devil—On the
Rocks in Desolation—Natural Windows—An Ancient House—On the Back
of the Dragon at Last—Cataracts and Cataracts in the Wonderful Cataract
Canyon—A Lost Pack-Train—Naming the Echo Peaks.

WITH one of the boats from the camp in Echo Park Powell went up the Yampa to see what might be there.
Though this stream was tranquil at its mouth, it proved to be
rough farther up, and the party, in the four days they were
gone, were half worn out, coming back ragged, gaunt, and
ravenous, having run short of food. The Monday following
their return, our boats were again carefully packed, life-preservers were inflated, and we went forth once more to the
combat with the rapids. A few minutes' rowing carried us to
the end of Echo Rock, which is a narrow tongue of sandstone,
about half a mile long and five hundred or six hundred yards
thick, and turning the bend we entered Whirlpool Canyon; the
cliffs, as soon as the other side of Echo Rock was passed,
shooting up into the air and enfolding us again in a canyon
embrace. The depth was quickly a couple of thousand feet
with walls very close together till, in three or four miles, we
came to a violent rapid. A landing was easily made and the
boats lowered by lines. Below this the canyon was much
wider, and the rapids were not difficult. By the time the

camping hour came, we had put behind seven miles with five
rapids and the extra bad one where the boats were lowered.
No whirlpools were encountered, the stage of water not being favourable for them.   As previously noted, every stage of
water produces different conditions, so that the navigator on
this river can never be certain of what he will find.   Our course
through Whirlpool was neither difficult nor dangerous, as we
were able to make landings at the few bad places and ran the

Island Park, Green River.
Between Whirlpool and Split-Mountain Canyons.
Photograph by E. O. BEAMAN, U. S. Colo. Riv. Exp.

rest of the rapids without damage of any kind.   Only one
camp was made in this beautiful gorge, and there we slept, or
tried to sleep, for two nights.   Myriads of ants swarmed over
the spot and made every hour more or less of a torment.
They extended their investigations into every article brought
out of the boats.   During the whole time their armies marched
and countermarched over, around, and through ourselves and
everything we possessed.   We saw a number of mountain sheep
in this canyon, but owing to the quickness of the sheep and the

difficulty of pursuing them over the wild cliffs, which they seemed to know well, we were unable to bring any down.

Our second day's run was uneventful through a superb gorge about twenty-four hundred feet deep, and at·a late hour in the afternoon, just after we had run our worst rapid in fine style,

Entrance to Split-Mountain Canyon, Right Hand Cliffs.
Height about 2000 feet.
Photograph by E. O. BEAMAN, U. S. Colo. Riv. Exp.

we perceived the great walls breaking away, and they soon melted off into rounded hills, exquisitely coloured, as if painted by Nature in imitation of the rainbow. The river spread out, between and around a large number of pretty islands bearing thick cottonwood groves. The shallowness of the water caused our keels to touch occasionally, but the current was comparatively slow and we were not disturbed over it. Powell hesitated as to calling this place Rainbow or Island Park, the choice eventually falling to the latter. The valley is only three or four miles long in a straight line. Shortly before sunset we had the disappointment of reaching the end of it, and immediately below the place where we camped the rocks closed sharply together once more. Here Powell determined that he would push ahead of the main party, in order to make his way, as

In Split-Mountain Canyon.
Highest walls 2700 feet.
Photograph by E. O. Beaman, U. S. Colo. Riv. Exp.

soon as possible, to the Uinta Ute Agency, in order to communicate with the outer world and ascertain if his plans for supply-trains were moving on to success. He took the *Dean*, but Bishop was put in my place because of his considerable experience in the Western country, for there was no telling what they might encounter. On the morning of July 7th, at daybreak, therefore, they were off, and speedily disappeared from our sight within the rocks that arose below our camp. A

number of the remaining men climbed to the top of the left-
hand side of the "gate," an altitude of about three thousand
feet above camp, and from there were able to see the *Emma
Dean* for a long distance, working down through the rapids.
The view from that altitude over the surrounding country and
into the canyon was something wonderful to behold. A wild
and ragged wilderness stretched out in all directions, while
down in the canyon—more of a narrow valley than a canyon

Split-Mountain Canyon.
Looking down from top near entrance, 3000 feet.
Photograph by E. O. BEAMAN, U. S. Colo. Riv. Exp.

after the entrance was passed—the river swept along, marked,
here and there, by bars of white we knew to be rapids. Crags
and pinnacles shot up from every hand, and from this circumstance it was at first uncertain whether to call the canyon
Craggy or Split-Mountain. The latter was decided on, as the
river has sawed in two a huge fold of the strata—a mountain
split in twain. When we entered it with our boats to again
descend, we had gone but a little distance before massive beds
of solid rock came up straight out of the water on both sides

and we were instantly sailing in a deep, narrow canyon, the beds at length arching over, down stream, high above our heads.   It was an extraordinary sight.   While we were looking at the section of the great fold, we discovered some mountain sheep far up the rocks.   Though we fired at them the circumstances were against our hitting, and they scampered scornfully away from crag to crag, out of our sight.   Then the canyon widened at the top, and at the same time rapids appeared. They came by dozens, but there were none that we could not master with certainty by hard work.   Wet from head to foot

Men of the 1871 Expedition at an Abandoned Cabin Opposite the Mouth of the Uinta River.
Photograph by E. O. Beaman U. S. Colo. Riv. Exp.

we continued this labour for three days, and then the rocks, the "Ribbon Beds," turned over and disappeared beneath the water just as they had come out of it above.   The low stage of the river made this canyon difficult, so far as exertion was concerned, and the rapids would perhaps be far easier during the spring flood.

We were now in Wonsits Valley, the longest expansion of the walls above Black Canyon.   Near our camp, which was on a soft, grassy bank beside smooth-flowing waters, some picture writings were found, the first indications, since the wreckage at Disaster Falls, outside of occasional signs of Powell's other party, that human beings had ever been in the country. The tail-piece at the end of the preface to this volume is a reduction of a drawing I made of the largest figure, which was about four feet high. The river now flowed gently between low banks covered in many places with cottonwoods, and it required hard labour of a different kind to get the boats along. Signs of Utes began to appear, and one morning a fine fellow, gaily dressed, and mounted on a splendid horse, rode into camp with a " How—how!" Farther on we came to him again, with his squaw, a good-looking young woman, very well dressed in a sort of navy blue flannel, and wearing numerous ornaments. We ferried them across the river, and afterwards found they were runaways from White River, —an elopement in reality.

The Runaways. White River Utes.
Photograph by E. O. Beaman, U. S. Colo. Riv. Exp.

After a good deal of hard rowing we finally reached the mouth of the Uinta. Thompson went up to the Agency, about forty miles away, and found that Powell had gone out to Salt Lake. When the latter came back to the Agency it was to direct Thompson to go on with our party, while Powell went out again to see about the ration-supply at the mouth of the Dirty Devil. The men sent there had been unable to find the place, or, indeed, to get anywhere near it. Powell was to meet us again at the foot of Gray Canyon, about one hundred and fifty miles farther down. When our supplies had been brought from the Agency and all was ready, we proceeded on our way, passing the elopers near the end of the valley, where they were very happy in a good camp with a fresh deer and plenty of vermilion, which they used liberally on their faces.   Below this the river was full of beaver, and had Pattie or some of the early trappers been there, they could have reaped a rich harvest.   The current was slow, and Thompson read Emerson aloud as we drifted.   Gradually the hills began

Canyon of Desolation.
Walls 2000 feet.
Photograph by E. O. BEAMAN, U. S. Colo. Riv. Exp.

to grow rocky, and then distinct low cliffs appeared, till finally we discovered ourselves fairly within the walls of another canyon, which from the barren character of its cliffs is called the Canyon of Desolation.   It is ninety-seven miles long, and immediately at its foot is Gray Canyon, thirty-six miles long. Then comes Gunnison Valley, and it was there that Powell was to return to us.   The first indication of descending waters was a slight swiftness, the river having narrowed up to its can-

yon-character.   At one place it doubled back on itself, forming
in the bend a splendid amphitheatre which was called after
Sumner of the former party.   This beautiful wall, about one
thousand feet high, was carved and sculptured by the forces of
erosion in a most wonderful manner.   It is shown on page 205.
After a few miles between such walls we began to expect

A Halt for Observations.
Second Powell Expedition.
Photograph by E. O. BEAMAN, U. S. Colo. Riv. Exp.

rapids, and hardly had the expectation been formed when it
was gratified.   An increasing roar came to our ears, and as we
rounded a bend three were discovered before us within the
space of half a mile.   The water had been continually falling
till now it was so low that these rapids exhibited a startling
number of rocks amidst the foam.   We believed we could run
them, and we did.   The first was cleared easily.   In the second
the *Nell* struck a submerged rock, but glanced over it without

damage, while our boat landed squarely on the top, for it could not be seen from above, and, after a momentary quiver, hung there as the wave which lifted us upon it receded. The water roared and boiled furiously about us, but did not quite come into the boat. It was impossible to dip the oars from the stationary boat on account of the force of the current. At last Hillers perceived that the sticking point was almost

Uinta Ute Tipi and a Summer Shelter and Outlook, Showing the Old-time Notched Log for a Ladder.
Photograph by J. K. HILLERS, U. S. Geol. Surv.

under the extremity of the keel. Getting out cautiously over the stern he succeeded in touching the top of the rock, and, thus lightened, the *Dean* shot forward, though not before Hillers, who had not let go of the stern rowlock, was able to leap on board. The *Cañonita* fared still worse. Following us too close, she tried to pass, but struck another rock, crushing in her side, though floating down nevertheless. An hour and a half spent on her put her in good order again, and away we went, running a third and a fourth with no trouble. The walls were now about two thousand feet high and we felt quite at home. Through some of the upper narrow promontories of sandstone there were large holes, or arches, some of them probably a hundred or more feet in diameter. They were similar to the Hole in the Wall, shown in the cut on page 41, only on a much larger scale. The next day, before stopping for dinner, we ran nine rapids with no accident. The river was

Dellenbaugh Butte, Green River near the San Rafael.
Photograph by E. O. BEAMAN, U. S. Colo. Riv. Exp.

wider than in the upper canyons, and while the low state of the water made harder work and pounded the boats more, I believe that on the whole it was an advantage. The current was less fierce and consequently the boats were always more controllable. Yet when the water falls below a certain point the danger of striking rocks is so much increased that a rapid which, at a little higher stage would be easy to run must be avoided entirely by a portage or a let-down. The waves at low water are also smaller and hence less likely to upset a boat.

In many places we would lower a boat by lines near the shore, with two men in her, and when a rock appeared they fended her off, or jumped into the water and eased the craft along, touching bottom where they could.   This worked very well for this place and the stage of water, though on this river one must ever be ready to adapt himself to differing conditions. Rapids were very numerous, but we succeeded in passing them in one way or another without seriously injuring the boats. The walls grew to magnificent proportions.   At one camp we could see, on the very top of the cliff opposite, an object that from our position was the counterpart of a log cabin.   Tall pines grew around it and the deception was complete.   The cliff being twenty-four hundred feet high, the "cabin" must in reality have been of huge size; but we applied the name "Log-Cabin Cliff" to the place.   At a heavy descent, where the *Emma Dean* of the first expedition was swamped, we took no chances and made a careful let-down; a little farther on we did the same thing again.   This method of passing a rapid is not romantic, but our object was not to perform spectacular feats but to accomplish the work in hand; so wherever there was any doubt as to the safety of running a rapid we adopted the prudent course.   It was difficult to decide sometimes just where to draw the line; in one rapid we tried to go through, the *Nell* struck a rock, knocking Thompson out and nearly capsizing, but no real harm was done.   The walls increased to nearly three thousand feet, and the rapids followed each other in quick succession every day.   At one point we saw, a couple of thousand feet above on the right a gigantic example of the natural arches.   Beyond this the walls began to grow somewhat lower.   Our life through this gorge, as well as through some others, might be described by the monotonous phrase, "Got up, ran rapids, went to bed."   There was no time to do anything else.   At night we were always sleepy and tired. Fortunately there were here fine places to camp—plenty of room, with smooth sand to sleep on.   As soon as we halted for the night we would don our dry clothes from the rubber bags, and, when supper was over, would prepare a bed.   If any kind of boughs or willows were to be had, we cut a quantity

and, laying them in regular order near together, formed a sort
of mattress which was very comfortable. If these were not to
be had, the softest spot of sand was the next choice. In putting
the river suit on in the morning, there was often something of
a shock, for it was not always thoroughly dry. At length the
welcome end of Desolation came, indicated by a lowering of

Gunnison Butte.
Head of Gunnison Valley and foot of Gray Canyon.
Powell Expedition of 1871 repairing boats.
Photograph by E. O. Beaman, U. S. Colo. Riv. Exp.

the walls and a break, where we were surprised to see a solitary
lame horse, but the next canyon, Gray, formed immediately.
This was at first called Lignite Canyon, but was afterwards renamed on account of the grey colour of the walls; an unusual
feature. The work here was similar to that in Desolation, and
we were not sorry when we came to the foot of it, there going
into camp to await the return of Powell. One of our flags was
planted at the end of an island below the canyon mouth, so

that he might see it. Opposite our camp was a very striking pinnacle then called Cathedral Butte, but later changed to
Gunnison.   Here we took the boats out and gave them a good
overhauling, which they badly needed.   The descent through
Desolation and Gray had been nearly six hundred feet.

Fishing one evening, Hillers thought his hook had caught
in a snag, but he was greatly surprised after carefully pulling in
his line, to find on the end of it a sluggish fish four feet long,
and as large around as a stovepipe.   We were to wait here till
the 3d of September for Powell, but on the 29th of August
three shots were heard in the valley outside; the Major's signal.   W. C. Powell and I were sent to investigate.   We found
him, with a companion, on the other bank, opposite the flag
we had put up.   Arriving near our station, a man was sent to
take their horses down to their camp, about five miles below,
and they went with us on the boats.   Hamblin, the man with
Powell, was not altogether comfortable in some of the swift
places.   As we cleared the high butte marking the end of Gray
Canyon, we perceived, stretching away to the westward from it,
a beautiful line of azure-blue cliffs, wonderfully buttressed and
carved.   At first these were called the Henry Cliffs, but afterward Henry was applied to some mountains and the cliffs were
called Azure.   At the camp we found another man, like the
first a Mormon and, as we learned later by intimate acquaintance,
both of fine quality and sterling merit.   The supplies Powell had
brought were three hundred pounds of flour, some jerked beef,
and about twenty pounds of sugar, from a town on the Sevier
called Manti, almost due west of our position about eighty
miles in an air line.   The pack-train having failed to reach the
mouth of the Dirty Devil, these additional rations were to
carry us on to the next station, the Crossing of the Fathers;
but they were not enough.   The other man with Hamblin was
a cousin of the same name, and when they rode away one
evening as the sun was going down, we were sorry to part with
them.   Their course lay through a wild, desolate country, but
we learned later that they had no trouble, though the day after
leaving us they ran upon a large camp of Utes.   Fortunately
the Utes were friendly.

For our part, we pushed off in our boats and headed for the Crossing of the Fathers with some misgivings on the food question. A large amount of mail had been brought in, and we enjoyed the newspapers, although they were weeks old.

Labyrinth Canyon, Trinalcove.
Photograph by E. O. BEAMAN, U. S. Colo. Riv. Exp.

Some monthly magazines were a great boon. For a time the stream was placid, allowing us to tie the boats together and drift again for a little while. Thompson and the Major read aloud from Whittier, the men sang "Sweet Evelina," and all appreciated the opportunity for this brief relaxation. Here

and there evidences of crossings were noticed, for it was in
this valley that Gunnison went over on the trip that proved
fatal to him, and here for years the Old Spanish Trail, which
Wolfskill inaugurated, led many eastward and westward, while
Utes and other Amerinds had used it long before that.   Indeed, as before mentioned, it was for a long time the first
locality, coming up from the Grand Wash, where the stream
could easily be crossed; a distance of about six hundred miles.
Many strangely eroded cliffs and buttes appeared as we descended, and one of these, near the mouth of the San Rafael,

Bonito Bend, between Labyrinth and Stillwater Canyons.
Photograph by E. O. BEAMAN, U. S. Colo. Riv. Exp.

was named after me.   At one place we saw some springs bub-
bling up from the bottom of an inlet, one of which was remarkable because of its size and power.   Its jet was five or
six inches in diameter, and rose six or eight inches above the
surface, the water being two or three feet in depth.   They
were called Undine Springs.   At the San Rafael a heavy rain-
storm came up, and presently we detected a loud roaring we
could not account for.   At last, however, it was discovered to
arise from the accumulated rain-water which was pouring over
a near-by cliff in a muddy torrent.   The whole country was

extremely bare and barren, mostly rock, and the rain gathered
as on the roof of a house. The river had narrowed up before
we reached the San Rafael and had entered low, broken walls.
The current was rather swift, but there were no rapids. As
we went on, the sight of the rain cascades falling with varying volume and colour, some chocolate, some amber, was very

The Butte of the Cross, between Labyrinth and Stillwater Canyons.
Photograph by E. O. BEAMAN, U. S. Colo. Riv. Exp.

beautiful. They continued for a time after the rain had ceased,
and then, as if the flood-gates had been closed, they vanished,
to reappear every time it began to rain afresh. Before long
the cliffs had reached one thousand feet in altitude, and we
were fairly within Labyrinth Canyon, which begins its existence at the mouth of the San Rafael. Many of the rain

cascades in the afternoon of this day were perfectly clear, and often fell several hundreds of feet, vanishing in spray, and presenting varied and exquisite effects in combination with the rich tones of the wet brown sandstone, and the background of dark grey sky. They ever increased in number, and directly opposite that night's camp one fell straight down for about two hundred feet, disappeared in mist to gather again on a ledge below, and shot out once more, a delicate silvery thread against the dark mass of the cliff. The next day we passed a group of three canyons entering at one point, to which the name Trinalcove was given, as they appeared from the river like alcoves rather than canyons. The river was now very winding with walls frequently vertical. There were no rapids, though the water as a rule moved somewhat swiftly. The days were growing short, and the night air had an autumnal chill about it that made the camp-fire comforting. At the end of sixty-two miles the walls broke up into buttes and pinnacles, thousands of them, suggesting immense organs, cathedrals, and almost anything the imagination pictured. One resembling a mighty cross lying down was in consequence called the "Butte of the Cross." This was practically the end of Labyrinth Canyon, and sweeping around a beautiful bend, where the rocks again began to come together, we were in the beginning of the next canyon of the series, two years before named Stillwater. At the suggestion of Beaman, the bend was called Bonito. On leaving our camp at this place the walls rapidly ran up, the current grew swifter, but the river remained smooth. The canyon was exceedingly "close," the rocks rising vertically from the edge of the water. There were few places where a landing could be made, but luckily no landing was necessary, except for night. The darkness fell before we found a suitable camp-ground. Some of our supplies had now to be used with caution, for it became evident that we would run short of food before we could get any more.

Long ago, no one knows how long, we might have been able to purchase of the natives who, a few miles below this camp, had tilled a small piece of arable land in an alcove. Small huts for storage were found there in the cliffs, and on a promontory, about thirty feet above the water, were the ruins of stone buildings, one of which, twelve by twenty feet in dimensions, had walls still standing about six feet high. The canyon here was some six hundred feet wide; the walls about nine hundred feet high, though the top of the plateau through which the canyon is carved is at least fifteen hundred feet above the river. We discovered the trail by which the old Puebloans had made their way in and out. Where necessity called for it, poles and tree-trunks had been placed against the rocks to aid the climbers. Some of our party trusted themselves to these ancient ladders, and with the aid of a rope also, reached the summit.

Beyond this place of ruins, the river flowed between walls not over four hundred and fifty feet apart at the top. The current was about three miles an hour, with scarcely a ripple, though it appeared much swifter because of the nearness of the cliffs. At the end of seven miles of winding canyon, there came a sharp turn to the east, which brought into view, at the other end, another canyon of nearly equal proportions and similar appearance. In the bottom of this flowed a river of almost the same size as the Green. The waters of the two came together with a good deal of a rush, the commingling being plainly visible. Neither overwhelmed the other; it was a perfect union, and in some respects it is quite appropriate that the combined waters of these streams should have a special name to represent them. The new tributary was Grand River, and when our boats floated on the united waters, we were at last on the back of the Dragon. Away sped the current of the Colorado, swirling along, spitefully lashing with its hungry tongue the narrow sand-banks fringing the rugged shores, so that we scarcely knew where to make a landing. Finally we halted on the right, constantly watching the boats' lines lest the sand should melt away and take our little ships with it. Along the bases of the cliffs above the high waters were narrow strips of rocky soil, supporting a few stunted cottonwoods and hackberry trees, which, with some stramonium bushes in blossom, were the sum total of vegetation. In every way the Junction is a desolate place. It is the beginning of Cataract

Canyon, and forty-one miles must be put behind us before we would see its end—forty-one miles of bad river, too.   From a point not far up the Green, which we easily reached with a boat, a number climbed out by means of a cleft about fifty feet wide, taking the photographic outfit along.   The

Head of Cataract Canyon, Looking down from Top of Walls near the Junction of the Grand and Green.
Depth, 1300 feet.
Photograph by E O. Beaman, U. S. Colo. Riv. Exp.

country above was a maze of crevices, pinnacles, and buttes, and it seemed an impossibility for any human being to travel more than a few hundred yards in any direction.   The character of the place may best be illustrated by stating that Steward, who had gone up by a different route, was unable to reach us, though we could talk to him across a fissure.   Many of these breaks could be jumped, but some of them were too wide for safety. The surface was largely barren sandstone, only a patch of sand here and there sustaining sometimes a bush or stunted cedar. It is the Land of Standing Rocks, as the Utes call it.

The supplies were now gone over and carefully and evenly divided, so that an accident to one boat should not cripple us any more than possible, and on Tuesday, the 19th of September, our bows were headed down the Colorado. A few miles below the Junction, a trail was seen coming down a canyon on the left, showing that the Utes have always known how to find the place. If Macomb had been properly guided he could have reached it. The familiar roar of rapids soon came to our ears, and thenceforth there was no respite from them. The first was so ugly that the boats were lowered by lines, the second was much the same, and then we reached a third which was even worse. The water was now growing cold, and as one's clothes are always wet when running rapids or portaging on the Colorado, we felt the effects of the deep shadows, combined with the cold drenchings. Our dinners were quickly prepared, for we were on allowance and Andy was not bothered with trying to satisfy our appetites; he cooked as much as directed, and if there were hungry men around it was not his fault. We all felt that short rations were so much ahead of nothing that there was no grumbling. The volume of water was now nearly double what it had been on the Green, and the force of the rapids was greatly augmented. Huge boulders on the bottom, which the Green would have turned over only once or twice, here were rolled along, when they started, for many yards sensible to not the eye but to the ear. This was a distinct feature of Cataract Canyon and shows the declivity to be very great and the boulders to be well worn. The declivity for a few miles is greater than in Lodore, perhaps the greatest on the river. Sometimes in Cataract the rumble of these boulders was mistaken for distant thunder. At one rapid I remember that a rock many feet square was swaying from the current. After dinner, the boats were lowered over the rapid, fall, cataract, or whatever it might be called, before which we had paused, and then in short order over four more tremendous ones. When we had run a fifth, in which we received a violent shaking-up, we went into camp on the left bank at the head of another roarer, or pair of them, and hast-

Side Canyon of Cataract Canyon.
1500 feet deep—20 feet wide at bottom, 300 feet at top.
Photograph by E. O. Beaman, U. S. Colo. Riv. Exp.

ened to throw off our saturated clothes and put on the dry from out the friendly rubber sacks. I never before understood the comfort of being dry. The topographers recorded a good day's work: nine miles and eight powerful cataracts. Cataract, we decided was the proper name for these plunges, for though they were by no means vertical, they were more violent than what is ordinarily called a rapid. This was one part of the canyons where White, in his imaginary journey, found an easy passage! The next day Powell took me with him on a climb to the top. We had little trouble in getting out. On the way back the Major's cut-off arm was on the rock side of a gulch we had followed up, and I found it necessary, two or three times, to place myself where he could step on my knee, as his stump had a tendency to throw him off his balance. Had he fallen at these points the drop would have been four hundred or five hundred feet. I mention this to show how he never permitted his one-armed condition to interfere with his doing things. The walls here were eighteen hundred feet, a gain of three hundred feet over the Junction. While we were away the men below had lowered the boats over two rapids, in one of which the *Nell* broke loose and went down alone with her cargo on board. As good fortune will have it, there is frequently an eddy or two at the foot of a rapid and into one of these she ran. By a desperate exertion of Hillers in swimming she was regained.

A boat must never be allowed to move without men aboard or lines attached. This would seem to go without saying, but for fear it does not I mention it for the sake of any who may want to try their skill at this work. In the morning there was a pleasant smooth stretch for some distance, but it was soon passed, and cataract followed cataract till we counted ten. Seven we ran with exhilarating speed; the other three demanding more respectful treatment, we lowered the boats by lines, when the noon hour was at hand and a halt was made for refreshments, five miles from the starting-point of the morning. As soon as we had consumed the allowance of bread, bacon, and coffee, we took up our task by making two very difficult and tiring let-downs; that is, manœuvring the boats in and out, among and over, the rocks alongshore by lines, with one or two men aboard, always on the lookout to prevent being caught by outer currents. This brought us face to face with a furious fall, but one that seemed free from obstructions, and the order was to run it. Accordingly, over we went, the boats shipping the great seas below and each one tapping the keel on a submerged rock at the start. Owing to the trend of the canyon, and the lateness of the season, the sun now passed early from sight, the walls throwing the bottom of the gorge into deep shadow with a wintry chill that was quickly perceptible to us in our wet clothing. The result was that our teeth chattered in spite of all we could do to stop the uncomfortable performance, and our lips turned blue. To be soaked all day long near the end of September, in our climate, is not an agreeable condition. Though less than seven miles was made this day we were forced to stop when the shadow fell and make a camp at the first opportunity. It was only half-past three o'clock, but it had been sunset to us for half an hour. Thus each working day was sadly shortened, for even where the bends were most favourable, the warm sun shone upon us only for the middle hours. The walls were close together and very straight; they grew higher and more threatening with every mile of progress, so that it seemed as if another day or two would shut out the sun from the bottom altogether. On account of our limited larder, if for no other reason, we were obliged to push ahead as rapidly as possible. The next day we were at it early, easily running the first cataract, but just below it an immediate landing was imperative at the head of another which no man in his senses would think of running. Some hard work put us below that, and then came one far worse. The morning was gone before we saw its foam receding behind us. The following day, on summing up, after much severe toil, and stopping to repair boats, it was found that we had gone only a mile and a half! At this rate, we thought, when would we see the end of this gorge? But in the morning our wet clothes were put on without a murmur from any one, and once more we renewed the attack. The worst fall the next day was a drop of about twenty feet in twenty yards; a sharp plunge of the river in one mass. As it seemed free from rocks in the middle a run was decided on. We therefore pulled squarely into it. On both sides the river was beaten to solid foam amongst the rocks, but in the middle, where we were, there was a clean chute, followed by a long tail of ugly waves. We were entirely successful, though the waves broke over my head till they almost took my breath away. The walls reached a height of twenty-five hundred feet, seeming to us almost perpendicular on both sides. It was the narrowest deep chasm we had yet seen, and beneath these majestic cliffs we ourselves appeared mere pigmies, creeping about with our feeble strength to overcome the tremendous difficulties. The loud reverberation of the roaring

Side Canyon of Cataract Canyon.
See figures of men, centre foreground on brink of lower terrace.
Photograph by E. O. BEAMAN, U. S. Colo. Riv. Exp.

water, the rugged rocks, the toppling walls, the narrow sky, all combined to make this a fearful place, which no pen can adequately describe. Another day the Major and I climbed out, reaching an altitude, some distance back from the brink, of 3135 feet above the river. The day after this climb the walls ran up to about twenty-seven hundred feet, apparently in places absolutely vertical, though Stanton, who came through here in 1890, said he did not think they were anywhere perpendicular to the top. The tongue of a bend we found always more or less broken, but in the curve the cliffs certainly had all the effect of absolute perpendicularity, and in one place I estimated that if a rock should fall from the brink it would have struck on or near our boat. This shows, at any rate, that the walls were very straight. The boats seemed mere wisps of straw by comparison, and once when I saw one which had preceded ours, lying at the end of a clear stretch, I was startled by the insignificance of the craft on which our lives depended. Beaman tried to take some photographs which should give this height in full, but the place was far beyond the power of any camera. In this locality there seemed to be no possibility of a man's finding a way to the summit. I concluded that at high water this part of Cataract Canyon would probably anni- hilate any human being venturing into it, though it is possible high water would make it easier. Where there was driftwood it was in tremendous piles, wedged together in inextricable confusion; hundreds of tree-trunks, large and small, battered and cut and limbless, with the ends pounded into a spongy lot of splinters. The interstices between the large logs were filled with smaller stuff, like boughs, railroad-ties, and pieces of dressed timber which had been swept away from the region above the Union Pacific Railway. Picture this narrow canyon twenty-seven hundred feet deep, at high water, with a muddy booming torrent at its bottom, sweeping along logs and all kinds of floating débris, and then think of being in there with a boat!

We proceeded as best we could with all caution. Every move was planned and carried out with the exactness of a battle; as if the falls were actual enemies striving to discover our weakness. One practice was to throw sticks in above them, and thus ascertain the trend of the chief currents, which enabled us to approach intelligently. The river here was not more than four hundred feet wide. As we continued, the can- yon finally widened, and at one place there was a broad, rocky beach on the left. The opposite wall was nearly three thou- sand feet high. Beaman, by setting his camera far back on the rocks, was able to get a view to the top, with us in it by the river, while we were trying to work the boats past a rapid. This photograph is reproduced on this page, and the figures, though very small, may be plainly seen. Not far below this the walls closed in again. Powell and Thompson tried to

Cataract Canyon, Right-hand Wall toward Lower End.
Height about 2700 feet. Note figures of men near edge of water, lower right-hand corner. They show as very small upright dark lines.
Photograph by E. O. BEAMAN, U. S. Colo. Riv. Exp.

climb out, but they failed on the first trial and had no time to make a fresh start. They came back to camp and as soon as an early supper was over we started on—about five o'clock. The walls ran close together and at the water were perfectly vertical for a hundred feet or so, then there was a terrace. As we sailed down, the river was suddenly studded with pinnacles of rock, huge boulders or masses fallen from the heights. By steering carefully we could pass among these and, keeping in the dividing line of the current, make for the head of a rocky island, on each side of which the waters plunged against the cliffs with great force as they dropped away to a lower level. The danger lay in getting too far over either way, and it was somewhat difficult to dodge the pinnacles and steer for the island at the same time. The *Cañonita* went on the wrong side of one, and we held our breath, for it seemed as if she could not retrieve her position in the dividing current, but she did. As we approached the head of the island our keel bumped several times on the rocks, while the current changed from the simple dividing line and ran everywhere. At length we reached the shallow water, and as the keel struck gently on a rock we were overboard, soon pulling the boat on the island, where the others quickly followed. By hauling the craft down the right-hand side for about half the island's length, we were able to pull directly across the tail of waves from the right-hand rapid, and avoid being swept against the cliff on the left where the whole river set. So close did every boat go that the oars on that side could not be used for a moment or two; and then we were past. At a higher stage of water this place would be much simpler. The river became serene; night was falling; we drifted on with the current till a roar issuing from the darkness ahead admonished us to halt. Some broken rocks on the right gave a footing and there we remained till morning. In the night it rained, and the rain continued into the daylight till cascades came leaping and plunging from everywhere into the canyon. Two of these opposite our camp were exceedingly beautiful. One was about two feet wide and the other five. For one thousand feet they made a clear plunge, then vanished in spray, feathery and beautiful. These rain cascades are a delightful feature of the country and some day will be famous. Soon Millecrag Bend, marking the end of Cataract Canyon, came in sight. The walls were only broken by a deep canyon valley coming in on the left, and the next canyon, Narrow, then began, but it was not one with difficult waters, and, being only nine miles in length, we were soon through it.   At its foot was the mouth of the Dirty Devil and the beginning of Mound Canyon, which was later combined with Monument under the name of Glen.

Our rations were now very low.   For some time, each man had been allowed for a meal, only a thin slice of bacon, a chunk of bread about the size of one's fist, and all the coffee he desired.   At long intervals a pot of Andy's rare bean-soup was added to the feast.   It was necessary, therefore, to push on with all haste, or we would be starving.   The *Cañonita* was consequently taken out and "cached" under a huge rock which had fallen against the cliff, forming a natural house.   Filling her with sand to keep her from "drying" to pieces we left her, feeling sure the party which was to come after her the next spring would find her safe.   She was forty feet above low water.   We now went ahead with good speed, leaving as much work as possible for the prospective *Cañonita* party to perform. All through Glen Canyon we found evidences of Puebloan occupation: house ruins, storage caves, etc.   The river was tame, though the walls, about one thousand to sixteen hundred feet high, were beautiful, and often, in places, vertical.   The low stage of water rendered progress somewhat difficult at times, but nevertheless we made fairly good time and on the 5th of October passed the San Juan, a shallow stream at this season, entering through a wide canyon of about the same depth as that of the Colorado, that is, about twelve hundred or fourteen hundred feet.   A short distance below it we stopped at the Music Temple, where the Howlands and Dunn had carved their names.   Reaching the vicinity of Navajo Mountain, Powell thought of climbing it, but an inquiry as to the state of the larder received from Andy the unpleasant information that we were down to the last of the supplies; two or three more scant meals would exhaust everything edible in the boats.   So no halt was made.   On the contrary, the oars were plied more vigorously, and on the 6th we saw a burned spot in the bushes on the right,—there were alluvial bottoms in the bends,—and though this burned spot was not food, it was an indication that there

The Town of Bluff.

Upper valley of the San Juan River. Photograph by CHARLES GOODMAN.

were human beings about; we hoped it indicated also our near approach to the Crossing of the Fathers. Horses and men had recently been there. Noon came and the surroundings were as silent, unbroken, untrodden as they had been anywhere above

Glen Canyon Wall.
About 1200 feet high. Homogeneous sandstone on top of thin bedded sandstone.
Photograph by J. FENNEMORE, U. S. Colo. Riv. Exp.

the burned spot. Though there was little reason for it, we halted for a dinner camp, and Andy brought out a few last scraps for us to devour. Hillers threw in a line baited with a small bit of bacon and pulled out a fish, then a second and several. It was the miracle of the loaves and fishes over again!

Bend after bend was turned and left behind, and still no Crossing, but late in the afternoon a shot was heard; then we saw a
white rag on a pole; then we landed and beheld a large pile of

Glen Canyon.
Sandstone wall about 1200 feet high.
Photograph by J. Fennemore, U. S. Col. Riv. Exp.

rations, in charge of three men.   These men, Dodds, Bonnemort, and Riley, as we were days overdue, had about made
up their minds we were lost, and had contemplated departing in the morning and leaving the rations to their fate.

Riley and Bonnemort were prospectors, who remained only to see us and make some inquiries about the river above. They told me afterward we were the roughest - looking

Glen Canyon, Sentinel Rock.
Between the Crossing of the Fathers and Lee's Ferry—about 300 feet high.
Photograph by E. O. BEAMAN, U. S. Colo. Riv. Exp.

set of men they had ever seen. Our clothes were about used up.

Powell prepared to go to Salt Lake, about five hundred miles away, to make preparations for our winter's mountain work, and we all wrote letters to send out. On the 10th of

October they left us, Hillers going with Powell, while we were to run down thirty-five miles farther to the mouth of the Paria, and there cache the two boats for the winter. Steward was now taken sick, and though some Navajos who came along kindly offered to carry him with them to Kanab, he preferred to stay with us, so we stretched him out, during our runs, on one of the cabins. This was not entirely comfortable for him, but the river was smooth and easy as far as the Paria, so there was no danger of spilling him off, and he got on fairly well. At the Paria, Jones, who had made a misstep in one of the boats at the Junction and injured one leg, developed inflammatory rheumatism in it, and also in the other. Andy at Millecrag Bend had put on his shoe with an unseen scorpion in it, the sting of which caused him to grow thin and pale. Bishop's old wound troubled him; Beaman and W. C. Powell also felt "under the weather," so that of the whole party left here, Thompson and I were the only ones who remained entirely well. Arriving at the Paria, we hid the boats for the winter, and waited for the pack-train that was to bring us provisions, and take us out to Kanab, which would be headquarters. The pack-train, however, was misled by a man who pretended to be acquainted with the trail, and we ate up all the food we had before it arrived. It came over an extraordinary path. Lost on top of the Paria Plateau, it was only able to reach us by the discovery of a singular old trail coming down the two-thousand-foot cliffs three miles up the Paria. While waiting we had examined the immediate neighbourhood and had climbed to the summit of some sandstone peaks on the left, where the wall of Glen Canyon breaks away to the southward. The view was superb. Mountains, solid and solitary, rose up here and there, and lines of cliffs, strangely coloured, stretched everywhere across the wide horizon, while from our feet, like a veritable huge writhing dragon, Marble Canyon zigzagged its long, dark line into the blue distance, its narrow tributaries looking like the monster's many legs. I took it into my head to try to shoot from there into the water of Glen Canyon beneath us, and borrowed Bishop's 44-calibre Remington revolver for the purpose. When I pulled the trigger I was positively startled by the violence of the report, a deafening shock like a thousand thunder-claps in one; then dead silence. Next, from far away there was a rattle as of musketry, and peal after peal of the echoing shot came back to us. The interval of silence was timed on another trial and was found to be exactly twenty seconds. The result was always the same, and from this unusual echo we named the place Echo Peaks.

I had made Jones a pair of crutches, by means of which he was able to hobble painfully around, and by the time the pack-train was ready to start for the settlement, about one hundred miles away, he could bear being lifted upon a horse. Steward, also, was able to ride, and with a number of us walking we left the Paria behind.

November's sharp days were upon us. We had only the remains of our summer clothing and few blankets, so that when the thermometer registered 11° F. above zero we did not dispute it.

CHAPTER XII

Into the Jaws of the Dragon—A Useless Experiment—Wheeler Reaches Diamond Creek Going Up-stream—The Hurricane Ledge—Something about Names— A Trip from Kanab through Unknown Country to the Mouth of the Dirty Devil.

WHILE our party, in September, was battling with the cataracts, another, as we afterwards learned, was starting from Camp Mohave on a perilous, impracticable, and needless expedition up the Colorado. How far this party originally expected to be able to proceed against the tremendous obstacles I have never understood, but the after-statement mentions Diamond Creek as the objective point. That such a wild, useless, and costly struggle should have been allowed by the War Department, which authorised it, seems singular, more particularly as little new was or could be, accomplished by it. The War Department must have known that Powell, two years before, had descended the river from Wyoming to the mouth of the Virgen, and that he was now more than half-way down the river on his second, more detailed exploration, authorised and paid for by the Government. Lieutenant Ives had also years before completely explored as high as the Vegas Wash, and there were therefore only the few miles, about twenty-five, between that Wash and the mouth of the Virgen, which might technically be considered unexplored, though only technically, for several parties had passed over it. Then why was this forlorn hope inaugurated? What credit could any one expect to obtain by bucking for miles up the deep, dangerous gorge filled with difficult rapids, which Powell had found hazardous and well-nigh impossible, coming down with the current? The leader of this superfluous endeavour was Lieutenant Wheeler, of the Topographical Engineers, who had been roaming the Western country for several years with a large escort. For some reason, Wheeler seems to have been disinclined to give Powell credit for his masterly achievement. On the map

The Grand Canyon.
Cliffs opposite the mouth of Diamond Creek. The highest point visible is about 3500 feet above the river.
Photograph by T. H. O'SULLIVAN, Wheeler Exp.

published in his Report, under the date 1879, *ten years after Powell's triumph*, he omits his name entirely, and he also fails to give Ives credit on the river, though he records his land trail. In the text I fail to find any mention of Powell in the regular order, and only towards the end of the volume under a different heading. As the book gives an admirable and detailed review of explorations in the West, one is completely at a loss to understand the omission of credit to two of the most distinguished explorers of all. Wheeler accepted White's story because one of his men who knew White at Camp Mohave, "corroborated" it. How could a man who knew nothing about the canyons give testimony worth consideration, for or against? Wheeler had also been informed by O. D. Gass, who, with three others, had worked his way up the Grand Canyon some few miles in 1864, that in his opinion it was impossible to go farther than he had gone. Yet White had reported this whole gorge as having only smooth water; his difficulties had all ended at the mouth of the Little Colorado. Gass's experience was worth a good deal as a gauge of White's story, and it proved the story false. But Wheeler did not so consider it, and therefore prepared to make the attempt to go beyond Gass. The latter was about right in considering it impossible to go above his highest point, but when Wheeler found himself trapped in the chasm, he was desperate, and, being at the time favoured by a low stage of water, he finally managed to get through.

Wheeler's boats were built in San Francisco and sent by way of the mouth of the Colorado to Camp Mohave. No details are given of their construction, but from Dr. Gilbert I learn that they were flat-bottomed. They were apparently about eighteen feet long. See page 302. There were three, and in addition a barge was taken from the quartermaster's department at Camp Mohave. There were two land parties with supplies, and the river party, the latter composed of the following persons: First Lieutenant George M. Wheeler, U. S. Topographical Engineers; G. K. Gilbert, geologist; W. J. Hoffman, naturalist; P. W. Hamel, topographer; T. H. O'Sullivan, photographer; E. M. Richardson, assistant topographer and artist; Frank Hecox, barometrical assistant; Frederick W. Loring, general assistant; six boatmen, six soldiers (one sergeant and five privates from Co. G, 12th Infantry, stationed at Mohave) and "Captain" Asquit, and thirteen other Mohaves—in all thirty-four. It was the fate of three of these, after escaping from the dangers of the great chasm, to be killed by an attack of Apaches on the Wickenburg stage.

These were Loring, Hamel, and Salmon.   Loring was a brilliant young literary man from Boston, whose career was thus
sadly ended.

The boats appear not to have been regularly named, though
two of them, at least, received titles before long, one, the boat
Gilbert was in, being called the *Trilobite*, and the other, the
photographic boat, was termed the *Picture*.   Leaving Mohave
on September 16th (1871) they proceeded with little difficulty
by towing and rowing, as far as Ives
had taken the *Explorer*, to the foot
of Black Canyon.
From here the
work was harder,
but by the 18th
they had arrived in
the heart of this
canyon.   The rapids were now more
severe, but as Ives
had gone up easily,
and also Johnson
with his steamboat, and Rodgers
with his, there was
nothing to prevent
the ascent of this

The Beginning of a Natural Arch.
Photograph by C. R. SAVAGE.

party.   On the tenth day, therefore, they passed Fortification
Rock and reached Las Vegas Wash, the termination of the
Ives exploration.   From here to the mouth of the Virgen was
the stretch that had, *technically*, never been explored, though
it had been traversed, at least, several times.   There is one
small canyon in the distance, called Boulder.   Passing the
mouth of the Virgen, Wheeler entered the canyon through the
Virgen Mountains, and this he named Virgin Canyon because,
as he says, it was his "first canyon on entirely new ground."
I am at a loss to understand his meaning.   If he intended **to**

convey the impression that he was the first to traverse this portion, it is an unwarranted assumption, and must be emphatically condemned. Powell had descended as far as the Virgen, and thus Wheeler was simply following his course backwards.

Passing through another small unnamed canyon, to which he applied the term Iceberg on account of the contour of its northern walls, he finally, on October 3d, came to the Grand Wash. On the next day the Ute Crossing near the beginning of the Grand Canyon was reached. Two or three days before this he could see what seemed to be a high range of mountains apparently perpendicular, which was, as he surmised, the foot of the Grand Canyon. Progress was now very slow, for the river was swifter than it had been below. Perceiving the impossibility of taking such a craft farther, the barge was left behind at the Crossing, to form a base of supplies in case the difficulties of ascending necessitated falling back. Relief parties from the rendezvous at Truxton Springs were to go, one to the mouth of the canyon and the other to the mouth of Diamond Creek, about thirty-five miles distant from the Springs, but the situation was complicated by these parties having no orders to wait at these points. Putting all of his land force who were at the canyon mouth on the south side of "this turbid, unmanageable stream," and picking three crews of nine persons each, with rations for fifteen days, he was ready to go ahead with this unwise enterprise, "imagining," as he admits, "but few of the many difficulties that were to be met." It was on October 7th that they entered the mouth of the great gorge. At length "a full view, magnificent beyond description, of the walls of the Grand Canyon " was had, and they were fairly on the road; as rough a road, going down, as one can well imagine, but going up in the teeth of the torrential rapids, hemmed in by close granite walls, it is about as near the impossible as anything that is not absolutely so could be. Wheeler certainly deserves credit for one thing in this haphazard affair, and that is for a splendid courage and abundant nerve, in which he was well supported by Gilbert's cool fortitude and indomitable spirit. Once when I was discussing this journey with Stanton, who,

at a later period, came down the gorge, he would hardly admit
that Wheeler actually did reach Diamond Creek: he thought
the ascent impossible. The second day in the canyon five
rapids were passed within two miles, and, on the next, nine
were overcome before noon, and before sunset, fifteen, showing that the party were working with all the nerve and muscle
they possessed. On this day they passed the monument Gass
and his companions had erected at their farthest point in 1864.
The rapids were now "more formidable" than any yet seen,
and Wheeler was "satisfied" that no one had ever gone higher.
This was true, and it is probable no one will ever try to go up
this portion again. The way to make the passage is from
above, the work being less and the danger no greater. Wherever a portage can be made going up it can also be made going
down. The river was compressed to seventy-five feet in one
place on this day. On the 10th they made about five miles,
and met with a serious accident: two of the boats were carried
back over a rapid, but were luckily secured again without having suffered damage. The declivity was now very great, and
the stream flowed along between solid granite, where footing
was both difficult and dangerous, and pulling the boats up over
the rocks taxed the combined strength of the crews. Everything had to be unloaded at one bad place and the first boat
was nearly swamped. All could not be taken up before dark,
so a "dreary camp is made among the débris of the slopes,
where, cuddled up Indian-fashion, the weary hours of the
night are passed." The labour was tremendous, and two of
the party became ill: one, a Mohave, who was badly bruised by
being thrown upon the rocks. Wheeler now began to despair
of reaching Diamond Creek, and well he might, but he concluded that he could get there if the men and the boats would
but hold together. The next day, another series of rapids
was surmounted, and then came a particularly bad-looking one.
The first boat was filled instantly with water, swamped, and
thrown back against the rocks "almost a perfect wreck, and
its contents were washed down below the overhanging rocks."
A package of Wheeler's valuable papers was lost, also a lot of
expensive instruments, the astronomical and meteorological

observations, and the entire cargo of rations.   This was a discouraging disaster, and came near compelling the retreat of the whole party.   Darkness came on, and they were obliged to

The Grand Canyon.
Near mouth of Diamond Creek.
Photograph by T. H. O'SULLIVAN, Wheeler Exp.

drop back about half a mile to make a camp.   Wheeler was weary and dispirited, though he maintained an outward show of cheerfulness toward the men, and the next morning the

Dragon was faced again.   They tried to find some remnant of
the lost cargo, but it had completely vanished.   Everything
had been swept away forever.   All the party were despondent,
one boat was badly damaged, and the diminution of the rations made the outlook gloomy.   The damaged boat was
therefore sent with a crew back to the place at the mouth of
the canyon where the barge had been left.   With the exception of Wheeler and Gilbert none of the party believed the
cataracts now ahead could be surmounted.

" Mr. Gilbert and myself," writes Wheeler, " propose to reas-
sure the men by taking the first boat across the rapids.   Portage of
the stores is made to the wash at the head of the rapids, which con-
sumes the greater share of the day, and half an hour before twilight
a rope is stretched and the emergency prepared for.   The entire
force is stationed along the line, and the cast-off is made.   In five
minutes the worst part of the rapid is over, and just as the sun sinks
gloomily behind the canyon horizon, the worst rapid is triumphantly
passed amid the cheers and exultations of every member of the
party."

The following day, October 13th, they reached the narrowest
part of the river, a channel less than fifty feet wide, but the
canyon on top is, of course, very broad.   With many portages
and other arduous toil the party slowly climbed up the river,
sometimes making less than three miles, sometimes a little
more.   The rapids grew worse and worse, and the smooth
stretches in between shorter and shorter.   On the 15th Gilbert's boat broke away, and he and Hecox were swept so far
down the stream that the rest could not reach them.   They
were obliged to remain where they were through the night
with nothing to eat.   The main camp was at a place where
there was barely room for the men to sleep amongst the rocks.
They were all gloomy enough, and starvation was beginning to
show its dreaded shadow amidst the spray.   On the 16th they
were compelled to carry the tow-line fully a hundred feet above
the water to get it ahead.   At another portage the rope broke
and the boat was instantly thrown out into the rapid by the
fierce current.   Fortunately she was not capsized, and they

managed again to secure her and make a second attempt, which succeeded. Climbing to the top of the granite they discovered it was comparatively level, and they believed they could travel over it, if necessary, as far as Diamond Creek. The rations for some time had to be dealt out on allowance, and at night, for safety, Wheeler put the entire stock under his head as a pillow. On the 17th they met with particularly bad rapids, one with a fall of ten and a half feet where the river was only thirty-five feet wide. The force of such pent-up waters may be imagined. The party had here one advantage over the river farther north,

The Crew of the " Trilobite."
At the mouth of Diamond Creek.
Photograph by T. H. O'SULLIVAN, Wheeler Exp.

at this season; it was much warmer in this part of the Grand Canyon.

"Each day," writes Wheeler of this portion, "seems like an age, and the danger of complete disaster stares one so plainly in the face that a state of uneasiness naturally prevails." On the 18th, at one of the descents, a boat was again torn loose, and Gilbert and Salmon were thrown into the raging waters. They fortunately succeeded in getting out, and the party pushed ahead, making three and one-half miles. The boats were now in a dilapidated condition, leaking badly. On October 19th two messengers were started, by way of the summit of the granite, to Diamond Creek to catch the relief party there, and

return with some food. Meanwhile Wheeler planned, if no
relief came, to abandon the river on the 22nd, but on the evening of that same day, having made six miles up the river, the
party had the joy of finally reaching Diamond Creek with the
two boats. Wheeler had succeeded in a well-nigh hopeless
task. "The land party had left at ten in the morning," so
Gilbert writes me, "and their camp was reached by our messengers on foot at 1 P.M. These facts were announced to us
by a note one of our messengers sent down the river on a
float." A number of the boat party were then sent out to the
rendezvous camp, while the remainder turned about and began
the perilous descent, having now to do just what would have
been necessary if the start had been made from Diamond
Creek. Mohave was reached in safety *on the evening of the
fifth day*, whereas it had required about four weeks of extremely hard work to make the same distance against the current. This is all the comment necessary on the two methods.
The whole party that reached Diamond Creek was as follows:
Lieutenant Wheeler, G. K. Gilbert, P. W. Hamel, T. H.
O'Sullivan, E. M. Richardson, Frank Hecox, Wm. George
Salmon, R. W. James, Thos. Hoagland, George Phifer, Wm.
Roberts, Privates Drew, Flynn, and Keegan, and six Mohaves,
making twenty in all.

"The exploration of the Colorado River," says Wheeler,
"may now be considered complete." The question may fairly
be asked, Why was the exploration now any more complete
than it was before Wheeler made this unnecessary trip? Powell,
two years before, had been through the part ascended, and
Wheeler, so far as I can determine, added little of value to what
was known before. If he thought Powell had not completed
the work of exploration, as his words imply, the exploration
was still not complete, for there remained the distance to the
Little Colorado, and to the Paria, and so on up to the source
of the river, which Wheeler had not been over. If he accepted
Powell's exploration *above* Diamond Creek, why did he not accept it below? His nerve and pluck in accomplishing the ascent
to Diamond Creek deserve great praise, but the trip itself
cannot be considered anything but a needless waste of energy.

Meanwhile, as noted in the last chapter, our own party had passed the Crossing of the Fathers, had arrived at the mouth of the Paria, and, according to our plans, had cached our boats there for the winter while we proceeded to inaugurate our land work of triangulation. A number of us were left for a while in camp in a valley lying between the Kaibab Plateau, then called Buckskin Mountain, and what is now called Paria Plateau, at a spring in a gulch of the Vermilion Cliffs. Two

The Dining-table in Camp.
Dutch oven, left foreground.
Photograph by F. S. Dellenbaugh.

large rocks at this place had fallen together in such a way that one could crawl under for shelter. This was on the old trail leading from the Mormon settlements to the Moki country, travelled about once a year by Jacob Hamblin and a party on a trading expedition to the other side of the river. Somebody on one of these trips had taken refuge beneath this rock, and on departing had written, in a facetious mood, along the top with a piece of charcoal, "Rock House Hotel." Naturally, in referring to the spring it was called, by the very few who knew it, Rock House Spring, and then the spring where the House Rock was, or House Rock Spring. From this came House Rock Valley, and the name was soon a fixture, and went on our maps. And thus easily are names established in a new country. All around were evidences of former occupation by the Puebloans, and I became greatly interested in examining the locality. At length, we were ordered across the Kaibab to the vicinity of Kanab, and I shall never fail to see distinctly the wonderful view from the summit we had of the bewildering cliff-land leading away northward to the Pink Cliffs. The lines of cliffs rose up like some giant stairway, while to the south-eastward the apparently level plain was separated by the dark line of Marble Canyon. On top of the plateau, which was covered with a fine growth of tall pines, we came about camping time to a shallow, open valley, where we decided to stay for the night. As it was on the top of the mountain Bishop recorded it in his notes as Summit Valley, and so it ever afterward remained. There was no spring, but a thin layer of snow eked out the water we had brought in kegs on the packs, and we and the animals were comfortable enough. The trail had not been travelled often, and was in places very dim, but we succeeded in following it without delay. The Kaibab, still frequently called the Buckskin Mountain, must have received this first name from its resemblance to a buckskin stretched out on the ground. The similarity is quite apparent in the relief map opposite page 41. As it was the home of the Kaibab band of Pai Utes, Powell decided to rename it after them. We arrived within eight miles of Kanab, where we made a headquarters camp at a fine spring, and trips from here and from a camp made later nearer Kanab were extended into the surrounding country. The Mormons had a year or two before come out from the St. George direction and established this new settlement of Kanab, composed then of a stockaded square of log houses and some few neat adobe houses outside; about fifty in all. The settlement was growing strong enough to scatter itself somewhat about the site marked off for the future town. One of the first things the Mormons always did in establishing a new settlement was to plant fruit and shade trees, and vines, and the like, so that in a very few years there was a condition of comfort only attained by a non-Mormon settlement after the lapse of a quarter of a century.

In the valley below Kanab a base line was measured nine miles long, and from this starting-point our work of triangulating the country was carried on. Trips with pack-trains to establish geodetic stations and examine the lay of the land

Renshawe, Riley, Dellenbaugh, Thompson, Mrs. Thompson.
Winter Headquarters at Kanab, 1872-3.   U. S. Colo. Riv. Exp.
Central Tent.
Photograph by J. K. HILLERS.

were made in all directions. Of course the reader understands that up to this time no map had been made of this vast region north of the Colorado, and that many parts of it were entirely unknown. The Mormons had traversed certain districts, but they only knew their own trails and roads and had as yet not had time to carry on any unnecessary examinations away from the lines they travelled. Some of our experiences were interesting, but I have not the space here for recording many of them. It was my first winter out of doors, and sleeping in snow-storms and all kinds of weather was a novelty; though the climate is fine and dry. It was only in the higher regions that we encountered much snow, yet the temperature in the valleys was quite cold enough. In leading the open-air life from summer to winter and to summer again, the system be-

The Uinkaret Mountains at Sunset, from the North-east.
Mt. Trumbull in middle, Mt. Logan in the far distance.
Oil sketch by F. S. DELLENBAUGH.

comes adjusted, and one does not suffer as much as at first glance would seem probable; in fact, one suffers very little if any, provided there are plenty of good food and warm clothing.

On one occasion, when we were coming away from a snowy experience in the Uinkaret Mountains, we were enveloped in a severe flurry one morning soon after starting. When we had gone about a mile and a half, the whole world seemed to terminate. The air was dense with the fast-falling snowflakes, and all beyond a certain line was white fog, up, down, and sideways. A halt was imperative, as we knew not which way to turn except back, and that was not our direction. Descending from our horses we stepped out in the direction of the illimitable whiteness, only to find that there was nothing there to travel on. The only thing to do was to camp, which we did forthwith. By our holding up a blanket at the four corners, and chopping some dry wood out of the side of a dead

Major Powell and a Pai Ute.   Southern Utah, 1872.
Photograph by J. K. HILLERS, U. S. Colo. Riv. Exp.

tree, Andy was able to start a fire, and we waited for atmospheric developments. Presently there were rifts in the white, and as we looked we could discern, far, far below our position, another land. As the storm broke away more and more, it was seen that we had arrived at the edge of a cliff with a sheer drop of one thousand feet. At last we were able to go on and hunted for a way to descend, which we did not find. Consequently we continued northwards and finally, on the second day, met with a waggon-track which we followed, reaching at last the edge where the cliff could be descended by way of a waggon-road the Mormons had cut out of the face for a mile and a quarter. This was the Hurricane Ledge, which extends across the country northwards from the Uinkaret Mountains to the Virgen River. Its course is well seen on the map opposite page 41, and also on the one on page 37. As the traveller comes to Hurricane Hill, the northern limit, from which the whole cliff takes its name, he has before him one of the most extraordinary views in all that region, if not in the

The Expedition Photographer in the Field.
Photograph by J. K. HILLERS, U. S. Geol. Surv.

world. Even the Grand Canyon itself is hardly more wonderful. To the right and below us lay the fair green fields of Toquerville, on the opposite side of the Virgen, and all around was such a labyrinth of mountains, canyons, cliffs, hills, valleys, rocks, and ravines, as fairly to make one's head swim. I think that perhaps, of all the views I have seen in the West, this was one of the weirdest and wildest. From Berry Spring in this valley a party of us returned to the Uinkaret district by following the country to the west of the Hurricane Ledge. On this occasion we again climbed Mt. Trumbull and some of the others of the group; and Dodds and I descended at the foot of the Toroweap to the river at the rapid called Lava Falls. It was a difficult climb.

In triangulating I often had occasion to take the bearings of two large buttes lying to the north-west, and in order that my recorder could put down the readings so that I might identify them later I was obliged to give him titles for these. They had no names in our language, and I did not know the native ones, so, remembering that at the foot of one I had found some ant-hills covered with beautiful diamond-like quartz crystals, I called it Diamond Butte, and the other, having a dark, weird, forbidding look, I named on the spur of the moment Solitaire Butte. These names being used by the other members of the corps, they became fixtures and are now on all the maps. I had no idea at that time of their becoming permanent. This was also the case with a large butte on the east side of Marble Canyon, which I had occasion to sight to from the Kaibab. It stood up so like a great altar, and, having in my mind the house-building Amerinds who had formerly occupied the country, and whom the Pai Utes called Shinumo, I called it Shinumo Altar, the name it now bears. Probably there are people who wonder where the altar is from which it was named. It was the appearance that suggested the title, not any archæological find. Once when we were in the Uinkaret country, Powell came in from a climb to the summit of what he named Mt. Logan, and said he had just seen a fine mountain off to the south-west which he would name after me. Of course I was much pleased at having my name thus perpetuated. The mountain turned out to be the culminating point of the Shewits Plateau. None of us visited it at that time, but Thompson went there later, and I crossed its slopes twice several years afterward. On the summit is a circular ruin about twenty feet in diameter with walls remaining two feet high.

It will be remembered that we had left one of our boats near the mouth of the Dirty Devil River. A party was to go overland to that point and bring this boat down to the Paria, and on the 25th of May (1872) Thompson started at the head of the party to try to explore a way in to the mouth of the Dirty Devil, at the same time investigating the country lying in between and examining the Unknown or Dirty Devil Mountains which had been seen from the river, just west of the course of the Dirty Devil River, now named Frémont River. We went west to a ranch called Johnson after the owner, thence north-westerly, passing the little Mormon settlement of Clarkson, and then struck out into the wilderness. Keeping a north-westerly course we crossed the upper

Lake on the Aquarius Plateau.
Photograph by J. K. Hillers, U. S. Colo. Riv. Exp.

waters of the Paria and made our way to the head of a stream flowing through what was called Potato Valley, and which the party of the previous year had followed down, endeavouring to find a trail by which to bring rations to us, under the impression that it was the head of the Dirty Devil. We also turned our course down it with the same idea. We had taken with us a Pai Ute guide whom we called Tom, but as we advanced into this region so far from his range, Tom got nervous and wanted to go back, and we saw him no more till our return. Six years before a Mormon reconnoitring party had penetrated as far as this, and in one place en route we passed the spot where one of their number who had been killed by the Utes had been buried. The grave had been dug out by the wolves, and a few whitened bones lay scattered around. It was a place where there was no water and we could not stop to reinter them. Several days after this we reached a point where progress seemed to be impossible in that direction, and Thompson and Dodds climbed up on high ground to reconnoitre. When they came back they said we were not on the headwaters of the Dirty Devil at all, and would be obliged to change our course completely. The Dirty Devil entered the Colorado on the other side of the Unknown Range and the stream we were on joined it on this side, the west, therefore it was plain that we had made a mistake. Accordingly, our steps were retraced to a point where we managed to ascend to the slopes of what is now called the Aquarius Plateau. Three men were sent back to Kanab after more rations, while Thompson with the other six pushed on around the slopes, trying to find a way to cross the labyrinth of canyons to the Unknown Mountains. On the 9th of June we were at an altitude of ten thousand feet above sea-level, with all the wilderness of canyons, cliffs, and buttes between us and the Colorado spreading below like a map, or rather like some kaleidoscopic phantasm. The slopes we were crossing were full of leaping torrents and clear lakes. They were so covered with these that the plateau afterwards was given the name Aquarius. Beaman, who had been photographer on our river trip, had left us, and we now had a new man from Salt Lake, named Fennemore. He was a frail man and the trip was almost too much for him. Down below we saw the smokes of native fires in several places, but we could not tell by what tribe they were made. At last we came to a point where the plateau broke back to the north, and we paused to search for a way to continue. I was sent out in one direction with one man, and Thompson went in another. I had not gone half a mile before I found an old trail which had very recently been travelled by natives, and when I had followed it far enough to get its trend, and as far as I dared, for I feared running on the camp at any point, I returned to report. Thompson decided to take this trail. It led us across strange country, and in one place for a long distance over barren sandstone into a peculiar valley. Here we camped about three miles from a great smoke, and the next morning ran right on top of a Ute encampment. At first we expected trouble, but there were only seven of the warriors, and they were, as we learned later, out of powder, so when they sighted us they disappeared. At last they returned, and we had a talk with them, trying to induce one to

Butte in Grand Gulch.

A tributary of the San Juan.
Photograph by CHARLES GOODMAN.

go with us as guide. They described the trails, but refused to go along.

We camped one night near them, and then went on, arriving finally, after a great deal of trouble at the Unknown Mountains, since called the Henry Mountains, having taken a wrong trail. At one place we were obliged to take the whole pack-train up a cliff fifteen hundred feet high, making a trail as we went. On the top were some water-pockets. We watered the stock at one of these the next morning, when we were obliged fairly to lift the horses out of the gulch by putting our

shoulders to their haunches.   At last, however, we got to the
mountains, and though it was now the 17th of June water
froze one half inch thick in the kettles in our camp about
fifteen hundred feet up the slopes.   Thompson climbed one of

Repairing Boat Near Mouth of Frémont River on the Colorado, 1872.
Photograph by J. FENNEMORE, U. S. Colo. Riv. Exp.

the mountains, and I started up another, but my companion
gave out.   We crossed through a pass, and on the 22d, after
pursuing a winding and difficult road through canyons, succeeded in getting the whole train down to the Colorado a
short distance below the mouth of the Dirty Devil.   The

Colorado was high, and swept along majestically. We found it had been up as far as the *Cañonita*, and had almost washed away one of the oars. We soon ran her down to our camp, and there put her in order for the journey, which from here to the Paria could be nothing more than a pleasure trip. Thompson, Dodds, and Andy left the rest of us and returned on the trail towards Kanab. Those left for the boat's crew besides myself were Hillers, Fennemore, the photographer, and W. D. Johnson. The latter was from Kanab, and was a Mormon, as was also the photographer, and both were fine fellows. The river was at flood and we had an easy time of it so far as travelling was concerned. Our investigations and photographing sometimes consumed half a day, but in the other half we made good progress, eight or nine miles without trying.

Major Powell in the Field, 1872.

The rations were limited in variety, but were abundant of their kind, being almost entirely bread and black coffee. When we tried, we made great runs, one day easily accomplishing about forty miles. The San Juan was now a powerful stream, as we saw on passing. At the Music Temple we camped, and I cut Hillers's and my name on the rocks. Fennemore made a picture of the place, given on page 215. On the

13th of July we reached the Paria, where we expected to find several of our party, but they were not there. We discovered that some one had come in here since our last visit, and built a house. It proved to be John D. Lee, of Mountain Meadow Massacre notoriety, who had established a home here for one of his two remaining wives. He called the place Lonely Dell, and it was not a misnomer. It is now known as Lee's Ferry. Mrs. Lee XVIII. proved to be an agreeable woman, and she and her husband treated us very kindly, inviting us, as we had nothing but bread and coffee, to share their table, an offer we gladly accepted. Here Johnson and Fennemore left us, going out with Lee to Kanab, and two days later we were relieved to see some of our men arrive with a large amount of supplies and mail. We then waited for the coming of Powell and Thompson with the others, when we were to cast off and run the gauntlet of the Grand Canyon.

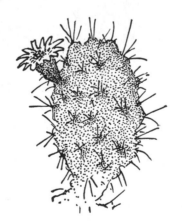

CHAPTER XIII

A Canyon through Marble—Multitudinous Rapids—Running the Sockdologer—A Difficult Portage, Rising Water, and a Trap—The *Dean* Upside Down—A Close Shave—Whirlpools and Fountains—The Kanab Canyon and the End of the Voyage.

BY referring to the relief map opposite page 41, the mouth of the Paria is seen a trifle more than half-way up the right-hand side. The walls of Glen Canyon here recede from the river and become on the south the Echo Cliffs, taking the name from the Echo Peaks which form their beginning, and on the north the Vermilion Cliffs, so called by Powell because of their bright red colour. The latter, and the canyon of the Paria, make the edges of the great mesa called the Paria Plateau, and, running on north to the very head of the Kaibab uplift, strike off south-westerly to near Pipe Spring, where they turn and run in a north-west direction to the Virgen River. Between the receding lines of these cliffs, at the Paria, is practically the head of the Grand Canyon. The river at once begins an attack on the underlying strata, and the resulting canyon, while at first not more than two hundred feet deep, rapidly increases this depth, as the strata run up and the river runs down. The canyon is narrow, and seen from a height resembles, as previously mentioned, a dark serpent lying across a plain. As the formation down to the Little Colorado is mainly a fine-grained grey marble, Powell concluded to call this division by a separate name, and gave it the title it now bears, Marble Canyon. There is no separation between Marble Canyon and the following one, the Grand Canyon, except the narrow gorge of the Little Colorado, so that topographically the chasm which begins at the Paria, ends at the Grand Wash, a distance of 283 miles, as the river runs, the longest, deepest, and altogether most magnificent example of the canyon formation to be found on the globe. With an average depth of about four thousand feet, it reaches for long stretches between five thousand and six thousand. At the Paria (Lee's Ferry) the altitude above the sea is 3170 feet, while at the end of the canyon, the Grand Wash, the elevation is only 840 feet. The declivity is thus very great (see the diagram on page 57, which gives from the Little Colorado down), the total fall being 2330 feet. Further comment on the character of the river within this wonderful gorge is unnecessary. Powell had been through it on his first expedition, and was now to make the passage again, to examine its geological and geographical features more in detail.

Navajos in Characteristic Dress.
Photograph by F. S. DELLENBAUGH.

Meanwhile, as recorded in the last chapter, Lieutenant Wheeler had made an effort, apparently to forestall this examination, and had precariously succeeded in reaching Diamond Creek, which is just at the south end of the Shewits Plateau, lower left-hand corner of the map facing page 41.

Powell and Thompson arrived at our camp at the mouth of the Paria on the 13th of August (1872) accompanied by Mrs. Thompson, who had been at Kanab all the previous winter, and had pluckily made several trips with Thompson into the mountains, and Professor De Motte. They had come in by

way of the south end of the Kaibab, and it was on this occasion that the valley on the southern part of the summit was
named De Motte Park. Preparations for our descent through
the great chasm were immediately begun. The boats had been
previously overhauled, and as the *Nellie Powell* was found un-
seaworthy from last season's knocks, or at least not in condition to be relied on in the Grand Canyon, she was abandoned,
and Lee kept her for a ferry-boat. Perhaps she might have
been repaired, but anyhow we had only men enough to
handle two boats. Steward's trouble had not sufficiently improved to warrant his risking further exposure, so he had returned to his home in Illinois. Bishop was in a similar plight,
and went to Salt Lake to regain his health, and Beaman had
started off to carry on some photographic operations of his
own. He came to the river and crossed on his way to the
Moki country, while we were preparing to depart from the
Paria. Johnson and Fennemore, who had been with us part
of the winter, were too ill to think of entering the great canyon, with all the uncertainties of such a venture, and as before
noted they, too, had left. Our party, then, consisted of seven:
Powell, Thompson, Hillers, Jones, W. C. Powell, Hattan, and
Dellenbaugh, all from the first season's crew. No one else was
available, as the trip was regarded in that region as extremely
desperate. On the 14th, the boats, *Emma Dean* and *Cañonita*,
were in readiness, and we loaded and took them down a mile
and a half to the point near where the road came in from
Kanab, whence our final departure would be made as soon as
Powell, who needed a little extra time for arranging his papers
and general affairs, should say the word. Everything was
carefully attended to, as if we were preparing our last will
and testament, and were never to be seen alive again, and I
believe this was the firm conviction of most of those not going
with the boats. Those who were going had abundant respect
for the dragon, and well knew that no holiday excursion
was before them. Their spirit was humble, and no precaution was to be neglected; no spirit of bravado permitted to
endanger the success of the undertaking. Mrs. Thompson and
De Motte ran down with us through two small rapids that exist

at the mouth of the Paria, and which we had to pass to reach
the camp mentioned. Mrs. Thompson would willingly have
gone all the way through if her husband had consented to it.

On the 15th it was "all ashore not going"; we said our
farewells to those leaving for Kanab, and turned our attention
to the river. We would see no one after starting till we arrived at the mouth of the Kanab, where we had discovered,
during the winter, that a pack-train, with some difficulty, could
be brought in with supplies. It was not till the 17th that we
were able to leave, as the boats needed some further attention.
On that day, about nine o'clock, we cast off and went down
some five miles, running one little rapid and another of considerable size before we halted for dinner. The walls were
still not high, only about five hundred feet, and I climbed out
to secure a farewell glance at the open country. On starting
again we had not gone far before we came to a really bad
place, a fall of about eighteen feet in seventy-five yards, where
it was deemed respectful to make a portage. This accomplished, another of the same nature, with an equally fierce growl,
discovered itself not far below, and a camp was made where
we landed at its head. This was ten miles below our starting-
point, and seemed to be the spot where a band of ten mining
prospectors were wrecked about a month before. They had
gone in to the mouth of the Paria on a prospecting trip, and
concluded they would examine the Grand Canyon. Consequently they built a large raft, and after helping themselves to
a lot of our cooking utensils and other things from some caches
we had made when we went out from the river for our winter's
work, they sailed away, expecting to accomplish wonders.
Ten miles, to the first bad rapids, was the extent of their
voyage, and there they were fortunate to escape with their
lives, but nothing else, and by means of ladders made from
driftwood, they reached once more the outer world, having
learned the lesson the Colorado is sure to teach those who regard it lightly. We made a portage at the place and enjoyed a
good laugh when we looked at the vertical rocks and pictured
the prospectors dismally crawling out of the roaring waters
with nothing left but the clothes on their backs. Our opinion

Marble Canyon.

Photograph by J. K. HILLERS, U. S. Colo. Riv. Exp.

was, they were served just right: first, because they had stolen
our property, and, second, because they had so little sense.
The walls had rapidly grown in altitude, and near the river
were vertical so that climbing out at this place was a particularly difficult undertaking.   The river was still very high, but
not at the highest stage of this year, which had been passed
before the *Cañonita* party had come down to the Paria from
Frémont River.   But the canyon was even yet uncomfortably
full and we were hoping the water would diminish rapidly, for
high tide in such a place is a great disadvantage.   The stream
was thick with red mud, the condition from which it derived
its name, and it swept along with a splendid vigour that be-
tokened a large reserve flood in the high mountains.   The
marble composing the walls of this canyon for most of its
length is of a greyish drab colour often beautifully veined, but
it must not be supposed that the walls are the same colour
externally, for they are usually a deep red, due to the dis-
coloration of their surface by disintegration of beds above full
of iron.   Except where high water had scoured the walls,
there was generally no indication of their real colour.   In places
the friction of the current had brought them to a glistening
polish; the surface was smooth as glass, and was sometimes cut
into multitudinous irregular flutings as deep as one's finger.
The grinding power of the current was well shown in some of
the boulders, which had been dovetailed together till the
irregular line of juncture was barely perceptible.

The next day was begun by accomplishing the portage over
the rapid which had punished the prospectors for their temerity
and for their lack of proper morals, and then we made most
excellent progress, successfully putting behind us eleven lively
rapids free from rocks before we were admonished to pause
and make a let-down.   Then camp was established for the
night with the record of ten and three-eighths miles for our
day's work.   At one place we passed a rock in the water so
large that it almost blocked the entire stream, which had averaged about two hundred feet in width, though narrowing
at many places to no more than seventy-five.   The current
was always extremely swift, while many whirlpools added

their demands, though they gave us no serious trouble. It is exasperating, however, to be turned around against one's will. The canyon at the top for a considerable distance was not over three-quarters of a mile wide. The depth was now from fifteen hundred to eighteen hundred feet. There were always rapids following quickly one after another, but so often they were free from rocks, the dangerous part of most rapids, that we were able to sail through them in triumph. On the 20th, out of thirteen sharp descents, we easily ran twelve, all in a distance of less than seven miles. The average width of the river was one hundred and twenty-five feet, while the walls rose to over two thousand feet, and at the top the canyon was about a mile and a quarter from brink to brink. This brought us to Vesey's Paradise, so named after a botanist friend of his, by Powell on the first descent. It was only a lot of ferns, mosses, and similar plants growing around two springs that issued from the cliffs on the right about seventy-five feet above the river, and rippled in silver threads to the bottom, but as it was the first green spot since leaving the Paria its appearance was striking and attractive to the eye that had been baffled in all directions except above, in a search for something besides red. Now the narrow, terraced canyon, often vertical on both sides for several hundred feet above the water, grew ever deeper and deeper, two thousand, twenty-five hundred, three thousand feet and more, as the impetuous torrent slashed its way down, till it finally seemed to me as if we were actually sailing into the inner heart of the world. The sensation on the first expedition, when each dark new bend was a dark new mystery, must have been something to quite overpower the imagination, for then it was not known that, by good management, a boat could pass through this Valley of the Shadow of Death, and survive. Down, and down, and ever down, roaring and leaping and throwing its spiteful spray against the hampering rocks the terrible river ran, carrying our boats along with it like little wisps of straw in the midst of a Niagara, the terraced walls around us sometimes fantastically eroded into galleries, balconies, alcoves, and Gothic caves that lent to them an additional weird and wonderful aspect, while the reverberating turmoil of the ever-descending flood was like some extravagant musical accompaniment to the extraordinary panorama flitting past of rock sculpture and bounding cliffs.

The 22d was a day to be particularly remembered, for the walls, though more broken at the water's edge, were now some thirty-five hundred feet high and seemed to be increasing by leaps and bounds, for at one place, through a side gorge on the right, we could discern cliffs so far above our heads that

tall pine trees looked no larger than lead pencils. It was the end of the Kaibab, whose summit was more than five thousand feet higher than the river at this point. Cataract followed rapid and rapid followed cataract as we were hurled on down through the midst of the sublimity, which, parting at our advance, closed again behind like some wonderful phantasmagoria.

Marble Canyon near the Lower End.
Walls about 3500 feet.
Photograph by J. K. HILLERS, U. S. Colo. Riv. Exp.

At times in the headlong rush the boats could barely be held in control. Once, a wild mass of breakers appeared immediately in the path of our boat, from which it was impossible to escape, even though we made a severe effort to do so. We thought we were surely to be crushed, and I shall not forget the seconds that passed as we waited for the collision which never came, for when the boat dashed into the midst of the spray, there was no shock whatever; we glided through as if on oil,—the rocks were too far beneath the surface to harm us. So constant was the rush of the descending waters that our oars were needed only for guidance.

Late in the day there came a long straight stretch, at the bottom of which the river appeared to vanish. Had any one said the course was now underground from that point onward, it would have seemed entirely appropriate. In the outer world the sun was low, though it had long been gone to us, and the blue haze of approaching night was drawing a veil of strange uncertainty among the cliffs, while far above, the upper portions of the mighty eastern walls, at all times of gorgeous hue, were now beautifully enriched by the last hot radiance of the western sky. Such a view as this was worth all the labour we had accomplished. When the end of this marvellous piece of canyon was reached a small river was found to enter on the left through a narrow gorge like the main canyon. It was the Little Colorado, and beside it on a sand-bank we stopped for the night, having ended one of the finest runs of our experience, about eighteen miles with but a single let-down; yet in this distance there were eighteen rapids, one of which was about two and one half miles long. It was a glorious record, and I do not recall another day which was more exhilarating. We had arrived at the end of Marble Canyon and the beginning of the Grand Canyon, there being nothing to mark the division but the narrow gorge of the Little Colorado. In Marble Canyon we had found sixty-nine rapids in the sixty-five and one half miles, with a total descent of 480 feet. Of these we ran sixty, let down by lines five times, and made four portages. Here at the mouth of the Little Colorado was the place where White's imagination pictured overwhelming terrors and his worst experience in a whirlpool opposite. But in reality the Colorado at this particular point is very tame, and when we were there the Little Colorado was a lamb.

Now the Grand Canyon, as named by Powell on his former trip, was before us, and soon we were descending through the incomparable chasm. Three or four miles below the Little Colorado the walls break away, and the canyon has more the appearance of a valley hemmed in by beetling cliffs and crags which rise up in all directions over 5000 feet, distant from the line of the river five or six miles.   On the right were two minor valleys within the canyon called Nancoweap and Kwagunt, named by Powell after the Pai Utes, who have trails coming down into them.[1] As we went on, the canyon narrowed again, becoming wilder and grander than ever, and on the 28th,

F. S. Dellenbaugh, 1872.
The exploring costume consisted of a shirt as above, a pair of cotton overalls, heavy hobnailed shoes, and a felt hat.
Tintype by J. K. HILLERS.

late in the day, we came to the first bad fall in this division, where a portage was necessary, and we made a camp. A short distance below this camp the granite ran up. To any one who has been in this chasm with a boat, the term "the granite runs up" has a deep significance. It means that the First Granite Gorge is beginning, and this First Granite Gorge, in the Kaibab division of the canyon, less than fifty miles in length as the stream runs, contains the wildest, swiftest, steepest piece of river on this continent except a portion in Cataract Canyon.   The declivity is tremendous.   Between the Little Colorado and the Kanab the total fall is 890 feet, and the bulk of this drop occurs in the granite.   In one stretch of ten miles the descent is 210 feet.   All through this granite the character of the river is different from anything above.   The falls are short and violent, while the stretches in between are smooth

[1] Kwagunt was the name of a Pai Ute who said he owned this valley—that his father, who used to live there, had given it to him.

and not always swift. But the moment a break occurs the turbulence and commotion are instantly very great. The summer is the wet season here, and to add to our troubles we were treated to frequent rains. The next day toward

Granite Falls, Grand Canyon.
Photograph by J. K. HILLERS, U. S. Colo. Riv. Exp.

noon, as we were sailing along between the black walls, on a rather sluggish current, a deep-toned roar was borne up to our ears. Nothing could be seen of the cause of it, but a complete disappearance of the river from our sight warned us to make a landing as soon as possible. Some broken rocks

protruding a few feet above the water at the base of the right-
hand wall afforded the desired opportunity, and running in we
stepped out and mounted them.   The cause of the roaring
was immediately apparent.   For a third of a mile the river was a
solid mass of huge waves and foam and plunges, and on each
side the granite came down so precipitously that a footing was
impossible.   It took no second glance to tell us that, at least
with this stage of water, there was but one course, and that
was to run the place.   There is nothing like having the inner
man fortified for exertion, therefore with a few bits of driftwood a fire was built, by means of which Andy prepared dinner.
When this had been disposed of operations were begun.   The
Cañonita was to remain here till our boat was well through.
In case we smashed up they would have a better chance, as
they might profit by our course, and if we went through safely,
we would be prepared to pick them up should disaster overtake
them.   At last we were ready.   The crew of the *Cañonita*
placed themselves where they could carefully watch our fort-
unes, and we pulled up the river very close to the right-hand
wall in slack current, for about a quarter of a mile, when we
turned the bow out and struck for the middle, heading there
straight for the descent.   I pulled the bow oars, and my back
was toward the terrific roar which, like the voice of some awful
monster, grew louder as we approached.   It was difficult to
refrain from turning round to see what it looked like now, but
as everything depended on the promptness with which Hillers
and I handled our oars in obedience to Powell's orders, I waited
for the plunge, every instant ready to execute a command.
We kept in the middle of the stream, and as we neared the
brink our speed began to accelerate.   Then of a sudden there
was a dropping away of all support, a reeling sensation, and
we flew down the declivity with the speed of a locomotive.
The gorge was chaos.   The boat rolled and plunged.   The
wild waters rolled over us, filling the open spaces to the gunwale.   With the camp kettles that were left out of the cabins
for that purpose, Hillers and I bailed as hard as we could, let-
ting the boat go with the current, but it seemed to do little
good, for every moment the waves broke over the craft from

Running the Sockdologer, Grand Canyon.
Fall 80 feet in ½ mile.
Studio painting by F. S. DELLENBAUGH.

end to end, and our efforts might as well have been made with a teaspoon, though in many other rapids the kettles had proved effective. Here and there, as we shot down, I could look back under a canopy of foam and see the head of a great black rock. Fortunately we safely cleared everything, and in probably less than a minute we were at the bottom, lying to in an eddy, bailing fast and watching for the other boat. No sign of any living thing could be discovered as we peered up the rapid, which from below had the appearance of an almost vertical fall. Presently at the top of the foam a white speck moved, clearly seen against the dark background. It was the *Cañonita* on the edge of the fall. I can see her yet, pausing for an instant, apparently, and then disappearing completely amidst the plunging waters. A minute later she reappeared at the bottom and ran alongside of us in good order. Owing to the large amount of water there seemed to be not much danger of striking a rock, and our boats did not capsize easily. After the plunge was begun we did not try to guide the boats— it would have been useless. The fall here was about eighty feet in a third of a mile. Some of the men called it the Sockdologer. The picture of it from above, on page 219, does not give a correct impression, as the plate was too slow, but it was the best that could be done at the time. The canyon continued very narrow at the bottom, the river averaging about one hundred and fifty feet. Late in the afternoon we arrived at a much worse place than the Sockdologer, though the fall was not so great. Landing on the left on some broken rocks, we saw no chance of getting around the rapid there, so we crossed to the right and landed on another little pile of rocks in a small alcove. The walls rose vertically, or nearly so, from the water's edge. We saw the only thing to do was to lower one boat, with two men on board, by her line for some distance (a hundred feet of best Manila rope were attached to each boat by a strong iron ring; in the stern was also an iron ring), and from the stern let the other cautiously down to the very head of the fall, where there was a second pile of rocks which received the boat between them and held her fast. The upper boat was then pulled back to where we had remained, the line from the second being tied to her stern. Entering her we clung to projections of the wall with our hands, to prevent the current from swinging the boat out, while the men who were in the lower boat carefully hauled on the stern line till at last we also reached the rocks. With a great deal of labour we then worked both boats from these rocks to some others nearer the right wall, from which they were manœuvred across to a pile about two hundred feet away against the foot of the cliff. This ended our struggle for the day, as night was upon us. The black rocks towering so far above made the gorge darken early, and rain began to fall. A little damp driftwood was collected with which a fire was started in order that Andy might prepare supper. When this was almost ready peal after peal of thunder suddenly crashed among the cliffs, which seemed to collapse and fall down upon us, and a flood from the sky descended. The fire died without a sputter, everything not in rubber was soaked, and all we could do was to stand in the darkness, cold and hungry, and wait for the deluge to cease. At last we were able to start the fire once more, and had a half-cooked supper before hunting the soft sides of the rocks for beds. The next day it required hard work till one o'clock to get the boats down two hundred yards farther. At one place to keep the bow in, I was in one of the boats, being lowered along the wall, while the other men were a hundred feet above my head, holding the end of two hundred feet of rope, as they clambered along a ledge. The situation all around was rather precarious, but we had no accident. This brought us to a small alcove where there was a limited talus. The boats were so much bruised that we were obliged to halt on these rocks for repairs, instead of starting out again into the current as we intended. This work took so long that darkness approached before all was done. At the same time we discovered that the river was rising rapidly, at the rate of three or four feet an hour, submerging the rocks. Fortunately, about twenty feet up the cliff was a narrow shelf, and to this the rations were passed to guard them from the rising waters. Then there was danger of the boats pounding to pieces, as the space they were on was rapidly decreasing, and waves from the rapid swept into the cove, so it was decided to raise them up on the side of the wall as far as necessary.   By means of the ropes we succeeded in swinging them at a height of about six feet and there made them fast for the night.   There was not room on the ledge for a camp, but by going out around a projection a talus was available, though there was a dearth of wood and level spots.   I managed to find enough half-dead mesquite bushes for a fire, and Andy did his best on the supper.   One hundred feet above the river I found driftwood.   To add to the discomfort of the occasion the rain began again, and the river continued its rise.   Through the night a watch was kept on the boats, so that they could be lifted farther if necessary. The morning of August 31st was wet and gloomy in the black gorge.   Some of the rocks were still above water, against the wall.   When the boats were lowered they pounded about at a frightful rate on the surges that swept into the alcove.   Then it was found that a hole in the *Dean* had been forgotten or overlooked, and she was leaking badly in the middle compartment.   But there was no chance to stop longer here for repairs, as the river seemed to be still rising.   A bag of flour was jammed against the hole, the boat was loaded, the hatches were battened down, we grasped our oars, and while the *Cañonita* crew held our stern to give us a fair start we pulled straight out as hard as we could to clear a huge rock just below, upon which the current was fiercely dashing.   Our boat was so wet and full of water that the gunwales were barely above the surface as we rolled heavily along through large waves.   I felt very uncertain as to whether or not she would remain afloat till we could make a landing, but luckily she did, and we halted at the first opportunity.   This was at a talus on the right where the entire cargo was spread out on the rocks to dry in the sun which now cheered us by its warm rays, and the leak in the boat was stopped.   The *Cañonita* soon came down safely. She was of a slightly better build than the *Dean*, and, with one less man in her, was able to ride more buoyantly.   It was after four o'clock before we were ready to go on, and we started once more with a fairly tight boat, dry inside.   Then we had a wild ride.   The descent was steady.   For eight miles there was a continuous rapid, accentuated by eight heavy falls. The boats sped along at high speed, but the way being clear we did not often stop, passing two places where the former expedition made portages. We had a glimpse of a creek coming in

Looking up a Side Canyon of the Grand Canyon in the Kaibab Division.
Photograph by J. K. HILLERS, U. S. Colo. Riv. Exp.

on the right which looked interesting, but it was left behind in a moment as the boats shot along between the dark granite walls. At a quarter past five we ran up to a sand-bank where a lone willow tree was growing. Here we made a camp. The canyon spread a little and the wide sand-bank appeared to our eyes like a prairie. Just below our camp there came in a muddy stream, which on the other trip was clear and was then named Bright Angel to offset the application of Dirty Devil to the river at the foot of Narrow Canyon.

It was now the beginning of September, but the water and the air were not so cold as they had been the year before in Cataract Canyon, and we did not suffer from being so constantly saturated. Running on the next day following the Bright Angel camp, we found the usual number of large rapids, in one of which a wave struck the steering oar and knocked Jones out of the boat all but his knees, by which he clung to the gunwale, nearly capsizing us. We found it impossible to help him, but somehow he got in again. The river was everywhere very swift and turbulent. One stretch of three and a half miles we ran in fifteen minutes. There were numerous whirlpools, but nothing to stop our triumphant progress. On the 2d of September there were two portages, and twenty rapids run, in the fifteen miles made during the day. Many of these rapids were very heavy descents. That night we camped above a bad-looking place, but it was decided to run it in the morning. Three-quarters of a mile below camp there was a general disappearance of the waters. We could see nothing of the great rapid from the level of the boats, though we caught an occasional glimpse of the leaping, tossing edges, or tops, of the huge billows rolling out beyond into the farther depths of the chasm. About eight o'clock in the morning all was ready for the start. The inflated life-preservers, as was customary in our boat, were laid behind the seats where we could easily reach them. The Major put his on, a most fortunate thing for him as it turned out, but we who were at the oars did not for the reason before mentioned,—that they interfered with the free handling of the boat. The men of the *Cañonita* took positions where they could observe and profit by our movements. Then out into the current we pushed and were immediately swept downward with ever-increasing speed toward the centre of the disturbance, the black walls springing up on each side of the impetuous waters like mighty buttresses for the lovely blue vault of the September sky, so serenely

A Capsize in the Grand Canyon.
Drawing by F. S. DELLENBAUGH.

quiet. Accelerated by the rush of a small intervening rapid, our velocity appeared to multiply till we were flying along like a railway train. The whole width of the river dropped away before us, falling some twenty-five or thirty feet, at least, in a short space. We now saw that the rapid was of a particularly difficult nature, and the order was given to attempt a landing on some rocks at its head, on the left. At the same instant this was seen to be impossible. Our only safety lay in taking the plunge in the main channel. We backwatered on our oars to check our speed a trifle, and the next moment with a wild leap we went over, charging into the roaring, seething, beating waves below. Wave after wave broke over us in quick succession, keeping our standing-rooms full. The boat plunged like a bucking broncho, at the same time rolling with fierce violence. As rapidly as possible we bailed with our kettles, but the effort was useless. At length, as we neared the end, an immense billow broke upon our port bow with a resounding crack. The little craft succumbed. With a quick careen she turned upside down, and we were in the foaming current. I threw up my hand and fortunately grasped a spare oar that was fastened along the outside of the boat. This enabled me to pull myself above the surface and breathe. My felt hat had stuck to my head and now almost suffocated me. Pushing it back I looked around. Not a sign of life was to be seen. The river disappeared below in the dark granite. My companions were gone. I was apparently alone in the great chasm. But in a moment or two Powell and Hillers, who had both been pulled down by the whirlpool that was keeping all together, shot up like rockets beside me, and then I noticed Jones clinging to the ring in the stern. As we told Powell, after this experience was over, he had tried to make a geological investigation of the bed of the river, and this was not advisable. Hillers and I climbed on the bottom of the upturned boat, and by catching hold of the opposite gunwale, and throwing ourselves back, we brought her right-side up. Then we two climbed in, an operation requiring nice calculation, for she rolled so much with the load of water that her tendency was to turn over again on slight provocation. We bailed with our hats rapidly. There was need for expeditious work, for we could not tell what might be around the corner. Presently enough water was out to steady the boat, and we then helped Powell and Jones to get in. Our oars had fortunately remained in the rowlocks, and grasping them, without waiting to haul in the hundred feet of line trailing in the current, we made for the left wall, where I managed to leap out on a shelf and catch the rope over a projection, before the *Cañonita*, unharmed, dashed up to the spot; her only mishap was the loss of a rowlock and two oars.

Starting once more on the swift current, we found rapids sometimes so situated that it was difficult to make a landing for examination. At one of these places, towards evening, a good deal of time was spent working down to the head of an ugly looking spot which could not be fairly seen. An enormous rock lay in the very middle at the head of the descent. There was no landing-place till very near the plunge, and in dropping down when we came to the point where it was planned that I should jump out upon a projecting flat rock, a sudden lurch of the boat due to what Stanton afterwards called fountains, and we termed boils, caused me, instead of landing on the rock, to disappear in the rushing waters. The current catching the boat, she began to move rapidly stern foremost toward the fall. Powell and Jones jumped out on rocks as they shot past, hoping to catch the line, but they could not reach it, and Jones had all he could do to get ashore. Meanwhile I had come to the surface, and going to the boat by means of the line which I still held, I fairly tumbled on board. Hillers handed me one of my oars which had come loose, and we were ready to take the fall, now close at hand, albeit we were stern first. As we sped down, the tide carried us far up on the huge rock, whose shelving surface sank upstream below the surging torrent, and at the same moment turned our bow towards the left-hand bank. Perceiving this advantage we pulled with all our strength and shot across the very head of the rapid, running in behind a large rock on the brink, where the boat lodged till I was able to leap ashore, or rather to another rock where there was a footing, and make fast the line.

It was a close shave.   The *Cañonita,* forewarned, was able to let
down to this place, from whence we made a portage to the bottom the next morning.   When once started again, we found ourselves in a very narrow gorge, where for four or five miles it was
impossible to stop on account of the swift current which swept
the boats along like chaff before a gale, swinging them from

The Grand Canyon. Looking down from Mouth of Kanab Canyon in Winter.
Photograph by E. O. BEAMAN.

one side to the other, and often turning them round and round
in the large whirlpools despite every effort we made to prevent
this performance.   In fact, we had no control of the craft in
this distance, and it was fortunate that there was nothing
worse to be here encountered.   The whirlpools were the most
perfect specimens I ever saw.   Usually they were about twenty

feet in diameter, drawing evenly down toward the vortex, the centre being probably about eighteen inches to two feet below the rim. The vortex at the top was about six to ten inches in diameter, diminishing in five or six feet to a mere point at the bottom. Our boats were twenty-two feet long, and as they were turned around in these whirls they about reached across them, while we could look over the side and see the vortex sucking down every small object. The opposite of these was the fountains, or boils, where the surface was exactly the reverse of the whirls: a circular mass of water about twenty feet in diameter would suddenly lift itself a foot or two above the general surface with a boiling, swirling movement. As I remember them they were usually the forerunners of the whirlpools.

The Outlet of the Creek in Surprise Valley, near the Mouth of Kanab Canyon, Grand Canyon.

Photograph by E. O. BEAMAN.

The river was still on the rise, scoring at the last camp another three feet. With such a dashing current the time we made where we were not compelled to move cautiously was admirable. On this day fourteen miles were traversed, we ran twenty-three rapids, and, what pleased us most, we saw the granite disappear, and the comfortable-looking red strata were again beside us. The river widened somewhat, and was now about two hundred and fifty feet. A cascade was passed on the 7th, which we recognized as one Beaman, who had climbed up to it during the winter, from the mouth of the Kanab, had photographed. From here to the Kanab was ten miles, and we sailed along with lightened hearts, knowing that our sadly depleted and half-ruined stock of rations would soon be replenished, and that mail from the world would be delivered by the pack-train we expected to find there. Late in the afternoon we arrived

Mouth of Kanab Canyon.
Abandoned boats of the U. S. Colo. Riv. Exp., 1872.
The Colorado flows just beyond the points on the left and right.
Photograph by J. K. HILLERS, U. S. Colo. Riv. Exp.

at the narrow cleft, and our men, who had waited long, were overjoyed to greet us once more, for, as we were several days overdue, they had been filled with forebodings, and had made up their minds they would never see us again.

From the Little Colorado we had travelled one hundred and eight miles, run one hundred and thirty-one rapids, made seven portages, and let down six times. The water had now fallen again some three feet, but it was still so high that it had backed up into the side canyon, where we ran the boats on account of an excellent camping-place. Sunday was spent resting here, and Thompson took observations for time. On Monday morning we expected to pack up again and proceed down the gorge, but Powell, instead of directing this course, announced that he had decided to end the river work at this point on account of the extreme high water, which would render impassable the rapid where the Howlands and Dunn had left. In addition, word was brought that the Shewits were in a state of war and had resolved to ambush us as we came down, a plot that had been revealed by a friendly member of the tribe to Jacob Hamblin. The ambush plan did not disturb us much, however, but the stage of water for the beginning of the Second Granite Gorge was another matter, and there was no telling when it would fall. It had been demonstrated by our winter's explorations that it would not be absolutely necessary for us to continue below this point so far as perfecting the topographic work was concerned, and as we were there for geographic purposes and not for adventure, the decision was against unnecessary risk. This decision then was, and ever since has been, a matter of great disappointment to me, for I was ready to finish up the Grand Canyon. It was with mingled feelings of regret and relief that I helped unload the boats, those faithful friends, which had carried us safely over so many miles of turbulent river, and from the constant hourly association had almost taken on a personality, till they seemed like members of the party. Sadly I turned my back on their familiar lines and followed the pack-train up the narrow gorge in the direction of Kanab.

CHAPTER XIV

THE topographic, geologic, and geodetic work of the survey did not cease with our departure from the river, but was continued in the remarkable country shown in the relief map opposite page 41, till the relationships and distances of the various features were established and reduced to black and white. That autumn, while we were engaged in these labours, Wheeler, with an elaborate outfit, entered the region, pursuing his desultory operations; and, drifting along the north side of the Grand Canyon for a little distance, he proceeded to the neighbourhood of St. George. The following year, for some unknown purpose, he crossed the Colorado at the Paria, though he knew that Powell's parties had previously mapped this area. When the winter of 1872–73 had fairly set in we established a permanent camp at Kanab, where, under Thompson's always efficient direction, our triangulations and topographic notes were plotted on paper, making the first preliminary map of that country. When this was ready, Hillers and I took it, and crossing the southern end of the High Plateaus, then deep with snow, we rode by way of the Sevier Valley to Salt Lake, where the map was sent on by express to Washington, whither Powell had already gone.

Seventeen years passed away before any one again tried to navigate the Colorado. The settling of the country, the knowledge of it Powell had published, the completion of the Southern Pacific Railway to Yuma in 1877, and of the Atlantic

and Pacific from Isleta to The Needles, in 1880–83, and of the
Rio Grande Western across the Green at Gunnison Valley,
simplified travel in the Basin of the Colorado.   A new railway
was then proposed from Grand Junction, Colorado, down the
Colorado River, through the Canyons to the Gulf of California,
a distance of twelve hundred miles.   At that time coal was a
difficult article to procure on the Pacific Coast, and it was
thought that this "water-level" road, crossing no mountains,

Camp at Oak Spring, Uinkaret Mountains.
Photograph by J. K. HILLERS, U. S. Colo. Riv. Exp.

would be profitable in bringing the coal of Colorado to the
Golden Gate.   At present coal in abundance is to be had in
the Puget Sound region, and this reason for constructing a
Grand Canyon railway is done away with.   There is nothing
to support a railway through the three hundred miles of the
great gorge (or through the other two hundred miles of canyon
to the Junction), except tourist travel and the possible development of mines.   These are manifestly insufficient at the present time to warrant even a less costly railway, which, averaging

about four thousand feet below the surface of the surrounding country, would be of little service to those living away from its immediate line, and there is small chance to live along the line. In addition the floods in the Grand Canyon are enorm-

Mukoontuweap Canyon, North Fork of the Virgen.
Ten miles long, 3500 feet deep.
Photograph by J. K. HILLERS, U. S. Geol. Surv.

ous and capricious. Sometimes heavy torrents from cloud-bursts plunge down the sides of the canyon and these would require to be considered as well as those of the river itself. To be absolutely safe from the latter the line would probably require, in the Grand Canyon, to be built at least one hundred and twenty feet above low water, so that for the whole distance through the Marble-Grand Canyon there would seldom be room beside the tracks for even a station. But Frank M. Brown had faith, and a company for the construction of the Denver, Colorado Canyon, and Pacific Railway was organised. Brown

Looking down the Canyon de Chelly, a Tributary of the San Juan and Containing many Cliff Houses.
Photograph by BEN. WITTICK.

was the president, and in 1889 he formed an expedition to survey the line.

On March 25th the preliminary party, consisting of F. M. Brown, F. C. Kendrick, chief engineer, and T. P. Rigney, assistant engineer, left Denver for Grand Junction, a station on the Rio Grande Western (near the C of Colorado, State name on map, p. 51), and the next morning set the first stake for the new railway which was to cost the president so dear. Then they bought a boat from the ferryman, and after repairing it laid in a supply of rations, engaged some men, and ran a half-mile down Grand River. Brown then left to go East in order to perfect his arrangements for this attempt to survey a railway route through the dangerous canyons. The boat party continued down Grand River to the head of the canyon, twenty-four miles, and then more slowly descended over rougher water, averaging five or six miles a day. At a distance of forty-three miles from the start the rapids grew very bad, and at one place they were forced to make a portage for twelve miles. At the end of one hundred miles they came to the little Mormon settlement of Moab. From here to the Junction of the Grand and Green was a distance of sixty miles, and the water was the same as it is just above the Junction, in the canyons of the Green, Stillwater, and Labyrinth, that is, comparatively smooth and offering no obstacles except a rather swift current. Nowhere had the cliffs risen above one thousand feet, and the river had an average fall of five feet to the mile. This was the first party on record to navigate, for any considerable distance, the canyons of Grand River. From the Junction they proceeded up the Green, towing the boat, desiring to reach the Rio Grande Western Railway crossing, one hundred and twenty miles away. By this time their rations were much diminished and they allowed themselves each day only one-half the ordinary amount, at the same time going on up the river as fast as possible, yet at the end of about eight days, when still thirty miles from their destination, they were reduced to their last meal. Fortunately they then arrived at the cabin of some cattlemen, Wheeler Brothers, who, discovering their plight, put their own ample larder, with true Western hospitality, at the surveyors' disposal. Thus opportunely fortified and refreshed, the men reached the railway crossing the following night.

In reviewing all the early travels through this inhospitable region, one is struck by the frequent neglect of the question of food-supplies. In such a barren land, this is the item of first importance, and yet many of the leaders treated it apparently as of slight consequence. Great discomfort and suffering and death often followed a failure to provide proper supplies, or, when provided, to take sufficient care to preserve them.

On the 25th of May, 1889, Brown's party was ready and started from the point where the Rio Grande Western crosses Green River. There were sixteen men and six boats. Five of the boats were new; the sixth was the one Kendrick and Rigney had used on the Grand River trip. The chief engineer of the proposed railway was Robert Brewster Stanton, and that he was not in the very beginning given the entire management was most unfortunate, for Brown himself seems not to have had a realisation of the enormous difficulties of the task before him. But the arrangements were completed before Stanton was engaged. All the men were surprised, disappointed, dismayed, at the character of the boats Brown had provided for this dangerous enterprise, and Stanton said his heart sank at the first sight of them. They were entirely inadequate, built of cedar instead of oak, only fifteen feet long and three feet wide, and weighed but one hundred and fifty pounds each. They would have been beautiful for an ordinary river, but for the raging, plunging, tumultuous Colorado their name was suicide. Then not a life-preserver had been brought. This neglect was another shock to the members of the party and their friends. Stanton was urged to take one for himself, but he declined to provide this advantage over the other men. Since then he has been disposed to blame Powell for not telling Brown that life-preservers are a necessity on the Colorado. He also says that Powell even declared to Brown that they were not imperative, and he consequently censures him for the subsequent disasters. There was certainly a misunderstanding in this, for Powell, knowing the situation from such abundant experience, never could have said life-preservers were not necessary, though on his first trip he did not have any. In this connection Thompson writes me: "The Major sent for me at once when Mr. Brown called at the office. I think we talked —we three, I mean—for half an hour, then the Major said, 'Professor Thompson knows just as much about the river as I do, and more about what is necessary for such a trip; you talk with him.' I took Mr. Brown to my room and we had a long talk. I think the next day Mr. Brown came again. I had two interviews with him alone. I told him distinctly that life-preservers were necessary. I probably told him we did not wear them all the time, but I told him we put them on at every dangerous rapid, and I showed him the picture in the Major's Report where we were wearing them. I clearly remember telling him to have one arm above and one below the preserver. I am positive about this, for after we received word of the loss of Brown we talked it over and I recalled the conversation. He impressed me as thinking we exaggerated the dangers of the river. He made a memorandum of things I said. I think he also talked with Hillers, and I have no doubt the latter told him to take life-preservers. But he had the Report, and there is no excuse for his neglecting so indispensable an article of the outfit. He was warned over and over again to neglect no precaution. I distinctly remember that the Major told him in so many words, 'not to underestimate the dangers of the river, and to never be caught off guard.'" On a previous page I have remarked that proper boats and a knowledge of how to handle them are more important than life-preservers, but that does not mean that a party should leave the life-preservers behind. In descending the Colorado every possible precaution must be taken. The first of these is the right kind of boats, second, proper arrangement as to food-supplies, and, third, life-preservers, etc. The New York *Tribune*, after the collapse of this Brown expedition, quotes Powell in an interview as saying that he would not have ventured in the boats Brown selected and that he thought Brown "failed to comprehend the significant fact that nothing can get through the Colorado Canyon that cannot float. Boats are repeatedly upset and inferior boats are mashed like egg-shells." Brown, undoubtedly, was rather inclined to look upon the descent somewhat lightly. Being a brave, energetic man it was hard for him to believe that this river demanded so much extra prudence and caution, when Powell had successfully descended it twice without, so far as the water was concerned, losing a man. However, the ill-fated expedition went on its way.

The boats were so frail that the journey by rail, some ten days, had opened their sides in a number of places, and they had to be immediately recalked. The bottoms were covered with copper. The party consisted of the following persons: Frank M. Brown, president; Robert Brewster Stanton, chief engineer; John Hislop, first assistant engineer; C. W. Potter, T. P. Rigney, E. A. Reynolds, J. H. Hughes, W. H. Bush, Edward Coe, Edward — —, Peter Hansborough, Henry Richards, G. W. Gibson, Charles Potter, F. A. Nims, photographer, and J. C. Terry. The baggage of each man was limited to twenty-five pounds. The cargoes were packed in air-tight zinc boxes three feet long, with one of which each boat was provided, but these were found to be cumbersome and heavy, the

A Cave-Lake in a Sandstone Cliff near Kanab, S. Utah.

The depth from front to rear is about 125 feet. The outer opening is the whole front of the arch. It belongs to the class of natural arches, alcoves, bridges, "holes in the wall," etc., common in this kind of sandstone throughout the Southwest.

Photograph by J. K. HILLERS, U. S. Colo. Riv. Exp.

boats being down to within one inch of the gunwales in the water, so they were taken out and all lashed together, forming a sort of raft. This carried about one-third of all the supplies, and all the extra oars and rope, a most unwise arrangement from every point of view. The nondescript craft hampered their movements, could not be controlled, and if once it got loose everything was sure to be lost. It would have been better to throw these boxes away at once and take what the boats could carry and no more, but this was apparently not thought of. All things considered, it is a wonder this party ever got through Cataract Canyon alive. At some little rapid, after leaving the railway crossing, the first boat stove a hole in her side, but this was readily repaired and the party ran without further accident over the smooth stretches of river preceding the Junction, arriving at this latter point in four days. They were now on the threshold of Cataract Canyon. Stopping to adjust instruments and repair boats for a day, they proceeded to the battle with the cataracts on May 31st. For forty-one miles they would now have their courage, muscle, and nerve put to the full test. Stanton records seventy-five rapids and cataracts, fifty-seven of them within a space of nineteen miles, with falls in places of sixteen to twenty feet. This, then, was what they were approaching with these frail craft. Two miles down they heard the roar of falling water and the place was reconnoitred, with the result that a large rapid was found to bar the way. The raft of provisions, and the boat that had towed it, were on the opposite side of the river, which afforded no chance for a camp or a portage, and a signal was made for the party to come over. A half mile intervened between this boat and the head of the rapid, but with the encumbering raft it was drawn down so dangerously near the descent that, to save themselves, the rope holding the raft was cut. Thus freed the boat succeeded in landing just at the head of the fall, but the raft went over, and that was the end of it. The fragments were found scattered all the way through the canyon. The next twenty-eight miles were filled with mishaps and losses. Twelve miles farther down, the boat in which Brown, Hughes, and Reynolds were running a rapid capsized. The men clung to her for a mile and a half and then succeeded in getting ashore. The rapids in this part are very close together, and to these men it seemed like one continuous cataract, which it very nearly is. On the same day another boat containing the cooking outfit struck a rock and went to pieces. The provisions she carried were, most of them, contributed to the maw of the dragon to follow those of the unfortunate raft.

Sometimes the boats got away from the men altogether, running wild, finally lodging somewhere below to be found again with the contents missing.[1] Soon they had so many large holes in them that one, No. 3, had to be broken up to obtain materials for repairing the others. Thus the party, by the time they had fairly arrived at the deepest and worst portion of this splendid chasm, were in a sad plight, but a plight mainly due to the original bad planning and mismanagement, and not necessary in navigating this gorge. They seldom attempted to cross the river, working down along one side and never entering the boats at all except where absolutely necessary. Thus they were greatly hampered in their movements. With our boats we never gave the crossing of the river a thought, and were in them continually, except where a portage was demanded. We could therefore always choose our course with as much freedom as is possible. But it must not be forgotten that the Brown party were in Cataract Canyon about the time of high water, while we passed through at a lower stage. This would make a difference, low water being in all the canyons far safer, though the work is harder on the men and the boats. By the 15th of June all provisions had disappeared except a sack and a half of flour, presumably one hundred pounds to the sack, a little coffee, some sugar, and condensed milk. The flour was all baked and divided equally, each man receiving two and one half pounds of bread, one pound of sugar, and four ounces of coffee. At one point they fortunately found a barrel of cut loaf-sugar amongst the driftwood. This had been lost from some army-supplies crossing at Gunnison Valley up the Green, or up Grand River, and they also found, a little below this, pieces of a waggon with the skeleton of a man. These also had, of course, come from at least a hundred miles above the Junction on the Green, or sixty miles up the Grand, as no waggon could get to the river at any place nearer to Cataract Canyon. The waggon-box had probably acted as a raft, bearing its gruesome passenger all these long miles into the heart of the mighty gorge, where the dragon stored

[1] With boats built on the model we used nothing could be lost of the contents even if the boat rolled over, for everything was under cover.

his prize, and for many a year treasured it among the deep
shadows.

They had still fifteen miles of Cataract Canyon and
the ten miles of the more kindly Narrow before them, and

In Marble Canyon, about Midway between Paria and Little Colorado.
Photograph by J. K. HILLERS, U. S. Colo. Riv. Exp.

Brown was now to hurry along and attempt to reach some
placer mines at Dandy Crossing, near the mouth of Frémont
River, where there were a few miners and where some food
might be obtained.   Ancient dwellings were seen all along the
gorge in the side canyons, some completely ruined, others in a

fair state of preservation, but the inhabitants had gone long ago, and no help could be hoped for in this direction. Most of the men now became thoroughly discouraged at the dismal prospect and wished to abandon immediately and entirely the enterprise, but Stanton was not of that mind. The difficulties showed him how hard it would be to do this part over again, and he resolved to stay and finish the work as far as possible now. His first assistant, Hislop, G. W. Gibson, the coloured cook, and the coloured steward, H. C. Richards, volunteered to stand by him, and the next morning the eleven others pushed on, leaving a boat for these five to follow with. For six days this determined little crew worked along at the rate of about four miles a day, with a ration of one small scrap of bread, a little coffee, and some condensed milk for breakfast and supper, and three lumps of sugar for dinner. Stanton says there was not a murmur of discontent from the men "carrying the survey over the rocks and cliffs on the side of the canyon, and handling the boat through the rapids of the river. At night, when they lay down on the sand to sleep, after a meal that was nine-tenths water and hope and one-tenth bread and coffee, it was without complaint." Relief was had on the sixth day, when they met a boat being towed up with provisions. This was near the end of Narrow Canyon. At one point in the lower part of the gorge they passed a place where, on a rock surface about six feet above the level of the water, they saw the inscription, "I. JULIEN—1836." They thought it could have been cut only from a boat or raft, and concluded that it was done by a party of Canadians which they heard had tried to explore this country at that early day. This is possible; or it may have been one of the band of missionaries which Farnham mentions as having started down the canyons and never again being heard of, though some one may have gone in at Millecrag Bend and worked their way as far as this. At Dandy Crossing, the party rested a few days, the boats were repaired, and fresh supplies of food purchased. They met near here Jack Sumner, of Powell's first party. From this place to the head of Marble Canyon, the mouth of the Paria, it is plain and easy going, at least for any one who has been through Cataract Canyon. Brown and Stanton went ahead with six men, the others coming along later with the survey.

At Dandy Crossing three of the party left the river—J. N. Hughes, E. A. Reynolds, and T. P. Rigney. One man joined the party, Harry McDonald, a frontiersman and an experienced boatman. From Lee's Ferry, Brown went on horseback to Kanab for supplies, for Dandy Crossing was not a metropolis, and more rations were needed before venturing to enter the Grand Canyon. Only one transit instrument was left, and it was decided that Brown, Stanton, Hislop, McDonald, Hansborough, Richards, Gibson, and Nims, the photographer, should form the party to proceed, making an examination, taking notes and photographs, but not attempting an instrumental survey. Brown returned from Kanab by July 9th, and an immediate start was made with the three boats,—boats entirely unfitted for the work in Cataract Canyon, and tenfold more inadequate for the giant gorge, with its terrible descents, now before them. It seems a pity they did not realise this and leave the continuation of the work till proper boats could be had, but it appears as if they again underestimated the dangers of the river. At any rate they went bravely forward with a courage that deserved a better reward. The first ugly rapids in Marble Canyon are the two near together about ten miles below Lee's Ferry, where the prospectors met their punishment early in July, 1872. These the Brown party reached safely, and made the necessary portages, camping at the foot of the Soap Creek or lower fall. Brown appeared to feel lonely and troubled, and asked Stanton to come and sit by his bed and talk. They smoked and talked till a late hour about home and the prospect for the next day. Brown's wife and two children were at this time travelling in Europe and probably the thought of them so far away made him somewhat blue. Then, if he had before thought that this canyon would be easy, the nature of the rapids around him served to undeceive his mind. The deepening gorge, inadequate boats, and increasingly bad rapids probably affected his nerves, for that night he dreamed of the rapids, and this troubled him so much that he mentioned it to Stanton in the morning. Breakfast

over, they went on. We had camped at the head of the Soap
Creek Rapids, and this party at the foot. In the first rapid
below, which was one of five that we easily ran before stopping
for dinner, Brown's boat was capsized. He and his oarsman,
McDonald, were thrown out on opposite sides, McDonald into
the current and Brown unfortunately into the eddy, where he
was drawn under by one of the whirlpools numerous in this
locality, and was never seen again. A half-minute later

Marble Canyon, Lower Portion.
Walls about 3500 feet.
From photograph by J. K. HILLERS, U. S. Colo. Riv. Exp.

Stanton's boat passed the spot, but all he saw was the lost
leader's note-book on the surface of the angry waters which
had so suddenly swallowed up its owner. The whole day long
the party sat sadly watching the place to see if the treacherous
river would give up the dead, but darkness fell in the gorge,
and the Colorado dashed along toward the sea as if no boat
had ever touched its relentless tide. What was one man more
or less to this great dragon's maw! For three days after the
others battled their way along without further disaster, and
then came Sunday, when they rested. On Monday, while

Stanton and Nims were making notes and photographs, the men were to finish up the lower end of the second of two very bad rapids where portages were made. Stanton's boat, containing Hansborough and Richards, was following the first boat, which had made the stretch with difficulty because the current

Looking West from Jacob's Pool on Road to Lee's Ferry. Vermilion Cliffs in Distance.
The "Jacob" after whom the pool was named was Jacob Hamblin.
This is the country Stanton was in after leaving the river.
Photograph by W. BELL.

set against the left-hand cliff. The second boat was driven against the foot of this wall under an overhanging shelf, and in the attempt to push her off she was capsized and Hansborough never rose again. Richards, who was a strong swimmer, made some distance down-stream, but before the first boat could reach him he sank, and that was the end for him. This terrible disaster, added to the death of Brown, and the foolhardiness of proceeding farther with such boats as they had, forced the decision which should have been made at Lee's Ferry. Stanton resolved to leave the river, but with the determination to return again to battle with the dragon at the earliest opportunity. The next thing was to get out of the canyon. They searched for some side canyon leading in from the north, by means of which they might return to the world, and just above Vesey's Paradise they found it and spent their last night in Marble Canyon at that point. From the rapid where Brown was lost, to Vesey's Paradise, my diary records that on our expedition of 1872 we ran twenty-six rapids, let down four times, and made two portages, all without any particular difficulty. I mention this merely to show the difference proper boats make in navigating this river, for the season was nearly the same; Brown was there in July and we in August, both the season of high water. The night passed by Stanton and his dishcartened but courageous band at Vesey's Paradise was long to be remembered, for one of the violent thunder-storms frequent in the canyon, in summer, came up. The rain fell in floods, while about midnight the storm culminated in a climax of fury. Stanton says that in all his experience in the Western mountains he never heard anything like it. "Nowhere has the awful grandeur equalled that night in the lonesome depths of what was to us death's canyon." The next day was fair, and by two in the afternoon, July 19th, they were on the surface of the country, twenty-five hundred feet above the river, and that night reached a cattle ranch.

By November 25th of the same year (1889) the indefatigable Stanton had organised a new party to continue the railway survey. He still had confidence in the scheme, and he refused to give up. And this time the boats were planned with some regard to the waters upon which they were to be used. McDonald was sent to superintend their building at the boatyard of H. H. Douglas & Co., Waukegan, Illinois. There were three, each twenty-two feet long, the same as our boats, four and one-half feet beam, and twenty-two inches deep, and each weighed 850 pounds. They were built of half-inch oak, on plans furnished by Stanton, with ribs one-and-one-half by three-quarters of an inch, placed four inches apart, all copper fastened. Each boat had ten separate air-tight galvanised-iron

Tapeets Creek.
Character of some of the tributary valleys of the north side of
the Grand Canyon through the Kaibab section. The
extreme height of the north wall is seen in the
distance. A considerable valley intervenes
between it and the river.
Photograph by J. K. HILLERS, U. S. Colo. Riv. Exp.

compartments running around the sides, and they were so arranged that the canned goods could be put under the foot-boards for ballast. There was a deck fore and aft, and there were life-lines along the sides. They were certainly excellent boats, and while in some respects I think our model was better, especially because the two transverse bulkheads amidships in ours tended to make their sides very strong and stiff, yet these boats of Stanton's were so good that the men would be safe as long as they handled them correctly. Cork life-preservers of the best quality were provided, and the order was for each man to wear his whenever in rough or uncertain water. All stores and provisions were packed in water-tight rubber bags, made like ocean mail-sacks, expressly for the purpose. The expedition was thus well provided.

From the railway the boats were hauled on waggons to the mouth of Crescent Creek near Frémont River, so as to avoid doing Cataract Canyon over again. There were twelve men, of whom four had been with the Brown party. They were R. B. Stanton, Langdon Gibson, Harry McDonald, and Elmer Kane, in boat No. 1, called the *Bonnie Jean;* John Hislop, F. A. Nims, Reginald Travers, and W. H. Edwards in boat No. 2, called the *Lillie;* and A. B. Twining, H. G. Ballard, L. G. Brown, and James Hogue, the cook, in the *Marie*, boat No. 3. Christmas dinner was eaten at Lee's Ferry, with wild flowers picked that day for decoration. On the 28th they started into the great canyon, passed the old wreck of a boat and part of a miner's outfit, and on the 31st reached the rapid where Brown was lost. It was now the season of low water, and the rapid appeared less formidable, though on entering it the place was seen to be in general the same, yet the water was nine feet lower. The next day Nims, the photographer, fell from a ledge a distance of twenty-two feet, receiving a severe jar and breaking one of his legs just above the ankle. The break was bandaged, and one of the boats being so loaded that there was a level bed for the injured man to lie on, they ran down about two miles to a side canyon coming in from the north. By means of this Stanton climbed out, walked thirty-five miles to Lee's Ferry, and brought a waggon back to the edge. Nims was placed on an improvised stretcher, and carried up the cliffs, four miles in distance and seventeen hundred feet in altitude. At half-past three in the afternoon the surface was reached. Twice the stretcher had to be swung along by ropes where there was no footing, and twice had to be perpendicularly lifted ten or fifteen feet. No one was in-

The Grand Canyon.
In the First Granite Gorge.
Upper walls are not seen. Those in sight are 1000 to 1200 feet.
Above they rise in terraces to between 5000 and 6000.
Photograph by J. K. HILLERS, U. S. Colo. Riv. Exp.

jured. Nims was taken to Lee's Ferry and left with W. M. Johnson, who had been a member of our land parties during the winter of 1871–72, and who had come with the *Cañonita* party through Glen Canyon. Nims was in good hands. After this accident Stanton was obliged to assume the duties of photographer and took some seven hundred and fifty views without previous experience.

By January 13th they had arrived at Point Retreat, where the canyon had before been abandoned, and here they found the supplies and blankets they had cached in a marble cave in perfect condition. The new boats were so well suited to the river work that they were able to run most of the rapids just as we had done, often going at the rate of fifteen miles an hour, and sometimes by actual measurement, twenty. Ten miles below Point Retreat, and twenty-five miles above the Little Colorado, when they were going into camp one evening they discovered the body of Peter Hansborough. The next morning, with a brief ceremony, they buried the remains at the foot of the cliff, carving his name on the face of the rock, and a point opposite was named after the unfortunate man. From Point Hansborough the canyon widens, "the marble benches retreat, new strata of limestone, quartzite, and sandstone come up from the river," writes Stanton, "and the debris forms a talus equal to a mountain slope. Here the bottoms widen into little farms covered with green grass and groves of mesquite, making a most charming summer picture, in strong contrast with the dismal narrow canyons above." They then passed the Little Colorado and entered the Grand Canyon proper, meeting with a lone prospector in the wide portion just below the Little Colorado, the only person they had seen in any of the canyons traversed.

Arriving at the First Granite Gorge (Archæan formation), they were at the beginning of the wildest stretch of river of all, perhaps the wildest to be found anywhere, the fall in the first ten miles averaging twenty-one feet to the mile, the greatest average except in Lodore and a portion of Cataract, and as this descent is not spread over the ten miles, but occurs in a series of falls with comparatively calm water between, it is not hard to picture the conditions. Stanton also pronounces these rapids of the First Granite Gorge the most powerful he saw, except two in the Second Granite Gorge. On January 29th they had cautiously advanced till they were before the great descent some of our party had called the Sockdologer, the heaviest fall on the river, about eighty feet in a third of a mile. They proceeded all along in much the same careful fashion as we had done, and as everyone who hopes to make this passage alive must proceed.   The water being low, they were able to let their boats by line over the upper end of the Sockdologer with safety, but, in attempting to continue, the *Marie* was caught by a cross-current and thrown against the rocks, turned half over, filled with water, and jammed tightly between two boul-

The Great Unconformity.
Top of the Granite, Grand Canyon.
Photograph by T. MITCHELL PRUDDEN.

ders lying just beneath the surface.   In winter, the air in the canyon is not very cold, but the river coming so swiftly from the far north is, and the men with lines about their waists who tried to go through the rushing waist-deep water found it icy.   Taking turns, they succeeded with a grappling-hook in getting out the cargo, losing only two sacks of provisions, but though they laboured till dark they were not able to move the boat.   Giving her up for lost, they tried to secure a night's rest on the sharp rocks.   Had a great rise in the river occurred now the party would have been in a terrible predicament, but though it rose a few days later it spared them on this occasion.

It came up only two feet, and this was a kindness, for it lifted the *Marie* so that they were able to pull her out of the vise. When they saw her condition, however, they were dismayed for one side was half gone, and the other was smashed in. The keel remained whole. By cutting four feet out of the centre and drawing the ends together, five days' hard work made practically another boat. They were then able to proceed, and, going past Bright Angel Creek, arrived on February 6th at what Stanton describes as "the most powerful and unmanageable rapid" on the river. This, I believe, was the place where we were capsized. Thompson at that time, before we ran it, declared it looked to him like the worst rapid we had encountered but at the stage of water then prevailing we could not get near it. Stanton wisely made a portage of the supplies and let the boats down by lines. His boat, the *Bonnie Jean*, played all sorts of pranks, rushing out into the current, ducking and diving under water, and finally floating down sideways. Then they thought they would try what Stanton calls Powell's plan of shooting a boat through and catching it below. Such a harum-scarum method was never used on our expedition, and I never heard Powell suggest that it was on the first. Stanton evidently misunderstood some of Powell's phrases in his Report. At any rate in this instance it was as disastrous as might have been expected. The poor *Marie* was again the sufferer, and came out below "in pieces about the size of toothpicks." The *Lillie* was then carried down and reached the river beyond in safety. A day or two after this McDonald decided to leave the party, and started up a little creek coming in from the north, to climb out to the plateau, and make his way to Kanab. This he succeeded in doing after several days of hard work and tramping through the heavy snow on the plateau. The other ten men concluded to remain with Stanton and they all went on in the two boats. Several days later they passed the mouth of the Kanab. The terrible First Granite Gorge was well behind them. But now the river began to rise. Before reaching the Kanab it rose four feet and continued to rise for two days and nights, altogether some ten or twelve feet. A little below the Kanab, where the canyon is very narrow, they came upon a peculiar phenomenon. They heard a loud roar and saw breakers ahead. Thinking it a bad rapid, they landed immediately on some rocks, and, going along these to examine the place, the breakers had disappeared, but as they stood in amazement there suddenly arose at their feet the same huge waves, twelve or fifteen feet high and one hundred and fifty feet long, across the river, "rolling downstream like great sea waves, and breaking in white foam with a terrible noise." These waves, as was later ascertained, were the result of a cloudburst on the headwaters of the Little Colorado, and indicate what might be expected in here in the event of a combination of such waves with the highest stage of water. The next day they were diminished, and the river fell somewhat, but it was still so powerful they could barely control the boats and had a wild and tumultuous ride, sometimes being almost bodily thrown out of the boats. By this time their rations were getting low, but by pushing on as fast as possible they reached Diamond Creek on March 1st, where supplies were planned to meet them. Remaining there ten days to recuperate they went on with only eight men, three concluding to leave at this place. The Second Granite Gorge begins about eighteen miles above Diamond Creek, and is about thirty miles long. It is much like the First Granite Gorge, being the same formation, excepting that it is shorter and that the declivity of the river is not so great. From Diamond Creek down to the end of the canyon is about fifty miles. It is a bad stretch, and contains some heavy falls which, as the river was still somewhat high, were often impossible to get around, and they were obliged to run them. The stage of water in both these Granite Gorges makes a great difference in the character of the falls. For example, in the Second Gorge, when Wheeler made his precarious journey in 1871, he was able, coming from below, to surmount the rapids along the sides with two of his boats, because the water happened to be at a stage that permitted this, whereas Stanton found it impossible to pass some of them without running, and Powell found the one that split his party the same way. So it appears that one day finds these gorges

Looking up the Grand Canyon, at the Foot of Toroweap, Uinkaret Division.
Depth of inner gorge about 3000 feet—width, brink to brink, about 3500 feet.
Oil sketch by F. S. DELLENBAUGH

easier or harder than another; but at their easiest they are truly fearful places.　At one of the worst falls Stanton's boat suddenly crashed upon a rock that projected from the shore, and there she hung, all the men being thrown forward.　The

The Grand Canyon—Lava Falls.
Just below the Toroweap.
Total depth of canyon about 4500 feet.
Photograph by J. K. HILLERS, U. S. Colo. Riv. Exp.

boat filled and stuck fast, while the great waves rolled over her and her crew.　Stanton tried to straighten himself up, and was taken in the back by a breaker and washed out of the craft altogether into a whirlpool, and finally shot to the surface fifty feet farther down. He had on his cork jacket and was saved, though he was ducked again and carried along swiftly by the tremendous current. The second boat had better luck and came through in time to pick Stanton up. The damaged boat was gotten off with a hole in her side ten by eighteen inches, which was closed by a copper patch at the first chance, the air chambers having kept the craft afloat. After this the bad rapids were soon ended, and on the morning of March 17th (1890) the party emerged into an open country and upon a peaceful, quiet river. Continuing down through Black and the other canyons, and through the intervening valleys, they reached, on the 26th of April, the salt tide where Alarçon, three and a half centuries earlier, had first put a keel upon these turbulent waters, the only party thus far to make the entire passage from the Junction to the sea. And as yet no one has made the complete descent from Green River Valley to the counter-current of the Tidal Bore, so if there is any reader who desires to distinguish himself here is a feat still open to him.

On the Bright Angel Trail.
Photograph by T. MITCHELL PRUDDEN.

Stanton deserves much praise for his pluck and determination and good judgment in carrying this railway survey to a successful issue, especially after the discouraging disasters of the first attempt. He holds the data and believes the project will some day be carried out. From the foregoing pages the reader may judge the probabilities in the case.

Since the Stanton party I have found no record of any person venturing by boat into the depths of the Grand Canyon. There are statements that one or two lone individuals have recently traversed portions of the upper river, and even the whole line of canyons, but of these I have no authentic knowledge. In 1891, a steam launch, the *Major Powell*, thirty-five feet long, with twelve horsepower engines, was brought out from Chicago by way of the Rio Grande Western Railway to the crossing of Green River, and there launched in September of that year. The screw was soon broken, and the attempt to go down the river abandoned. In 1892 another attempt was made, but this also was given up after a few miles. But in 1893, W. H. Edwards, who had been with the Stanton party, together with some others, took the *Major Powell* down to the Junction and back, making a second trip in April. The round trip took four days, running time. They also went up the Grand some distance. Entering the head of Cataract Canyon the launch struck a rock and the party came near being wrecked, but had the good luck to get off without much damage.

A view of the Grand Canyon may now be had without risk or discomfort of any kind, as the Atchison, Topeka, and Santa Fé Railway runs trains to the Bright Angel Hotel at the very edge of the gorge at one of the grandest portions, opposite Bright Angel Creek. There are several trails in this region leading down to the river besides the one from the hotel. It is always a hard climb for those unaccustomed to mountaineering. From the north, for any who are fond of camping, a pleasant trip may be made from the end of the Union Pacific Company's southern extension to the Toroweap and the Kaibab country, though this is a matter of a couple of weeks.

In a general way we have now traced the whole history of the discovery and exploration of this wonderful river, which after nearly four centuries still flings defiance at the puny efforts of man to cope with it, while its furious waters dash on through the long, lonely gorges, as untrammelled to-day as

they were in the forgotten ages.   Those who approach it re-
spectfully and reverently are treated not unkindly, but woe
and disaster await all others.   The lesson of these pages is
plain, and the author commends it to all who hereafter may
be inspired to add their story to this Romance of the Colorado
River.

EPILOGUE

MAJOR POWELL had kindly consented to write an introduction to this volume wherein I have inadequately presented scenes from the great world-drama connected with the Colorado River of the West, but a prolonged illness prevented his doing any writing whatever, and on September 23, 1902, while, indeed, the compositor was setting the last type of the book, a funeral knell sounded at Haven, Maine, his summer home, and the most conspicuous figure we have seen on this stage, the man whose name is as inseparable from the marvellous canyon-river as that of De Soto from the Mississippi, or Hendrik Hudson from the placid stream which took from him its title, started on that final journey whence there is no returning. A distinguished cortege bore the remains across the Potomac, laying them in a soldier's grave in the National Cemetery at Arlington. Thus the brave sleeps with the brave on the banks of the river of roses, a stream in great contrast to that other river far in the West where only might be found a tomb more appropriate within sound of the raging waters he so valiantly conquered.

In the history of the United States the place of John Wesley Powell is clear.[1] A great explorer, he was also foremost among men of science and probably he did more than any other single individual to direct Governmental scientific research along proper lines. His was a character of strength and fortitude. A man of action, his fame will endure as much by his deeds as by his contributions to scientific literature. Never a seeker for pecuniary rewards his life was an offering to

---

[1] I am indebted to Major Powell's brother-in-law, Prof. A. H. Thompson, for many of the facts herein stated, and for revision of dates to his brother Prof. W. B. Powell.

science, and when other paths more remunerative were open to him he turned his back upon them. He believed in sticking to one's vocation and thoroughly disapproved of wandering off in pursuit of common profit. The daring feat of exploring the canyons of the Colorado was undertaken for no spectacular effect or pecuniary reward, but was purely a scientific venture in perfect accord with the spirit of his early promise. As G. K. Gilbert remarks in a recent number of *Science*[1] it was "of phenomenal boldness and its successful accomplishment a dramatic triumph. It produced a strong impression on the public mind and gave Powell a national reputation which was afterwards of great service, although based on an adventurous episode by no means essential to his career as an investigator." The qualities which enabled him so splendidly to perform his many self-imposed tasks were an inheritance from his parents, who possessed more than ordinary intelligence. Joseph Powell, his father, had a strong will, deep earnestness, and indomitable courage, while his mother, Mary Dean, with similar traits possessed also remarkable tact and practicality. Both were English born, the mother well educated, and were always leaders in the social and educational life of every community where they dwelt. Especially were they prominent in religious circles, the father being a licensed exhorter in the Methodist Episcopal Church. Both were intensely American in their love and admiration of the civil institutions of the United States and both were strenuously opposed to slavery, which was flourishing in America when they arrived in 1830. For a time they remained in New York City and then removed to the village of Palmyra whence they went to Mount Morris, Livingston County, New York, where, on March 24, 1834, the fourth of their nine children, John Wesley, was born. Because of the slavery question Joseph Powell left the Methodist Episcopal Church on the organisation of the Wesleyan Methodist Church and became a regularly ordained preacher in the latter. It was in this atmosphere of social, educational, political, and religious fervor that the future explorer grew up. When he was four or five years old the family moved to Jack-

[1] October 10, 1902.

John Wesley Powell.
1834–1902.

373

son, Ohio, and then, in 1846, went on westward to South Grove, Walworth County, Wisconsin, where a farm was purchased. They were in prosperous circumstances, and the boy was active in the management of affairs, early exhibiting his trait for doing things well. His ploughing, stack-building, and business ability in disposing advantageously of the farm products and in purchasing supplies at the lake ports received the commendation of the countryside.

His early education was such as the country schools provided. He later studied at Janesville, Wisconsin, earning his board by working nights and mornings. His parents ever held before him the importance of achieving the highest education possible. Thus he continually turned to books, and while his oxen were eating or resting, he was absorbed in some illuminating volume. In 1851 his family removed to Bonus Prairie, Boone County, Illinois, where a larger farm had been purchased. About 1853 the Wesleyan College was established at Wheaton, Illinois, and the family removed there in order to take advantage of the opportunities afforded. The father became one of the trustees and Powell entered the preparatory classes. With intervals of teaching and business pursuits, he continued here till 1855, when, largely through the influence of the late Hon. John Davis, of Kansas, he entered the preparatory department of Illinois College at Jacksonville, Illinois. Thus far he had shown no special apitude for the natural sciences, though he was always a close observer of natural phenomena. His ambition at this period, which was also in accord with the dearest wishes of his parents, was to complete his college course and enter the ministry. Illinois College not possessing a theological atmosphere after a year spent there he departed, and in 1857 began a course of study at Oberlin College, Ohio. Among his studies there was botany, and in this class Powell at last discovered himself and his true vocation— the investigation of natural science. He became an enthusiastic botanist and searched the woods and swamps around Oberlin with the same zeal and thoroughness which always characterised his work. He made an almost complete herbarium of the flora of the county, organising the class into a club to assist in its collection. In the summer of 1858, having returned to Wheaton, Illinois, where the family had settled in 1854, he joined the Illinois State Natural History Society, then engaged in conducting a natural history survey of the State through the voluntary labour of its members. To Powell was assigned the department of conchology. This work he entered upon with his usual application and made the most complete collection of the mollusca of Illinois ever brought together by one man. Incidentally, botany, zoölogy, and mineralogy received attention, and in these lines he secured notable collections. With the broad mental grasp which was a pronounced trait, he perceived that these studies were but parts of the greater science of geology, which he then announced, to at least one of his intimate friends, was to be the science to which he intended to devote his life. The next year was given to study, teaching, and lecturing, usually on some topic connected with geology.

In the spring of 1860, on a lecturing tour, he visited some of the Southern States, and while there closely observed the sentiment of the people on the subject of slavery, with the result that he expressed the conviction that nothing short of war could settle the matter. In the summer of 1860 he became principal of the public schools of Hennepin, Illinois. These he organised, graded, and taught with a vigour which was characteristic, yet never forgetting his geological investigations in the neighbouring country, where, on Saturdays and at other times when the schools were not in session, he made botanical and zoölogical collections.

Convinced that war was inevitable, the winter of 1860–61 found him studying military tactics and engineering. When the call came for troops, he was the first man to enroll, and largely through his efforts Company H of the 20th Regiment, Illinois Infantry, was raised in Putnam County. When the regiment was organised at Joliet, Illinois, he was appointed sergeant-major, and in this capacity went to the front. When the force was sent to Cape Girardeau, Missouri, his prescience in studying military engineering made him invaluable. He was practically given charge of planning and laying out and constructing the fortifications at that place, a work he executed so well that it received the unqualified commendation of General Frémont. The second lieutenant of Company H resigning, Powell was elected to fill the vacancy. After a service of a few weeks with his company he was put in charge of the fortifications he had constructed, being retained in this post after the departure of his regiment. In the early winter of 1861–62 he recruited a company of artillery, largely from loyal Missourians. This company was mustered into service as Battery F, 2d Illinois Artillery, John Wesley Powell, Captain. After drilling a few weeks he was ordered to proceed with his battery to Pittsburg Landing, Tennessee, where he arrived the latter part of March, 1862. The battery took part in the battle of Shiloh, April 6th of that year, and during the engagement, as Powell raised his arm, a signal to fire, a rifle ball struck his hand at the wrist glancing toward the elbow. The necessary surgery was done so hastily that later a second operation was imperative, which left him with a mere stump below the elbow-joint. Never for long at a time afterward was he free from pain and only a few years ago a third operation was performed which brought relief.

As soon as the original wound was healed he went back to his command, assisting as Division Chief of Artillery in the siege of Vicksburg. After the fall of this place he took part in the Meridian Raid. Then he served on detached operations at Vicksburg, Natchez, and New Orleans until the summer of 1864, when he was re-assigned to the former command in the Army of the Tennessee. In all the operations after the fall of Atlanta he bore an active part, and when Sherman commenced the march to the sea, Powell was sent back to General Thomas at Nashville, in command of twenty batteries of artillery. At the battle of Nashville he served on the staff of Thomas and continued with this command till mustered out in the early summer of 1865. As a soldier his career was marked by a thorough study and mastery not only of the details of military life, but of military science. Especially was he apt in utilising material at hand to accomplish his ends—a trait that was also prominent in his civil life. Bridges he built from cotton-gin houses, mantelets for his guns from gunny bags and old rope, and shields for his sharpshooters from the mould-boards of old ploughs found on the abandoned plantations. All this time wherever possible he continued his studies in natural science. He made a collection of fossils unearthed in the trenches around Vicksburg, land and river shells from the Mississippi swamps, and a large collection of mosses while on detached duty in Illinois. He also familiarised himself with the geology of regions through which the armies passed to which he was attached. Time and again he was commended for his services and declined promotion to higher rank in other arms of the service. "He loved the scarlet facings of the artillery, and there was something in the ranking of batteries and the power of cannon," writes Thompson, "that was akin to the workings of his own mind."

In 1862 he was married to his cousin, Miss Emma Dean, of Detroit, who still lives in Washington with their daughter, an only child. Mrs. Powell was often his companion in the army and early Western journeys. Upon the return of Powell to civil life in 1865 he was tendered a nomination to a lucrative political office in Du Page County, Illinois, and at the same time he was offered the chair of geology in the Wesleyan University, a struggling Methodist College at Bloomington, Illinois. There was no hesitation on his part. He declined the political honour and its emoluments and accepted the professorship, which he retained two years. At the session of the Illinois Legislature in 1867 a bill was passed, largely through his effort, creating a professorship of geology and natural history in the State Normal University at Normal, Illinois, with a salary of fifteen hundred dollars and an appropriation of one thousand dollars annually to increase the geological and zoölogical collections. He was elected to this chair and at about the same time was also chosen curator of the Illinois State Natural History Society, whose collections were domiciled in the museum of the Normal University. Attracted by the Far West as a field for profitable scientific research, the summer of 1867 found him using his salary and the other available funds to defray the expense of an expedition to the then Territory of Colorado for the purpose of securing collections.

He organised and outfitted at Plattsmouth, Nebraska. All
his assistants were volunteers except the cook. A. H.
Thompson, afterwards so closely associated with him in the
detailed exploration of the Colorado and in subsequent survey
work, was the entomologist of the party. They crossed the

Green River from the U. P. Railway to White River,
showing gorges through the Uinta Mountains.

plains with mule teams to Denver, worked along the east slope
of the Front Range, climbed Pike's Peak, and went westerly
as far as South Park. Without realising it, apparently, Powell
was all these years steadily approaching the great exploit of
his life, as if led on and prepared by some unseen power.
Now the project of exploring the mysterious gorges of which

he heard such wonderful tales dawned upon him. It was as near an inspiration as can be imagined. Henceforth his mind and energy were directed irresistibly toward the accomplishment of this conception. Again in 1868 he was in the field with the same financial backing, to which was added a small allotment from the Illinois Industrial University at Champaign, Illinois, a State school. All but Mrs. Powell and his brother Walter, of this 1868 party, returned East on the approach of autumn, while with these and several trappers and hunters, among whom were the two Howlands, William Dunn, and William Rhodes Hawkins, afterwards of his party to explore the canyons, he crossed the range to White River and wintered there near the camp of Chief Douglass and his band of Utes. When spring came in 1869 he went out to Granger, on the Union Pacific Railway, and there disposed of his mules and outfit, proceeding immediately to Washington, where he induced Congress to pass a joint resolution endorsed by General Grant authorising him to draw rations from Western army posts for a party of twelve men while engaged in making collections for public institutions. Never was assistance better deserved. Then he returned to Illinois and obtained from the trustees of the Normal University permission to again divert his salary and the other funds to Western work. The trustees of the Illinois Industrial University allotted him five hundred dollars, and the Chicago Academy of Sciences, through the influence of Dr. Andrews, the curator, also contributed two hundred and fifty or five hundred dollars. In addition some personal friends contributed small sums.

The object proposed was to make collections in natural history to be shared accordingly with the contributing institutions. While these collections were one of Powell's objects, others were the examination of the geology, and particularly the solution of the greatest remaining geographical problem of the United States, the canyons of the Green and Colorado rivers. The Green, as has been explained in preceding pages, was known as far as the Uinta Mountains, and here and there at widely separated points on down to about Gunnison Valley. But there were long gaps, and below Gunnison Crossing as far as the Grand Wash the knowledge of the canyons as already pointed out was vague in the extreme. The altitude of Green River Station, Wyoming, was known to be about six thousand feet above sea level, and that of the mouth of the Virgen less than one thousand. How the river made up this difference was not understood and this problem was what Powell now confronted. His fortitude, nerve, courage, and war experience served him well in this endeavour upon which he started, as previously described. in the spring of 1869. The War Department and perhaps the Smithsonian Institution, furnished some instruments. This expedition met with so many disasters that Powell deemed a second descent in the interest of science desirable, and for a continuation of his explorations, Congress voted in 1870 an appropriation of ten thousand dollars. This second expedition was successful, performing its work in the years 1871–72–73. At the Session of 1871–72 another appropriation was made by Congress for proceeding with the topographical and geological survey of the country adjacent to the river. These appropriations were expended under the supervision of the Smithsonian Institution and were continued annually for work under the titles, Exploration of the Colorado River and its Tributaries, and Survey of the Rocky Mountain Region, up to 1879, when the work was consolidated largely through Powell's endeavour, with two other surveys, Hayden's and Wheeler's. The latter thought all this work ought to be done by the War Department, but Powell believed otherwise and his view prevailed. Out of these grew by the consolidation the Geological Survey, of which Clarence King was made director, Powell, because of the earnest efforts he had made to bring about the consolidation, refusing to allow his name to be presented. The new Geological Survey was under the Interior Department, and in 1881, when King resigned the directorship, Powell was immediately appointed in his place. The results of Powell's original field-work were topographic maps of a large part of Utah, and considerable portions of Wyoming, Arizona, and Nevada, constructed under the direction of Powell's colleague, Prof. A. H. Thompson. There were also many volumes of reports and monographs, among them the account of the expedition of 1869, entitled, *The Exploration of the Colorado River of the West, 1869 to 1872; The Geology of the Uinta Mountains*, by Powell; *Lands of the Arid*

The Grand Canyon.
Boats of the second Powell Expedition, showing armchair
in which Powell sat.
Photograph by J. K. Hillers, U. S. Colo. River Exp.

Region, by Powell; *Geology of the High Plateaus of Utah*, by C. E. Dutton, of the Ordnance Department, U. S. A.; *Geology of the Henry Mountains*, by G. K. Gilbert; and four volumes of *Contributions to North American Ethnology*, one of which contained Lewis H. Morgan's famous monograph on "Houses and House Life of the American Aborigines." Early in his Western work Powell became interested in the native tribes. In the winter of 1868, while on White River, he studied language, tribal organisation, customs, and mythology of the Utes and from 1870 to 1873 he carried on studies among the Pai Utes, the Moki, etc., being adopted into one of the Moki clans. On his journeys during these periods he often took with him several of the natives for the purpose of investigating their myths and language. Eventually he became the highest authority on the Shoshonean tribes. In 1874 he was one of the commissioners to select and locate the Southern Pai Utes on a reservation in south-eastern Nevada.

North American archæology also claimed his interest and about the time of the consolidation of the Surveys Powell proposed the establishment of a Bureau of Ethnology to carry on investigations in this field as well as the ethnologic. This was done and the Bureau was attached to the Smithsonian Institution with Powell as director, an office that he held without salary till his resignation as head of the Geological Survey in 1894. After this he received a salary as chief of the Bureau of Ethnology in which office he remained till his death. The widely known extensive series of valuable volumes published by the Bureau, constituting a mine of information, attest the efficacy of his supervision. He contributed much to these and also wrote numerous papers on anthropological subjects and made many addresses. His labours as a pioneer in and organiser of the science of ethnology have been recognised by learned institutions and societies throughout the world. The results of his direction of the Geological Survey are seen in the maps, reports, bulletins, and monographs, constituting an imperishable monument to his ability as an organiser and administrator.

He delivered many lectures and once, when he appeared on the platform at the University of Michigan, an incident occurred which illustrates his tact and his faculty for seizing means at hand to accomplish his end. At this time it was the habit of the students at public lectures to guy the speaker, even Charles

Sumner having been a victim. Powell had been warned of this practice. As he advanced in evening dress a voice called out "How are your coat tails?"—a greeting which was repeated from all parts of the house. During a momentary lull he exclaimed with the peculiar squinting of the eyes and the half-laugh his friends so well remember: "Your greeting reminds me of Dave Larkins's reply when criticised for wearing a wamus[1] in July. Dave said, with his slow drawl, 'If you don't like my wamus I can take it off.' " The suggestion took with the students and when the laughter had ceased, cries of "You 'll do—go on," came from everywhere. The incident roused Powell, and he has often said he never talked better nor had a more attentive audience. He was rewarded with enthusiastic applause. With his closing sentence he said: "I have given you the finest account of the exploration of the Colorado River my command of language permits. I have been as dramatic and as eloquent as I thought this occasion demanded. If any one wishes a plain statement regarding the exploration, I will be happy to give it to him at my hotel." There was a hush for a moment as the students grasped the implication and cries of "Sold!" burst from them. A large number did call the next morning to discover whether he had actually stated facts, which of course he had.

He possessed absolute independence of thought and never accepted what was told him unless he could demonstrate its accuracy. Often in his explorations he was told he could not travel in certain places, but he went on just the same to find out for himself. He had a rare faculty of inducing enthusiasm in others, and by reposing complete confidence in the individual, impelled him to do his very best. Thus he became the mainspring for much that was never credited to him, and which was really his in the germ or original idea. Gilbert truly says, "it is not easy to separate the product of his personal work from that which he accomplished through the organisation of the work of others. He was extremely fertile in ideas, so fertile that it was quite impossible that he should personally develop them

[1] A wamus in old times was a very heavy woollen garment.

all, and realising this, he gave freely to his collaborators. The work which he inspired and to which he contributed the most important creative elements, I believe to be at least as important as that for which his name stands directly responsible.'' [1]

Pilling's Cascade.
Creeks of the High Plateaus.
Photograph by J. K. HILLERS, U. S. Geol. Surv.

In the field of geology he was particularly facile in the invention of apt descriptive terms, and indeed he was never at a loss for words to express new meanings, coining them readily

[1] *Science*, Oct. 10, 1902.

where none had existed that were appropriate. Some of his ideas have been developed by younger men, till they have become distinct divisions of the larger science to which they belong. His greatest work in the Geological Survey, that which was more the result of his personal effort, may be summed up under three heads: First, the development of a plan for making a complete topographic map of the United States; second, the organisation of a Bureau for the collection of facts and figures relating to the mineral resources of the country; and third, his labours to preserve for the people the waters and irrigable lands of the Arid Region. It is hard to say which of these is greater or which was nearer his heart. Together they constitute a far-reaching influence in the development of the country such as no one man heretofore has contributed. His studies and recommendations with regard to the arid lands of the West are of the greatest importance to that district and to the country at large and the nearer they can be carried out the better will it be for posterity. He perceived at once that the reservation of sites for storage reservoirs was of the first importance and this was one of the earliest steps he endeavoured to bring about.

Of late years when he might have relaxed his labours, he turned his attention to the field of psychology and philosophy, working till his malady, sclerosis of the arteries, produced his last illness. The result was two treatises in this line, *Truth and Error*, published in 1899, and "treating of matter, motion, and consciousness as related to the external universe or the field of fact," as Gilbert describes it, and *Good and Evil*, running as a series of essays in the *American Anthropologist*, treating of the same factors as related to humanity or to welfare. A third volume was planned to deal with the emotions, and he had also woven these ideas into a series of poems, of which only one has been published. Few understand these later products of Powell. Many condemn them; but Gilbert expresses his usual clear, unbiassed view of things and says (and I can do no better than to quote him, a man of remarkably direct thought, and for many years very close to Powell): "His philosophic writings belong to a field in which thought has ever found language inadequate, and are for the present, so far as may be judged from the reviews of *Truth and Error*, largely misunderstood. Admitting myself to be of those who fail to understand much of his philosophy, I do not therefore condemn it as worthless, for in other fields of his thought events have proved that he was not visionary, but merely in advance of his time."

One inexplicable action in his career, to my mind, was his complete ignoring in his report of the men and their work, of his second river expedition, particularly of his colleague, Prof. Thompson, whose skill and energy were so largely responsible for the scientific and practical success of the second expedition. The report embodied all the results achieved by this expedition and gave no credit to the men who with unflagging zeal, under stress and difficulties innumerable accumulated the data. This has ever appeared to me unjust, but his reasons for it were doubtless satisfactory to himself. The second expedition is put on record, for the first time in this volume, except for a lecture of mine printed some years ago in the *Bulletin* of the American Geographical Society.

The life of Powell is an example of the triumph of intelligent, persistent endeavour. Long ago he had formulated many of his plans and as far back as 1877, and even 1871, as I understood them, he carried them out with remarkable precision. Before the authorisation of the Bureau of Ethnology, its scope was developed in his mind and he saw completed the many volumes which have since been published. His power to observe the field ahead, standing on the imperfections of the present, was extraordinary. As a soldier he was a patriot, as an explorer he was a hero. As a far-seeing scientific man, as an organiser of government scientific work, as a loving friend, and a delightful comrade whether by the camp-fire or in the study, and as a true sympathiser with the aspirations and ambitions of subordinates or equals, there has seldom been his superior.

APPENDIX

The Canyons, Valleys, and Mouths of Principal Tributaries of the Colorado, in their order, from source to gulf, together with lengths and greatest depths of canyons, descent in feet, and altitudes above sea.

The altitudes from the Gulf to the Junction have been adjusted to spirit-levelling from the A. & P. Railway to Stone's Ferry, above the mouth of the Virgen.

ALTITUDE AT HEAD	NAMES OF CANYONS, VALLEYS, AND CHIEF TRIBUTARIES OF THE COLORADO	ALTITUDE AT FOOT	DESCENT IN FEET	LENGTH IN MILES	GREATEST DEPTH OF CANYON
13,790	Frémont Peak, Wind River Mts.				
10,160	Timber Line, Wind River Mts..		3,630		
6,900	*New Fork*, mouth (East)........		3,260		
6,240	*Big Sandy*, mouth (East)......		660		
6,075	Union Pacific R'y Crossing... ⎱		165		
....	*Bitter Creek*, mouth (East).... ⎰			62	
5,940	*Black's Fork*, mouth (West)...				
5,813	*Henry's Fork*, mouth (West).. ⎰		262		
5,813	FLAMING GORGE........ ⎱				1,300
....	HORSESHOE CANYON.... ⎬			9⅓	1,600
....	KINGFISHER CANYON... ⎰				1,200
....	Kingfisher Park..............				
....	RED CANYON	5,375	438	25⅔	2,500
....	Red Canyon Park..............				
5,375	Brown's Park................			35½	
....	SWALLOW CANYON.......				
....	*Vermilion Creek*, mouth (East)..				
5,375	Gate of Lodore..............				
5,375	CANYON OF LODORE......	5,100	275	20¾	2,700
5,100	*Yampa River*, mouth (East).....				
5,100	Echo Park			1	
5,100	WHIRLPOOL CANYON.....	4,940	160	14¼	2,400
4,940	Island Park........			9	
4,940	SPLIT-MOUNTAIN CANYON			8	2,700
....	Wonsits Valley..............			87¾	
....	*Ashley Fork*, mouth (West).....				
4,625	*Uinta River*, mouth (West).....		315		
....	*White River* (East)............				
....	CANYON OF DESOLATION.			97	2,700
....	GRAY CANYON.............	4,075	550	36	2,000
4,075	Gunnison Valley, at Crossing...			27¼	
....	*San Rafael*, mouth (West)......				
....	LABYRINTH CANYON......			62½	1,300

ALTITUDE AT HEAD	NAMES OF CANYONS, VALLEYS, AND CHIEF TRIBUTARIES OF THE COLORADO	ALTITUDE AT FOOT	DESCENT IN FEET	LENGTH IN MILES	GREATEST DEPTH OF CANYON
. . . .	Bonito Bend	. . . .	. . . .	. . . .	. . . .
. . . .	STILLWATER CANYON. . . .	3,860	215	42¾	1,300
3,860	*Grand River* (East).	. . . .	. . . .	. . . .	. . . .
3,860	CATARACT CANYON.	. . . .	. . . .	41	2,700
. . . .	Millecrag Bend.	. . . .	. . . .	. . . .	. . . .
. . . .	NARROW CANYON.	3,430	430	9½	1,300
3,430	*Frémont River*, mouth (West). . .	. . . .	. . . .	. . . .	. . . .
. . . .	Dandy Crossing.	. . . .	. . . .	. . . .	. . . .
3,430	GLEN CANYON.	3,170	260	149	1,600
3,300	*Escalante River*, mouth (West). .	. . . .	. . . .	. . . .	. . . .
3,280	*San Juan River*, mouth (East). .	. . . .	. . . .	. . . .	. . . .
3,220	Crossing of the Fathers.	. . . .	. . . .	. . . .	. . . .
3,170	*Paria River*, mouth (West).	. . . .	. . . .	. . . .	. . . .
3,170	Lee's Ferry.	. . . .	. . . .	. . . .	. . . .
3,170	MARBLE CANYON.	2,690	480	65½	3,500
2,690	*Little Colorado River*, mouth (E.)	. . . .	. . . .	. . . .	. . . .
2,690	GRAND CANYON.	840	1,850	217½	6,000
. . . .	*Bright Angel Creek*, mouth (West)	. . . .	. . . .	. . . .	. . . .
. . . .	*Tapeets Creek*, mouth (West). . . .	. . . .	. . . .	. . . .	. . . .
1,800	*Kanab Canyon*, mouth (West). . .	. . . .	. . . .	. . . .	. . . .
. . . .	*Havasupai Creek*, mouth (East). .	. . . .	. . . .	. . . .	. . . .
1,300	*Diamond Creek*, mouth (East). . .	. . . .	. . . .	. . . .	. . . .
840	*Grand Wash*, mouth (West)	. . . .	. . . .	. . . .	. . . .
. . . .	ICEBERG CANYON.	. . . .	. . . .	. . . .	. . . .
. . . .	VIRGIN CANYON. . . . . . . ; . .	. . . .	. . . .	. . . .	. . . .
700	*Virgen River*, mouth (West). . . .	. . . .	140	. . . .	. . . .
. . . .	BOWLDER CANYON.	. . . .	. . . .	20	2,000
. . . .	BLACK CANYON.	. . . .	. . . .	25	1,700
. . . .	PAINTED CANYON.	. . . .	. . . .	2	100
. . . .	Cottonwood Valley	. . . .	. . . .	. . . .	. . . .
. . . .	PYRAMID CANYON.	. . . .	. . . .	6	250
. . . .	Mohave Valley.	. . . .	. . . .	30	. . . .
. . . .	MOHAVE CANYON.	. . . .	. . . .	8	. . . .
. . . .	Chemehuevis Valley. . . . . . . ; ; .	. . . .	. . . .	12	. . . .
. . . . . .	MONUMENT CANYON. . , . . .	. . . .	. . . .	6	. . . .
375	*Bill Williams Fork*, mouth (East)	. . . .	325	. . . .	. . . .
. . . .	Great Colorado Valley.	. . . .	. . . .	107	. . . .
. . . .	CANEBRAKE CANYON.	. . . .	. . . .	10	. . . .
. . . .	Purple Hill Pass.	. . . .	. . . .	2	. . . .
. . . .	Explorer Pass.	. . . .	. . . .	. . . .	. . . .
120	*Gila River*, mouth (East).	. . . .	255	. . . . . .	. . . . .
. . . .	PUERTO DE LA PURISIMA .	. . . .	. . . .	⅛	50
0	Gulf of California.	. . . .	120	. . . .	. . . .

The longest stretch of unbroken canyon walls is the Marble and Grand, 283 miles, with a total river fall of 2330 feet.

The entire length of the river, counting the Green as the Upper Colorado, is about 2000 miles. The area drained is some 300 to 500 miles wide by 800 miles long, and contains approximately about 300,000 square miles. To the Gulf from the Grand Wash is in the neighbourhood of 600 miles; from Lee's Ferry, 900; from the mouth of Grand River, about 1100.

In the Marble and Grand Canyons the fall is as follows.[1]   The vertical dotted lines of diagram on page 57 give these divisions, beginning at the left with 2.

SUB-DIVISIONS OF THE GRAND CANYON	DISTANCE IN MILES	FALL IN FEET	FALL IN FEET PER MILE
1. Marble Canyon.............................	65.2	510	7.82
2. Little Colorado to the Granite	18.2	110	6.04
3. Granite Falls................................	10	210	21.
4. To Powell's Plateau in the Granite............	26.4	320	12.13
5. Around western base of Powell's Plateau.......	10.8	100	9.26
6. Head of Kanab Division.....................	4.8	50	10.42
7. Main Kanab and Uinkaret Division..........	65.2	310	4.75
8. Shewits Division to Granite	12	70	5.83
9. Granite to Diamond Creek..	18	210	11.66
10. Granite below Diamond Creek................	7.2	25	3.47
11. Granite below Diamond Creek................	10.8	100	9.26
12. Shewits Granite to End of Canyon	35	175	5.
From Little Colorado to Kaibab Division.........	9.6	60	6.25
Kaibab Division	58	700	12.07
Kanab Division..............................	47.6	240	5.01
Uinkaret Division............................	19.2	100	5.21
Shewits Division.............................	84	540	6.43

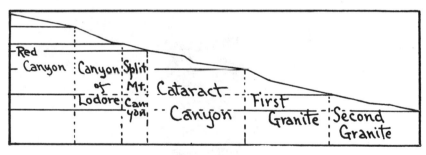

Consecutively arranged profiles of the greatest declivities on the Colorado and Green.
Same scales as diagram p. 57

The exact number of rapids cannot be given, as in some portions of Lodore, Cataract, Marble, and the Grand Canyon it is difficult to divide the almost continuous fall into parts.   The number also varies with the stage of water, a high stage covering up some of the smaller rapids.   I count 62 rapids in Cataract Canyon, but Stanton makes it 75.   The discrepancy arises in the way of dividing some of the descent in the worst portions.   Lodore for a large part of its length is so nearly one continuous rapid that it is difficult to count the special drops.   In Marble Canyon I counted 73, and in the distance from the Little Colorado to the mouth of the Kanab, 131.   We counted about 600 from Green River Valley to the Kanab Canyon, and Stanton's party counted 520 large rapids from Frémont

River to the Grand Wash, or about 600 from the Junction. From Green River Valley to the foot of Black Canyon something over 1000 would be a near estimate of the total number of rapids. The velocity is always tremendous.

The width of the river varies according to the locality. Green River is from 250 to 400 feet in the canyons, and 800 to 1000 in the valleys. The Colorado is from 75 to 400 or 500 in the canyons and from 1200 to 1500 in the valleys. In the Granite Gorges there are points where the distance between the buttresses at the water is no more than 50 feet. In Marble Canyon there are a dozen places where the width is not over 60 to 75 feet. The depth varies from several feet to an unknown quantity in the narrow parts. There is also a variation of depth with the year and the season. Years when the high mountains receive an abnormal snow-fall the river rises to abnormal heights and at such times the depth of water in the Grand Canyon is enormous and the velocity appalling. The current varies from three miles per hour to twenty or more.

[1] After Dutton, *Tertiary History*, p. 240.

INDEX

A CATALOG OF SELECTED
DOVER BOOKS
IN ALL FIELDS OF INTEREST

A CATALOG OF SELECTED DOVER
BOOKS IN ALL FIELDS OF INTEREST

CONCERNING THE SPIRITUAL IN ART, Wassily Kandinsky. Pioneering work by father of abstract art. Thoughts on color theory, nature of art. Analysis of earlier masters. 12 illustrations. 80pp. of text. 5⅜ x 8½. 23411-8 Pa. $3.95

ANIMALS: 1,419 Copyright-Free Illustrations of Mammals, Birds, Fish, Insects, etc., Jim Harter (ed.). Clear wood engravings present, in extremely lifelike poses, over 1,000 species of animals. One of the most extensive pictorial sourcebooks of its kind. Captions. Index. 284pp. 9 x 12. 23766-4 Pa. $12.95

CELTIC ART: The Methods of Construction, George Bain. Simple geometric techniques for making Celtic interlacements, spirals, Kells-type initials, animals, humans, etc. Over 500 illustrations. 160pp. 9 x 12. (USO) 22923-8 Pa. $9.95

AN ATLAS OF ANATOMY FOR ARTISTS, Fritz Schider. Most thorough reference work on art anatomy in the world. Hundreds of illustrations, including selections from works by Vesalius, Leonardo, Goya, Ingres, Michelangelo, others. 593 illustrations. 192pp. 7⅛ x 10¼. 20241-0 Pa. $9.95

CELTIC HAND STROKE-BY-STROKE (Irish Half-Uncial from "The Book of Kells"): An Arthur Baker Calligraphy Manual, Arthur Baker. Complete guide to creating each letter of the alphabet in distinctive Celtic manner. Covers hand position, strokes, pens, inks, paper, more. Illustrated. 48pp. 8¼ x 11. 24336-2 Pa. $3.95

EASY ORIGAMI, John Montroll. Charming collection of 32 projects (hat, cup, pelican, piano, swan, many more) specially designed for the novice origami hobbyist. Clearly illustrated easy-to-follow instructions insure that even beginning papercrafters will achieve successful results. 48pp. 8¼ x 11. 27298-2 Pa. $3.50

THE COMPLETE BOOK OF BIRDHOUSE CONSTRUCTION FOR WOODWORKERS, Scott D. Campbell. Detailed instructions, illustrations, tables. Also data on bird habitat and instinct patterns. Bibliography. 3 tables. 63 illustrations in 15 figures. 48pp. 5¼ x 8½. 24407-5 Pa. $2.50

BLOOMINGDALE'S ILLUSTRATED 1886 CATALOG: Fashions, Dry Goods and Housewares, Bloomingdale Brothers. Famed merchants' extremely rare catalog depicting about 1,700 products: clothing, housewares, firearms, dry goods, jewelry, more. Invaluable for dating, identifying vintage items. Also, copyright-free graphics for artists, designers. Co-published with Henry Ford Museum & Greenfield Village. 160pp. 8¼ x 11. 25780-0 Pa. $10.95

HISTORIC COSTUME IN PICTURES, Braun & Schneider. Over 1,450 costumed figures in clearly detailed engravings—from dawn of civilization to end of 19th century. Captions. Many folk costumes. 256pp. 8⅜ x 11¾. 23150-X Pa. $12.95

THE WIT AND HUMOR OF OSCAR WILDE, Alvin Redman (ed.). More than 1,000 ripostes, paradoxes, wisecracks: Work is the curse of the drinking classes; I can resist everything except temptation; etc. 258pp. 5⅜ x 8½. 20602-5 Pa. $5.95

SHAKESPEARE LEXICON AND QUOTATION DICTIONARY, Alexander Schmidt. Full definitions, locations, shades of meaning in every word in plays and poems. More than 50,000 exact quotations. 1,485pp. 6½ x 9¼. 2-vol. set.
Vol. 1: 22726-X Pa. $16.95
Vol. 2: 22727-8 Pa. $16.95

SELECTED POEMS, Emily Dickinson. Over 100 best-known, best-loved poems by one of America's foremost poets, reprinted from authoritative early editions. No comparable edition at this price. Index of first lines. 64pp. 5³⁄₁₆ x 8¼. 26466-1 Pa. $1.00

CELEBRATED CASES OF JUDGE DEE (DEE GOONG AN), translated by Robert van Gulik. Authentic 18th-century Chinese detective novel; Dee and associates solve three interlocked cases. Led to van Gulik's own stories with same characters. Extensive introduction. 9 illustrations. 237pp. 5⅜ x 8½. 23337-5 Pa. $6.95

THE MALLEUS MALEFICARUM OF KRAMER AND SPRENGER, translated by Montague Summers. Full text of most important witchhunter's "bible," used by both Catholics and Protestants. 278pp. 6⅝ x 10. 22802-9 Pa. $12.95

SPANISH STORIES/CUENTOS ESPAÑOLES: A Dual-Language Book, Angel Flores (ed.). Unique format offers 13 great stories in Spanish by Cervantes, Borges, others. Faithful English translations on facing pages. 352pp. 5⅜ x 8½. 25399-6 Pa. $8.95

THE CHICAGO WORLD'S FAIR OF 1893: A Photographic Record, Stanley Appelbaum (ed.). 128 rare photos show 200 buildings, Beaux-Arts architecture, Midway, original Ferris Wheel, Edison's kinetoscope, more. Architectural emphasis; full text. 116pp. 8¼ x 11. 23990-X Pa. $9.95

OLD QUEENS, N.Y., IN EARLY PHOTOGRAPHS, Vincent F. Seyfried and William Asadorian. Over 160 rare photographs of Maspeth, Jamaica, Jackson Heights, and other areas. Vintage views of DeWitt Clinton mansion, 1939 World's Fair and more. Captions. 192pp. 8⅞ x 11. 26358-4 Pa. $12.95

CAPTURED BY THE INDIANS: 15 Firsthand Accounts, 1750-1870, Frederick Drimmer. Astounding true historical accounts of grisly torture, bloody conflicts, relentless pursuits, miraculous escapes and more, by people who lived to tell the tale. 384pp. 5⅜ x 8½. 24901-8 Pa. $8.95

THE WORLD'S GREAT SPEECHES, Lewis Copeland and Lawrence W. Lamm (eds.). Vast collection of 278 speeches of Greeks to 1970. Powerful and effective models; unique look at history. 842pp. 5⅜ x 8½. 20468-5 Pa. $14.95

THE BOOK OF THE SWORD, Sir Richard F. Burton. Great Victorian scholar/adventurer's eloquent, erudite history of the "queen of weapons"–from prehistory to early Roman Empire. Evolution and development of early swords, variations (sabre, broadsword, cutlass, scimitar, etc.), much more. 336pp. 6⅛ x 9¼. 25434-8 Pa. $9.95

AUTOBIOGRAPHY: The Story of My Experiments with Truth, Mohandas K. Gandhi. Boyhood, legal studies, purification, the growth of the Satyagraha (nonviolent protest) movement. Critical, inspiring work of the man responsible for the freedom of India. 480pp. 5⅜ x 8½. (USO) 24593-4 Pa. $8.95

CELTIC MYTHS AND LEGENDS, T. W. Rolleston. Masterful retelling of Irish and Welsh stories and tales. Cuchulain, King Arthur, Deirdre, the Grail, many more. First paperback edition. 58 full-page illustrations. 512pp. 5⅜ x 8½. 26507-2 Pa. $9.95

THE PRINCIPLES OF PSYCHOLOGY, William James. Famous long course complete, unabridged. Stream of thought, time perception, memory, experimental methods; great work decades ahead of its time. 94 figures. 1,391pp. 5⅜ x 8½. 2-vol. set.
Vol. I: 20381-6 Pa. $12.95
Vol. II: 20382-4 Pa. $12.95

THE WORLD AS WILL AND REPRESENTATION, Arthur Schopenhauer. Definitive English translation of Schopenhauer's life work, correcting more than 1,000 errors, omissions in earlier translations. Translated by E. F. J. Payne. Total of 1,269pp. 5⅜ x 8½. 2-vol. set. Vol. 1: 21761-2 Pa. $11.95
Vol. 2: 21762-0 Pa. $12.95

MAGIC AND MYSTERY IN TIBET, Madame Alexandra David-Neel. Experiences among lamas, magicians, sages, sorcerers, Bonpa wizards. A true psychic discovery. 32 illustrations. 321pp. 5⅜ x 8½. (USO) 22682-4 Pa. $8.95

THE EGYPTIAN BOOK OF THE DEAD, E. A. Wallis Budge. Complete reproduction of Ani's papyrus, finest ever found. Full hieroglyphic text, interlinear transliteration, word-for-word translation, smooth translation. 533pp. 6½ x 9¼.
21866-X Pa. $10.95

MATHEMATICS FOR THE NONMATHEMATICIAN, Morris Kline. Detailed, college-level treatment of mathematics in cultural and historical context, with numerous exercises. Recommended Reading Lists. Tables. Numerous figures. 641pp. 5⅜ x 8½.
24823-2 Pa. $11.95

THEORY OF WING SECTIONS: Including a Summary of Airfoil Data, Ira H. Abbott and A. E. von Doenhoff. Concise compilation of subsonic aerodynamic characteristics of NACA wing sections, plus description of theory. 350pp. of tables. 693pp. 5⅜ x 8½. 60586-8 Pa. $14.95

THE RIME OF THE ANCIENT MARINER, Gustave Doré, S. T. Coleridge. Doré's finest work; 34 plates capture moods, subtleties of poem. Flawless full-size reproductions printed on facing pages with authoritative text of poem. "Beautiful. Simply beautiful."–*Publisher's Weekly*. 77pp. 9¼ x 12. 22305-1 Pa. $6.95

NORTH AMERICAN INDIAN DESIGNS FOR ARTISTS AND CRAFTSPEOPLE, Eva Wilson. Over 360 authentic copyright-free designs adapted from Navajo blankets, Hopi pottery, Sioux buffalo hides, more. Geometrics, symbolic figures, plant and animal motifs, etc. 128pp. 8⅜ x 11. (EUK) 25341-4 Pa. $8.95

SCULPTURE: Principles and Practice, Louis Slobodkin. Step-by-step approach to clay, plaster, metals, stone; classical and modern. 253 drawings, photos. 255pp. 8⅛ x 11.
22960-2 Pa. $11.95

CATALOG OF DOVER BOOKS

THE INFLUENCE OF SEA POWER UPON HISTORY, 1660–1783, A. T. Mahan. Influential classic of naval history and tactics still used as text in war colleges. First paperback edition. 4 maps. 24 battle plans. 640pp. 5⅜ x 8½. 25509-3 Pa. $12.95

THE STORY OF THE TITANIC AS TOLD BY ITS SURVIVORS, Jack Winocour (ed.). What it was really like. Panic, despair, shocking inefficiency, and a little heroism. More thrilling than any fictional account. 26 illustrations. 320pp. 5⅜ x 8½. 20610-6 Pa. $8.95

FAIRY AND FOLK TALES OF THE IRISH PEASANTRY, William Butler Yeats (ed.). Treasury of 64 tales from the twilight world of Celtic myth and legend: "The Soul Cages," "The Kildare Pooka," "King O'Toole and his Goose," many more. Introduction and Notes by W. B. Yeats. 352pp. 5⅜ x 8½. 26941-8 Pa. $8.95

BUDDHIST MAHAYANA TEXTS, E. B. Cowell and Others (eds.). Superb, accurate translations of basic documents in Mahayana Buddhism, highly important in history of religions. The Buddha-karita of Asvaghosha, Larger Sukhavativyuha, more. 448pp. 5⅜ x 8½. 25552-2 Pa. $12.95

ONE TWO THREE . . . INFINITY: Facts and Speculations of Science, George Gamow. Great physicist's fascinating, readable overview of contemporary science: number theory, relativity, fourth dimension, entropy, genes, atomic structure, much more. 128 illustrations. Index. 352pp. 5⅜ x 8½. 25664-2 Pa. $8.95

ENGINEERING IN HISTORY, Richard Shelton Kirby, et al. Broad, nontechnical survey of history's major technological advances: birth of Greek science, industrial revolution, electricity and applied science, 20th-century automation, much more. 181 illustrations. ". . . excellent . . ."–*Isis.* Bibliography. vii + 530pp. 5⅜ x 8¼. 26412-2 Pa. $14.95

DALÍ ON MODERN ART: The Cuckolds of Antiquated Modern Art, Salvador Dalí. Influential painter skewers modern art and its practitioners. Outrageous evaluations of Picasso, Cézanne, Turner, more. 15 renderings of paintings discussed. 44 calligraphic decorations by Dalí. 96pp. 5⅜ x 8½. (USO) 29220-7 Pa. $4.95

ANTIQUE PLAYING CARDS: A Pictorial History, Henry René D'Allemagne. Over 900 elaborate, decorative images from rare playing cards (14th–20th centuries): Bacchus, death, dancing dogs, hunting scenes, royal coats of arms, players cheating, much more. 96pp. 9¼ x 12¼. 29265-7 Pa. $11.95

MAKING FURNITURE MASTERPIECES: 30 Projects with Measured Drawings, Franklin H. Gottshall. Step-by-step instructions, illustrations for constructing handsome, useful pieces, among them a Sheraton desk, Chippendale chair, Spanish desk, Queen Anne table and a William and Mary dressing mirror. 224pp. 8⅛ x 11¼. 29338-6 Pa. $13.95

THE FOSSIL BOOK: A Record of Prehistoric Life, Patricia V. Rich et al. Profusely illustrated definitive guide covers everything from single-celled organisms and dinosaurs to birds and mammals and the interplay between climate and man. Over 1,500 illustrations. 760pp. 7½ x 10⅛. 29371-8 Pa. $29.95

Prices subject to change without notice.

Available at your book dealer or write for free catalog to Dept. GI, Dover Publications, Inc., 31 East 2nd St., Mineola, N.Y. 11501. Dover publishes more than 500 books each year on science, elementary and advanced mathematics, biology, music, art, literary history, social sciences and other areas.